Springer Series

FOCUS ON MEN

Daniel Jay Sonkin, PhD, Series Editor
James H. Hennessy, PhD, Founding Editor

Focus on Men provides a wide range of books on the major psychological, medical, and social issues confronting men today.

Frederick W. Bozett, RN, DNS, (born 6/20/31, died 9/10/90) was a Professor in the graduate program, College of Nursing, University of Oklahoma. He received his doctorate in nursing from the University of California, San Francisco in 1979. He edited *Homosexuality and the Family* (1989), *Gay and Lesbian Parents* (1987), and co-edited *Dimensions of Fatherhood* (1985). His research interests focused on gay fathers and their children, and he published widely in these areas. He was a member of Sigma Theta Tau and Sigma Xi, and was on the editorial boards of *Holistic Nursing Practice* and *Journal of Homosexuality*.

Shirley M. H. Hanson, RN, PMHNP, PhD, FAAN, is a Professor in the Department of Family Nursing at Oregon Health Sciences University in Portland, Oregon. She completed her academic work at Pacific Lutheran University, University of Alaska, University of Washington, and University of Pennsylvania. She has taught in several schools of nursing and has an extensive background in family nursing. Her research interests include families and health, single-parent families, fatherhood, and child/adolescent/family mental health and therapy. She is an active member of the American Nurses' Association, Sigma Theta Tau, Council of Nurse Researchers, American Association of Marriage and Family Therapists, and the National Council on Family Relations. In addition to her academic responsibility, she is in part-time practice as a child and family therapist in Portland. She has authored many articles and chapters in books and journals, and has co-edited issues of *American Behavioral Scientist* and *Family Relations*, and the book *Dimensions of Fatherhood* (1985). Presently she is an editorial board member or reviewer of *Nursing Research, Western Journal of Nursing Research*, and *Journal of Family Psychology*. Dr. Hanson is a fellow of the American Academy of Nursing.

Fatherhood and Families in Cultural Context

Frederick W. Bozett
Shirley M. H. Hanson

Editors

Springer Publishing Company
New York

Springer Publishing Company, Inc.
536 Broadway
New York, NY 10012

90 91 92 93 94 / 5 4 3 2 1

Library of Congress Cataloging-in-Publication Data

Fatherhood and families in cultural context / edited by Frederick W.
   Bozett, Shirley M. H. Hanson.
      p.   cm.—(Springer series, focus on men ; v. 6)
   Includes bibliographical references and index.
   ISBN 0-8261-6570-2
      1. Fatherhood—United States—Cross-cultural studies.   I. Bozett,
   Frederick W., 1931-1990.   II. Hanson, Shirley M. H., 1938-   .
   III. Series.
   HQ756.F375   1990
   306.874′2′0973—dc 20   90-9955
                                                               CIP

Printed in the United States of America

To the memory of my mother *Marie Jenkins Bozett*, and for my stalwart friend and brother *Charles*

With much love,
    FWB

I dedicate this book to two significant people in my life who died during the development of this book. First, *Frederick W. Bozett*, coauthor/coeditor, professional colleague, and friend, died on September 10, 1990. Fred became very ill during the middle development of this book and passed away just before the book went to press. Without Fred, our ten years of collaborative work on fatherhood and families would never have been so rich and successful. Fred's work contributed immensely to the theory and research base in the field of family nursing, gay fatherhood and families, and fatherhood in general. His prolific writing and publication will live way beyond his mortal life.

Second, my mother *Betty Harmon* died August 25, 1990 after a long illness. If I had one person to whom to give credit for my life's work on the "family," it was my mother. Family always came first in her life giving me impetus to re-enact that primary focus through my research, writing, and teaching.

With eternal gratitude to both,
    SMHH

Contents

Foreword

In 1975, I published an article entitled "Father: Forgotten Contributors to Child Development." This title reflected the contemporary disregard for paternal influences on children, but both the title and contents of that brief article also reveal much about disciplinary overspecialization, and the extent to which developmentalists often ignore the broader sociocultural context in which children are raised. Fathers, of course, may have been discovered anew by developmental (and clinical) psychologists in the 1970s, but their existence and importance had been well recognized in much earlier times. Paternal rights, duties, responsibilities, and patterns of influence were intensively described in the Bible and related religious tracts (such as the Gemorah); they pervade the writings of Roman, Greek, and Egyptian philosophers and Jurists—manuscripts that are universally recognized amongst the greatest treasures of human literature. Likewise, themes of filial piety and affection, as well as of paternal commitment, love, devotion, responsibility, neglect, and abuse run through many of the greatest novels ever written. The 19th century in England even brought sensitive accounts of foster and single fatherhood in such novels as George Eliot's *Silas Marner* and Emily Brontë's *Wuthering Heights*.

Since the late 19th century, of course, social scientists have yearned to be seen as scientists with their own empirical tradition rather than as the modern successors to philosophers and novelists, in the process overlooking the insightful observations of Henry James in favor of the more analytical systematization developed by his equally famous brother, William. Few would deny the success with which the social sciences have become established as independent scientific disciplines in scarcely more than a century—notably a century rent by periodic upheavals that have depleted entire national traditions and the intelligentsia. In seeking to define an independent identity, however, psychologists and sociologists have jealously protected their domain from outside incursions and have readily embraced the trends toward increasing specialization that continue to pervade the academy.

By the 1970s, furthermore, the "grand theories" of Freud, Piaget, Miller, and Dollard were politely ridiculed or ignored by scholars developing increasingly elegant but remarkably parochial theories. Fathers were assuredly not "forgotten contributors to child development" in the writings of Sigmund Freud; on the contrary, real and imagined paternal roles and behaviors were believed to play crucial formative roles. For reasons both good and bad, however, academic developmentalists frowned upon clinical interpretation as the source of information about developmental processes, instead preferring to gather information by systematically questioning the most readily available and verbally-competent informants about children—mothers, particularly literate, verbal, middle-class, white mothers in urban areas. It was implicitly assumed that formative importance was somehow a function of the amount of time spent together, and this assumption, coupled with the general cultural devaluation of fatherhood in the 1950s, led to the development of a literature based first on interviews with mothers and then on observations of mothers and children, or children and unfamiliar women. As Bronfenbrenner (1975, 1979) lamented, academic psychologists of the 1950s and 1960s completely ignored the social (including family) context in which children were raised, and it is little wonder that fathers too were forgotten.

Bronfenbrenner's ecological perspective assumed a major corrective significance; by ridicule and logic, he demanded that social scientists recognize the extent to which behaviors and values were directly and indirectly influenced by aspects of the multiple contexts in which people, their families, and their communities were embedded. One index of the rapidity with which developmentalists embraced the contextualist and ecological perspectives is evident in the evolution of the titles I gave to a series of books and lectures about fathers and children. In 1976, I edited *The Role of the Father in Child Development*; when the revised edition was published in

1981, I argued (unsuccessfully) that it be renamed *Fathers' Roles in Child Development* in recognition of the multiple roles that fathers can and do play in their families. By 1983, I was lecturing on "The Changing Roles of Fathers," and by 1984 often added "in Cultural Perspective" to this title.

My personal odyssey was by no means a solitary one, as is illustrated by the contents of this book and of many others published in the past decade. There is no single "father's role" that somehow transcends time, place, and social station; fathers play many roles in their families, and the nature and relative importance of these roles vary historically, intraculturally, and interculturally. Both the title and the content of this volume illustrate the widespread current attempts to develop broader, more inclusive, and more socioculturally—and historically—sensitive views of fatherhood. *Fatherhood* comprises a panoply of roles that must be viewed simultaneously from the perspectives of sociology, psychology, history, health sciences, child and family studies, social welfare, anthropology, gender studies, social policy, and biology if we are to advance our understanding of the many roles of fathers. Bozett and Hanson's collection represents a significant step in the development of this knowledge.

MICHAEL E. LAMB

References

Bronfenbrenner, U. (April 1975). *Social change: The challenge to research and policy*. Paper presented to the Society for Research in Child Development, Denver, Colorado.

Bronfenbrenner, U. (1979). *The ecology of human development*. Cambridge, MA: Harvard University Press.

Lamb, M. E. (1975). Fathers: Forgotten contributors to child development. *Human Development, 18,* 245–266.

Lamb, M. E. (Ed.) (1976). *The role of the father in child development*. New York: Wiley.

Lamb, M. E. (Ed.) (1981). *The role of the father in child development* (rev. ed.). New York: Wiley.

Introduction

Within the past two decades, a plethora of books and journal articles on fatherhood have appeared. Research on the multiple aspects of family roles played by men has been undertaken, as has research on different structural configurations and developmental stages within which fatherhood is enacted. Contrary to the situation in the early 1970s, there is now no paucity of knowledge about fathers, fatherhood, and fathering. There remains, however, gaps in our knowledge, and it is the intention of the editors of this volume to begin to fill one of these lacunae.

For purposes of this volume we have defined *culture* in its broadest sense to include the multiple facets that surround and influence men in the United States with regard to the paternal role with families. This includes the influence and impact of history and social economic status, variations induced by rural and urban environments, as well as ethnicity, religion, and organizations. Likewise, the importance of legal/political systems as they bear on fathers from various ethnic groups, and the effect of internal family culture and dynamics on father role enactment in families are considered.

When we compiled our previous work, *Dimensions of Fatherhood* (1985), we had wanted to include the cultural component. To do so would have made that book too lengthy and cumbersome. We, therefore, waited to compile the current volume until research had increased our knowledge about the subject, qualified authors for each of the chapters were available, and the time was right. The right time is *now*, and we have been fortunate to include work by outstanding experts in each of their respective disciplines.

There is no other single volume that focuses on the cultural influences and familial impact of American fatherhood. The work edited by Lamb, *The Father's Role: Cross-Cultural Perspectives* (1987) is an excellent text that has as its primary focus research on fatherhood in different countries—more of a cross-country/cultural perspective. Several other books on families, parenthood, and fatherhood include some aspects of culture, especially from the ethnic perspective. But none focus on the subject solely from the cultural viewpoint, nor do any contain a discussion of culture within the broad conceptual framework as herein considered.

This book synthesizes the empirical, theoretical, and contemporary literature about men as parents and the multiple cultural impacts that influence their socialization and consequent enactment of the fathering role in families. In order to obtain a broad representation of what we meant by culture, we sought family authors from various academic and practice disciplines so that this book would be useful to students, professionals, academicians, and practitioners in a variety of fields. The contributors come from many disciplines, all of which are attempting to understand and explain family culture: family social studies, family therapy, sociology, anthropology, social work, psychology, and the health professions, including nursing. Thus, it was our intent to have these contributing authors present an overview of the research on the topic, to suggest implications, and to recommend future research directions for each of the chapters. Depending on the writer and the availability of empirical data, our goal was largely met, although the amount of available research varied from topic to topic. Some of the areas discussed in this volume lack a solid research foundation; however, it was our intent to provide academicians, practitioners, researchers, and others interested in fatherhood and family science a beginning literature upon which further scholarship can be built.

This book has eleven chapters. Chapter 1 gives a broad overview of what constitutes culture, fatherhood, and families. Chapter 2 is on historical perspectives and the role of social change. Chapter 3 compares different ethnic cultures such as black, latino, Asian and Native American fathers. Chapter 4 discusses changes in legal view and implications for fathers in minority cultures. Social class and fatherhood is the focus of Chapter 5, and Chapter 6 addresses religion and its impact on fatherhood. Chapter 7 focuses on the impact of environment on fatherhood and compares rural and urban influences. The effects of organizational culture on fatherhood are examined in Chapter 8. Chapter 9 addresses the determinants of family culture and their effects on fatherhood, and Chapter 10 addresses the internal family culture of fathers and the family, or how different family dynamics play a role in how men father children. Finally, Chapter 11 concludes the book with a discussion about cultural change and the future of fatherhood and families. Although the book progresses from more general to specific views and from more external to internal factors, each chapter stands alone and can be read and understood without having to read another.

We believe this book fills a gap in the knowledge about culture, fatherhood, and families, and that this book will be found knowledgeable and stimulating by both professionals and students. We trust that readers will find this book as exciting and useful as we find it.

FREDERICK W. BOZETT
SHIRLEY M. H. HANSON

Acknowledgments

We wish to thank the contributing authors. Each has painstakingly produced creative work that makes this volume unique and on the cutting edge of fatherhood and family research. We are indebted to all of them for their dedication and commitment to this project and to this important topic. In addition, we want to acknowledge Dennis Orthner, who in the earlier days of development of this volume helped expand our vision and broadened our imagination as to what constitutes culture.

Frederick Bozett takes this opportunity to thank Drs. Betty Carmack, Francis Carter, and Eleanor Hein who have provided loving personal and professional support over many years and through difficult times. He is deeply indebted and profoundly grateful. He also thanks everyone at the University of Oklahoma College of Nursing who, over the past 10 years, has supported him in his dance.

Shirley Hanson wants to first acknowledge the love and support from her family of origin and family of procreation, for it was through them that she learned what "family" is about: parents KENNY and BETTY HARMON; inlaws RALPH and LOUISE HANSON; siblings ALBERT, BILL, MARG, PEGGY, and KATHY; husband LARRY; and children DEREK and GWEN. Many nursing friends and colleagues over the years from the University of Washington, Intercollegiate Center for Nursing Education, University of Pennsylvania and Oregon Health Sciences University have supported and been patient with her musings. Vivian G-O., Vivian W-W., Jean W., Kathryn B., Jo T., Gretchen D., Ann B., Joanne G-D., Thelma C., Doris J., Karen M-B., Marsha H., Victor M., Helene M., Carolyn G., Peggy J., and Merlin M., are just a few who helped her to soar to greater heights.

Contributors

Gary L. Bowen, PhD, ACSW, is an Associate Professor and Chairperson, Services to Families and Children Specialization, School of Social Work, the University of North Carolina at Chapel Hill. He received his PhD in Child Development and Family Relations from the University of North Carolina at Greensboro. He has consulted extensively with both civilian and government employers over the past decade concerning the nature of and response to work and family linkages. Under contract with the Department of Health and Human Services, he is currently conducting an investigation of the influence of government-supported daycare programs on the economic self-sufficiency of low-income parents with preschool children.

Steven F. Chapman, MS, is a doctoral student in Child and Family Development at the University of Georgia. With interests that range from the areas of ethnic families to family law, divorce, and remarriage, and human sexuality, he has contributed to texts and is currently engaged in several research and writing efforts.

John DeFrain, PhD, graduated from the University of Wisconsin–Madison in 1975 and has been a Professor of Family Science in the Department of Human Development and the Family, University of Nebraska–Lincoln for 15 years. He has co-directed a joint postgraduate training program in marriage and family therapy; was a cofounder of the National Symposium on Building Family Strengths; and has done extensive consulting for courts, universities, churches, agencies, and individual families on marriage, parenting, divorce, and custody issues. DeFrain has co-authored two dozen professional articles and five books: *Coping With Sudden Infant Death*; *Secrets of Strong Families*; *Stillborn*; *The Invisible Death*; *On Our Own: A Single Parent's Survival Guide*; and *Parents in Contemporary America* (with E. E. LeMasters).

Rebecca J. Erickson, MA, is currently finishing her PhD in Sociology at Washington State University. Her areas of interest include family, social psychology, and social theory. She is currently investigating the effects of emotionally demanding jobs on the emotional division of labor in the family.

Viktor Gecas, PhD, is Professor of Sociology and Rural Sociology at Washington State University, where he has taught since 1969. He received his PhD in sociology from the University of Minnesota in 1969. He has served on the editorial boards of *Social Psychology Quarterly*, *Journal of Marriage and the Family*, and *Symbolic Interaction*. Within the American Sociological Association, he has been a council member of the Social Psychology Section and the Family Sociology Section, and a member of the Committee on Freedom of Research and Teaching. Within the National Council on Family Relations, he has served as Chair of the Research and Theory Section, board member, and member of the Burgess Award Committee. His primary research interests are in socialization, self-concept formation, and parent–child relations.

Anthony P. Jurich, PhD, is a Professor of Human Development and Family Studies and Clinical Director of Marriage and Family Therapy at Kansas State University. He is the co-author of *Marriage and Family Therapy: New Perspectives in Theory Research and Practice* and has authored 95 journal articles and book chapters. He is a certified sex therapist with the American Association for Sex Education, Counseling, and Therapy. He is the 1976 Kansas State University Teacher of the Year and the 1987 Osborne Award winner from the National Council on Family Relations for being the National Outstanding Teacher of the Year in Family Relations. He has been nominated as a national member of Omicron Nu and is a Fellow in the American Association for Marriage and Family Therapy.

Michael E. Lamb, PhD, is Chief of the Section on Social and Emotional Development at the National Institute of Child Health and Human Development, where he directs comparative cross-cultural research on the development of individual differences among children, adolescents, and parents. He was previously Professor of Psychology, Psychiatry, and Pediatrics at the University of Utah, and has written or edited several books and articles on fathers and children, including *The Father's Role: Cross-Cultural Perspectives*; *The Role of the Father in Child Development*; *The Father's Role: Applied Perspectives*; and *Fatherhood and Social Policy*.

E. E. LeMasters, PhD, is Emeritus Professor of Social Work and Sociology at the University of Wisconsin–Madison. He received his PhD in sociology and anthropology from Ohio State University, his MS in psychiatric social work from Case Western Reserve University, and did his undergraduate work in sociology and English at Miami University of Ohio. Dr. LeMasters was previously Director of the Graduate School of Social Work at the University of Wisconsin–Madison. Prior to this he was Dean of Students at the Associated Colleges of Upper New York. His publications include *Courtship and Marriage, Parents in Modern Society*, and *Blue-Collar Aristocracy*. His study *Parenthood as Crisis* has been reprinted in over 80 publications.

Teresa Donati Marciano, PhD, is Professor of Sociology, Fairleigh Dickinson University, Teaneck, New Jersey. She received her BA from Barnard College, and her MA and PhD from Columbia University. Her research and publications have examined family pattern changes (structural, demographic, religious), and the impact of gender on fertility decisions and religious practices.

Alfredo Mirandé, PhD, has been professor of Sociology and Ethnic Studies at the University of California, Riverside since 1974, and is currently Chair of Ethnic Studies. He is on the Board of the Society for the Study of Social Problems (SSSP) and has served on the American Sociological Association Minority Fellowship Program Committee, on the Steering Committee of the National Association of Chicano Studies (NACS), and as Editor of the newsletter of the Caucus of Chicano Sociologists, *Noticias*. Dr. Mirandé received a senior National Research Council Postdoctoral Fellowship (1984–

85) and a Rockefeller Foundation Research Fellowship for Minority Group Scholars (1985–86). His publications include *The Age of Crisis* (1975), *La Chicana: The Mexican-American Woman* (1980), *The Chicano Experience* (1985), *Gringo Justice* (1987), and many journal articles dealing with race and ethnicity.

Richard A. Moody, BS, received his BS in Psychology from Brigham Young University. He is currently in the master's program in Marriage and Family Therapy at Kansas State University.

Dennis K. Orthner, PhD, is Professor and Director of the Human Services Research and Design Laboratory, School of Social Work, the University of North Carolina at Chapel Hill. He received his PhD in sociology from Florida State University and has conducted research on work and family issues in universities as well as in the private sector. Dr. Orthner serves on the editorial board of several major family and youth journals, and has provided testimony to state and national congressional committees on issues related to the work, family, and community concerns. He is currently editing a special issue of the *Journal of Early Adolescence* on the effects of parental work on early adolescent development.

Toni Tripp-Reimer, RN, PhD, FAAN, is Professor and Director of the Office for Nursing Research Development and Utilization at the University of Iowa College of Nursing. She received her PhD in anthropology from the Ohio State University in 1977. Her research integrates the themes of ethnicity, health behaviors, and aging.

Jan A. Schroff, BS, graduated from the University of Southern Mississippi in 1969. She is completing her master's degree at the University of Nebraska in the Department of Human Development and the Family. The emphasis of her research is on farm fathers and their family interrelationships.

Rudy Ray Seward, PhD, is an associate professor and the graduate advisor in the Department of Sociology and Social Work at the University of North Texas. He received his PhD in sociology from Southern Illinois University, Carbondale in 1974. Major research interests include various aspects of the family especially its history, perinatal care, and childhood. His memberships include the National Council on Family Relations, American Sociological Association, Society for Cross-Cultural Research, and the Committee of Family Research within the International Sociological Association. He has authored a book, chapters, journal articles, and reviews primarily dealing with the family. His dissertation, *The American Family: A Demographic History* (1978), was selected and published as part of the National Council on Family Relations' monograph series. Other publications have appeared in the *Journal of Marriage and the Family, International Journal of Sociology of the Family*, and *Sociology and Social Research*.

Peter N. Stearns, PhD, is Heinz Professor and Head, Department of History, Carnegie Mellon University. He received his doctorate in history from Harvard University, and has devoted his career in research and teaching to various facets of modern social history including masculinity and fatherhood. He is founder and editor of the *Journal of Social History* and author or editor of more than 30 books in the field. His book on men's history was one of the first in the field, soon to reemerge in a revised edition. Current research focuses on the history of emotions, including their relationship to gender and parenthood.

Lynda Henley Walters, PhD, is Associate Professor of Child and Family Development at the University of Georgia. She received her PhD in Child and Family development from the University of Georgia in 1978. Her research is in the areas of parent–child relationships, family law, and adolescence, with a particular interest in cross-cultural studies. Dr. Walters is a member of the National Council on Family Relations and has, in addition to holding other offices, served as Chair of the Family Law Focus Group and Chair of the Research and Theory Section.

Carmel Parker White, MS, received an MS in Human Development from Brigham Young University in 1987. She is currently a doctoral student in Life Span Human Development at Kansas State University.

Mark B. White, MS, received an MS in Marriage and Family Therapy from Brigham Young University in 1988. He is currently a doctoral student in Marriage and Family Therapy at Kansas State University.

Susan E. Wilson, RN, MSN, is a lecturer at the University of Iowa College of Nursing. She received her MSN in Community Health Nursing from the University of Nebraska Medical Center in 1983. Her research focuses on fathering and, specifically, adaptation to the role by fathers of newborn infants.

1

Cross-Cultural Perspectives on Fatherhood

Toni Tripp-Reimer
Susan E. Wilson

Historical Overview of Concept of Fathering

The ancient Roman author Livy tells a story that illustrates a father's power in Roman times. Later recounted by Geoffrey Chaucer in "The Physician's Tale" of *The Canterbury Tales*, the story, tells of the Roman Virginius, who had a pure and beautiful daughter. A judge with lustful intentions conspired to have the daughter declared a slave who had been stolen in infancy. Virginius, rather than allow his own honor to be sullied, told his daughter that he must cut off her head. Despite the child's pleas for mercy, he beheaded his innocent daughter and presented the head to the judge. This act inspired an uprising by the people against the judge. The people imprisoned the judge and planned to hang the judge's chief conspirator, but Virginius begged mercy for the conspirator, and the people only exiled the man. No one suggested any wrong doing by the father who killed his daughter; rather, Virginius lived on in great honor and respect.

According to historians, a father's authority in Roman society astonished the Greeks. In Roman law, not only could a father privately sentence a child to death, but a male child and an unmarried female child remained under the complete authority of the father until the father's death. At a Roman father's death his sons became heirs and independent adults, and his daughters became heiresses— although a strict paternal uncle, if he chose, could exercise control over the unmarried or divorced daughters. This pattern of authority prevailed even if a son became consul, the highest public official in the Roman government. Even as an adult, a son needed his father's consent to borrow money, sign a contract, free a slave, or draw up a will. In contrast, an 18-year-old male orphan could do whatever he pleased with his money (Veyne, 1987).

During the Christian Middle Ages the father's power to privately sentence his children to death was abolished, and his authority was limited in that he could not require his child to commit sin. However, in other areas, his wife and children were wholly subject to his authority throughout his life (De la Ronciere, 1988). For example, in the 11th and 12th century in Italy, the father, as sole trustee of the family property, managed his wife's dowry (and in some cases the dowries of his daughters-in-law) and his son's cash reserves. During these times, the father (*paterfamilias*) held power not only of the family property but also of all family members. Paternal authority in Europe only began to wane when the rise of commercial civilization gave sons greater opportunity to earn money independent of family holdings and to physically leave the family residence for employment in the city (Duby, 1988).

The anthropological literature offers a rich variety of holocultural ethnographic topics related to marriage and parenting such as sexual attitudes and practices, kinship structures and taboos, male-female dominance and autonomy in the domestic setting, and familial patterns and responsibilities (Broude & Greene, 1976; Levinson & Malone, 1980; Schlegel, 1972; Stephens, 1963). But, as Mackey (1985) points out, investigations of adult male–child interactions are sparse.

In 1970, as the study of fathers attracted initial interest, investigators focused on a wide variety of issues: psychological influences on daughters, father–infant interactions, parental preferences, male child care, fathers' role in child development, and beginning formulations that a father–child bond may parallel the mother–child bond in terms of emotion and intensity (Appleton, 1981; Lamb, 1976; Lamb, 1977a; Lamb 1977b; Lamb 1977c; Levine, 1976; Lynn, 1974; &

Yablonsky, 1982). While Mackey (1985) pinpoints the 1970s as the decade in which researchers first recognize the American father figure as a potentially important and significant parent most researchers concur that the modern notion of a male parent equally participating throughout a child's lifetime is only selectively practiced in pockets of American society. One of the challenges of current researchers is to identify under what conditions this emergent father role is thriving.

Purpose

This chapter is an overview of fathering in cross-cultural perspective. Initially, we will look broadly at knowledge that can be gleaned from cross-species and holocultural studies; we later discuss aspects of the fathering role as it is enacted in a variety of cultures. Specific attention is given to five fathering functions: endowment, provision, protection, caregiving, and formation.

Overview of Fathering in Cross-Cultural Perspective

Culture comprises values, beliefs and customs that are shared by members of a social group. It may also be viewed as a set of rules or behavioral standards that are learned through enculturation. Culture thus refers to learned lifestyle patterns. In every society, culture patterns the experience of persons on the basis of their age and sex. This is clearly true of parental roles. The experience of fatherhood varies dramatically across cultures. That is, the way in which a father is expected to behave, and the ways in which others treat the father are highly variable. Diversity in the experience of fatherhood may be linked culturally to variations in the social structure such as kinship patterns, family structure, and economic system.

The study of fathering behaviors has not been a major focus of anthropologists or other social scientists until recently. The majority of previous accounts of fathering are marred by theoretical or methodological problems. For example, heavy reliance has been placed on the wife as informant. Thus, we generally have reports on fathering behaviors from the perspective of the mother. In addition, for research conducted by social scientists in North America, there has been a general confounding effect of social class with ethnicity. Consequently, many fathering behaviors that have been associated with a particular cultural or ethnic group, may , in fact, only be an artifact related more to poverty. For example, most social scientists who investigate interactions in black families have focused on the most problematic, economically devastated neighborhoods. In pointing out this fact, McAdoo (1986) calls for us to "give up the matricentric scientific notions that describe Black fathers as invisible men, who are not active in and have no power, control, or interest in the socialization of their children" (p. 118).

However, two lines of investigation can illuminate the way in which cultural aspects of fathering have been approached. These lines include reports from ethological studies of primate social behavior, and ethnographic accounts as analyzed primarily by the "culture and personality school" of anthropology.

Cross-Species Studies of Fathers

Anthropologists have studied paternal behavior from a variety of perspectives. At the cross-species level, anthropologists had long focused on primate infant socialization. However, only recently has this line of investigation included intensive study of the male's role. Because physiological paternity is difficult to establish, Simonds (1974) points out that social paternity rather than biological paternity may be most salient. On the other hand, Passingham (1984) remarks that when paternity can be determined with relative certainty, it is in such monogamous groups that the most dramatic examples of paternal involvement exist.

Not surprisingly, different species exhibit a wide range of paternal behavior. According to Poirier (1972), the primate infant's relationship with adult males is highly variable in terms of amount and time of onset. He contends that the group's social structure largely determines contact and illustrates this point by comparing two species of monkeys. He points out that the langur of Southeast Asia minimizes the amount of infant–adult male contact, whereas the Japanese Macaque allows certain infants contact with dominant adult males. Occasionally, primate males may be more involved in infant care than mothers. Mitchell and Brandt (1972) point out that in some species of New World monkeys, the father assumes the major care of an infant, while the mother's primary contacts are short periods of nursing and cleaning. For example, among troops of titi monkeys, the male holds or carries the infant unless it is being nursed. Additionally, among some baboon species, males may adopt an infant or juvenile and fully assume its care (after it no longer needs to nurse).

Burton (1972) summarized the adult male's role in infant socialization among a macaque troop he observed. These roles are interesting, particularly in comparison to paternal behaviors of humans. Macaque paternal behaviors included encouraging infant motor development, orienting the infant outward (toward the troop), reinforcing socially appropriate behaviors through reward (e.g., embrace), and extinguishing socially inappropriate behaviors through punishment (e.g., threat).

Indicators of the level of involvement of the male in infant socialization have also been identified: social structure of the group; the number of males in a troop (adult males at all levels of the primate order have high infant interactions if they are in one-male groups or monogamous family groups); and the familiarity of a given male with a female (the more familiar that relation, the more protective attention is provided her infant). Additionally, infant characteristics also influence paternal behavior in that adult males seem to direct more paternalistic protective behavior toward female infants than toward male infants, and for a longer period of time (Mitchell & Brandt, 1972).

Holocultural Reports

In anthropology, primary documentation of cross-cultural patterning of fathering has been derived from investigations which have theoretical linkages to the earlier Culture and Personality School. Individuals from this theoretical orientation contend that there is a strong linear relationship between social structural components (such as household structure, economic patterns, division of labor) and childrearing practices (disciplinary techniques, number of caretakers, salience of mother and father). They further contend that as a result of these, childrearing practices lead to and reinforce particular adult values, norms, and "personality types." The adult features, then, are reflected in the projective systems of a culture, such as religious dogma, art and recreation, games and play activities, and magical beliefs. Particular focus has been to correlate particular childrearing practices and conditions with adult behavior and expressive systems. In a wide series of studies, father absence (or low authority) has been linked with couvade (Munroe, Whiting, & Hally, 1973), the segregation of males at puberty (Kitahara, 1975), deliberate social instruction (Herzog, 1962), and male initiation ceremonies (Whiting, Kluckhohn, & Anthony, 1958). Similar studies linked paternal authority or closeness with bride theft (Ayres, 1974), games of chance (Barry & Roberts, 1972), and the status of women (Coltrane, 1988). However, a major limitation of each of these reports is that they draw inferences based on correlations of cultural elements. They cannot be interpreted as establishing a causal relationship among any of the variables of interest.

Reisman (1983), however, questioned the usefulness of this correlational approach. Reisman compared two cultures in which childrearing practices are virtually indistinguishable, but in which the adult behaviors differ dramatically. He contends that it is not the childrearing practice per se that is important in influencing adult personality; rather, it is the interpretation of the behavior for the child. That is, childrearing events or patterns in themselves do not influence adult personality. What may have salience is the meaning of the event or practice from the standpoint of each participant. For application to cross-cultural fathering, then, the focus would not be on the actual fathering behavior, but on the meaning children, kin and others placed on that behavior.

Nature of Fathering

The nature of fathering can be described in terms of interactional social responsibilities and functions; however in so doing, its complexity must be acknowledged. In the sections that follow we discuss the nature of fathering under five separate and discrete functions: endowment, provision, protection, caregiving, and formation. All functions are overlapping and interacting more complexly than researchers yet understand.

Despite this complexity and the added factor of differences between cultures, one concept, "investment," has universal application. Trivers (1972) first introduced the concept of "male parental investment" which evolutionarily validates many of the functions we discuss. He defined the term as "any investment by the parent in an individual offspring that increases the offspring's chance of surviving (and hence reproductive success) at the cost of the parent's ability to invest in other offspring" (p. 139). Even considering the concept of male parental investment (Trivers, 1972), the fact remains that high male parental investment is rare among vertebrates, especially among mammals (West & Konner, 1976).

Endowment Function: Legal Versus Genetic

The link between legal and genetic endowment of fatherhood was not self-evident throughout history. In Roman times, birth alone did not guarantee a recognized position as a son or daughter in a family. The will of the father as head of the family determined the child's status. Indeed, the all-powerful position of the *paterfamilias*, derived from Roman law, gave a father the prerogative whether or not to socially recognize the infant as his own. For newborns, this option was formalized through the special rite of *amphidromies*, by which the father picked up the infant in his arms and, before witnesses, walked around the house three times. Under Roman law, anyone—newborns and freed slaves alike—gained full filial rights in a family only through the father's will, rather than by mere virtue of a biological circumstance. A citizen of Rome did not "have" a child, but "took" a child; as the special rite would explain, the Roman father literally "raised" him (Delaisi de Parseval & Hurstel, 1987; & Veyne, 1987).

Romans and earlier Greeks who refused to socially recognize an infant had an alternative recourse. They could abandon the child by literally exposing it to the natural elements. It is not known how often children died by this socially accepted custom. Sometimes, if the child was left in a public place, it may have been with the hope that someone else would adopt the infant. The custom of abandonment itself, however, would not bring criticism from society.

In fact, Greeks and Romans thought it peculiar that Egyptians, Germans, and Jews abandoned none of their children but raised them all.

Greeks more frequently left female infants exposed to the elements:

In 1 B.C. a Greek wrote his wife: "If (touch wood!) you have a child, let it live if it is a boy. If it is a girl, expose it." It is not at all clear, however, that the Romans shared this prejudice. They exposed or drowned malformed infants. This, said Seneca, was not wrath but reason: "What is good must be set apart from what is good for nothing." The Romans also exposed the children of their daughters who had "gone astray." More important, some Romans abandoned their legitimate children because they were poor, and others because they wished to bequeath a decent fortune to their suriviving heirs. The poor abandoned the children they could not feed. . . . Even the wealthiest Roman might have reasons not to keep an unwanted child, especially if the birth disrupted plans for division of his estate. A rule of law stated that "the birth of a son (or daughter) breaks a will" sealed previously, unless the father were willing to disinherit in advance any offspring that might be born after the will was sealed. Some fathers may have felt that it was better to do away with a child than to disinherit it. (Veyne, 1987, pp. 9–10)

Exposure was also used as a matter of principle. Any husband unsure of a wife's fidelity could, on principle alone, publicly indicate his suspicions about adultery by exposing the newborn. The issue was not biological paternity because the same man at will could resort to the common practice of adopting a totally unrelated child as an heir, with public approval. The principle at hand was the insult of cuckoldry. Sometimes political or religious principles were recorded: when the beloved prince Germanicus died, Plebs voiced their displeasure with the gods' government by smashing temples, and some parents apparently exposed their infants in protest. When Nero murdered his mother Agrippina, an unknown person "exposed his child in the middle of the forum with a sign on which he had written: *I will not raise you, lest you cut your mother's throat*" (Veyne, 1987, p. 11).

Although the "voice of blood" spoke very little in Rome and Greece, this contrasts sharply with the way that the biological function is assumed in current Western cultures. Modern societies formulated kinship patterns defined "by blood" as a concrete, biogenetic term; it designates that 50% of each person's genetic makeup comes from a father and 50% from a mother. Paternal responsibility, obligations, and commitment that bond or fail to bond to a child may derive from the degree of certainty of this "natural" sense of blood kinship; a sense of direct "blood linkage" from past ancestry to future generations may directly originate from notions of a common possession of

genetic substance. In 20th century Western culture, "The relationship
. . . can never be severed, whatever its legal position. Legal rights may
be lost, but the blood relationship cannot be lost." This "objective fact
of nature" is actually "culturally defined" (Schneider, 1968, p. 24).
Further, a blood relationship is a relationship of identity. Aspects of
temperament, build, physiognomy, habits, intelligence, beauty, and
disposition frequently provide confirmation or denial of biological
identities between father and child.

*"Paternity" Versus "Fatherhood": New Functional Implications
from Biological Issues.*   The French have taken the lead in wrestling
with contemporary legal issues raised by new options created by
modern biomedical technologies (Delaisi de Parseval & Hurstel,
1987). Genetically, paternity can now be proven with a success rate
of 99.8%; as a result, courts could recognize a form of scientific
paternity—a dramatic shift of control from Roman times when
paterfamilias had the prerogative to accept or decline paternity.
However, establishing the genitor of the child through biology alone,
is not the only legal consideration in establishing filial and paternal
rights related to the interest of the social father. Three phenomena
explain the new concepts of of paternity in France:

1.   Fatherhood [can be] split between several individuals,
     sometimes not seen as cumulative, sometimes considered as
     additional [a sharing of the traditional functions of fathers].
2.   Intentional fatherhood (psychologically or morally speak-
     ing)—in other words—fatherhood through preconcep-
     tional adoption.
3.   Delayed or delayable fatherhood [AID[1]—Artificial Insemina-
     tion with Donor—where the genitor is separated from the
     social (educator and name-giver) father]; artificial homolo-
     gous insemination (where the donor takes on fatherhood
     from his own donated but artificially inseminated semen);
     fatherhood after cancer treatment (from semen donated be-
     fore treatment); and postmortem fatherhood (from stored
     frozen semen). (Delaisi de Parseval & Hurstel, 1987, p. 77)

   In vitro fertilizations (IVF) present different implications from
other intentional but noncoital forms of fatherhood, because they can
depend on one or several women (source of egg and womb may be

different) and on an unknown sperm donor. "Straight" IVF techniques, however, where the father's sperm and mother's egg are
united in a test tube, do not separate the genitor function from the
social father. This is also true of fathering with a surrogate mother,
with or without artificial insemination. That is, genitor and social
father functions are not divided.

New implications for fatherhood arise from more discrete
delineations between the biological father, established through scientific paternity—and the social father, established through any of
several noncoital but intentional routes to fatherhood. Future social
scientists and legal scholars alike will be challenged by the far-
reaching implications for filial and parental rights.

The taken-for-granted aspect of the biological function is seen
in the establishment of paternity inheritance rights and in sexual
taboos such as restrictions on premarital and extramarital intercourse. The rules governing sexual behavior vary greatly between
cultures. But even in cultures where adultery is permitted, occasional
sexual taboos and incest taboos still apply. As Stephens (1963) notes,
in permissive societies the problem of jealousy exists when spouses
engage in extramarital intercourse even when such activity is socially
permitted. Therefore, any confusion in paternity may jeopardize the
father–child relationship.

Widespread cross-cultural extramarital sexual norms provide a
contradictory picture on the importance of the biological function of
the father. On the one hand, the double standards for males and
females, with more restrictive norms for wives, can be easily explained in terms of the sociobiological paradigm (Broude, 1980); that
is, one can be certain of maternal heredity, but not always of the
paternal. On the other hand, less restrictive norms favor nonbiologi-
cal fathering. Rosenblatt and Hillabrant (1972) speculate that although restrictive norms on adultery may not be consciously related
to societal concerns of childlessness, there is a tendency for less
restrictive norms for adultery in societies providing few alternatives
to childlessness such as adoption, fosterage, or the taking of an
additional spouse or inseminator.

To what degree does biological inheritance affect the individual?
The answer depends, in part, on the nature of the characteristic
under consideration. Acquired characteristics, such as knowledge or
specific skills, are obviously not transmitted. However, trait propen-
sities may have a biological component. For example, research on

alcoholism has widely supported the biological connection. For example, when researchers compared sons of alcoholics reared by adoptive families from infancy to their brothers raised by the alcoholic parent, the brothers eventually developed alcoholism at the same high rates (17% and 25% respectively) (Goodwin et al., 1974). The endowment function can be seen with this condition.

Provision Function

A consensus of anthropologists accept that our earliest ancestors relied upon hunting and scavenging to provide sustenance. They view hunting as a male activity either from the beginning of time or as being progressively assumed by males at the gradual exclusion of females who developed essential nonhunting skills and techniques for proscuring and storing food. The rationale for this explanation is evolutionary: As male and female divisions of labor developed, Mackey (1985) argues that successful evolution depended on a mutual cooperation between genders. Selection processes would encourage the parents to share the food they had procured. And he further argues that a positive father–child bond facilitated the likelihood of sharing willingly and more generously. Levinson and Malone (1980) agree with Mackey (1985) in that channeling food stuffs to dependent children, either directly or through the female mediator, is a universal consistency across cultures and throughout time. May (1978) reported that even in a group of minimally involved fathers—husbands who thought the newborn in the family was primarily for their spouse and therefore would only minimally change their life—made one exception: that they, as breadwinner, would need to make more money.

Modern Western Culture. Two trends may account for many of the recent changes in the provisioning style of fathers for their children: (1) an increase in the number of married women working outside the home; and (2) a rise in the divorce rate (Jackson, 1987).

The first trend can be seen in the United States. According to the U.S. Bureau of the Census, from 1975 to 1988, the labor force participation rates for wives, in families with a husband present, rose from 44.5% in 1975 to 56.7% in 1988. The trend has been consistently rising since 1950 when the rate was only 24.8%—less than half of the rate today (Eshleman, 1988, p. 130).

Similarly, in Great Britain, during the first half of the century British married women in the work force represented a small percent of all workers (10%). But since World War II, the rate of economically active married women gradually increased to 57% of those under age 60 in 1981—although over half were employed part-time (less than 30 hours a week) (Jackson, 1987). Although working mothers impact greatly on the nature of who contributes to the family income, an increase in the number of women workers in Great Britain has subsequently made little impact on the structure or expectations of the British family. Most mothers actively working outside the home consider themselves economically dependent on the father, and the traditional assumption prevails: Men work to sustain the family with basic and necessary provisions, and most women work to supplement the income and improve the standard of living. That men are the chief breadwinners and women are economic dependents is in Great Britain institutionally reinforced by the laws on employment, social security, and taxation, which define economic dependence as women's normal status (Land, 1986).

The second trend, the rise in the divorce rate, has forced a greater number of couples to restructure their economic interdependence. However, at every income level, divorced fathers have less financial problems than divorced mothers, who in most instances have primary custody of the children. A minority of divorced or separated men fully contribute to the support of their children (Bird, 1979):

> A study made by the National Commission on the Observance of International Women's Year found that only one out of five divorced fathers supported their children. Only 7 percent paid alimony, and most people thought a working wife whould not even ask for it. That meant that she was likely to have to live—and very likely support their children, too—on a paycheck that amounted to little more than half of his. (Bird, 1979, p. 16)

Protection Function

In specifying the functions of fathering, Lewis and Feiring (1978) highlighted protection as one of the more important ones. It includes "protection from potential sources of danger, including inanimate sources—falling off trees or being burnt in fires—and animate, as in being eaten by a predator or taken by a nonkin" (p. 55).

Contemporary researchers prefer a less overt interpretation of this theoretical role and phrase the analysis in terms of fathering "concerns"—or in psychological/role terminology such as protector of the "'infant-mother symbiosis" (McNall, 1976; Henderson, 1980). If one defines protection in these less restrictive terms, then the protection function could include any direct calming effect on maternal anxiety and thereby an indirect effect on the infant's sense of security (Henderson, 1980). The protective function is not directly observed but, rather, is inferred from expressed apprehension over the well-being for family members. Concern refers to a feeling state where the individual accepts responsibility (Winnicott, 1965).

Increasingly more fathering studies are including "concern" as a variable of investigation. One of the earliest of these studies, (Pedersen & Robson, 1969) reported a disproportionately higher measure of paternal concern for female infants than for male infants in a sample of homogeneous middle-class fathers. The investigators speculated that this finding reflected a cultural expectation that males (even infants) *should* be hardier and therefore the fathers did not need to demonstrate paternal concern. Some researchers doubt the existence of an inferred but unobserved universal protection function. Instead, the supposed protector of hearth and kin may be an indicator of male aggressiveness or quest for territorial dominance. When societies have a warrior group or class, it is predominantly composed of males (Ember & Ember, 1971). The protection is communal; all warriors defend the entire group rather than fathers individually protecting their own children (West & Konner, 1976).

Anthropologists studying the male supremacist complex in 112 societies connect male supremacist practices to population control rather than to fathers protecting their offspring (Divale & Harris, 1976). Researchers cannot even assume that most of the warriors, as husbands, would indirectly be fighting to protect their children. Excessive warfare (ostensibly to "protect" the group) leads to increased polygyny (as a reward for successful warring), which, according to Divale and Harris (1976), results in many male warriors being wifeless (when the most aggressive males acquire a disproportionate number of women). More startling, warfare is associated with increased female infanticide (as a means to regulate population growth in the absence of effective or less costly alternatives). Regardless of the rationale or acceptability of its practice, infanticide counteracts the nobler assumption of paternal protector of hearth and kin.

Caregiving Function

Attempts to document paternal caregiving patterns have addressed a variety of activities, ranging from prenatal classes and labor room participation through direct and indirect infant care tasks. Some studies refer to the father as a mother-surrogate figure (Henderson, 1980; Winnicott, 1965). Current trends distinguish the traditional, modern, and emergent fathering roles (Fein, 1978).

The traditional perspective maintained an instrumental/expressive dichotomy in paternal and maternal roles. The father remained aloof and distant, and rarely participated in direct caregiving activities. The modern perspective valued successful child development as a goal of fathering. Although the modern father recognized that a father's behavior influenced his children, researchers from this perspective emphasized the negative effects found in father-absent families rather than focusing on actual fathering behaviors. The emergent perspective recognizes the benefit of active paternal involvement with infant care. While some studies focus on the effects on the infants, most researchers acknowledge a benefit to fathers and mothers as well.

It should be noted, however, that social and cultural variables may confound the notion of these trends. For example, Bushmen fathers of Subsaharan Africa have been found to be affectionate and indulgent with their children—often holding and cuddling their infants—yet they rarely provide routine childcare, which is given by the mothers who follow the traditional paradigm (West & Konner, 1976).

Attendance in prenatal classes, low complexity of the task, female sex of the infant, positive past parental relationship, and the father's participation in the birth were factors associated with infant caretaking (Katsh, 1981; Manion, 1977). One report advocates a change in hospital policy which would include fathers when routine caregiving skills are taught to mothers in the postpartum nursery (Gollober, 1976). In a study of intact families, a major correlate of heavy paternal involvement in childcare was the wife's feelings about her own father and his role in her childrearing experience (Radin, 1981).

Other investigators studied caregiving as part of a male–female housework time study. While acknowledging that paternal infant-caregiving contributions may be gradually increasing, all report that mothers continue to maintain the primary responsibility, especially while the mother is employed (Pleck, 1979). When patterns of divisions of labor for childcare are cross-culturally documented, the data usually represents the average, or modal pattern—which may subsume the likelihood of a considerable range of active levels of involvement of fathers in caregiving. Many researchers in this area recognize the need for studies using time-use techniques or family observations—coupled with a longitudinal design (Russell, 1987).

Comparing maternal and paternal caregiving activities frequently assumes a biological argument that the mother and not the father is equipped for and thereby more nurturant toward the offspring. Frodi (1980) debunked this assumption in an experimentally designed study that differentiated between paternal capacity, performance, and the discrepancy attributed to sex-stereotyping pressures. The study concluded that a father's sensitivity to the infant's responsiveness was a consequence rather than a precursor of involvement with the infant. In reviewing studies of infrahuman animal species which suggested that parenting behaviors by males are rare, Howells (1971) suggests that "the main lesson to be found from the study of the care given to young animals is that nature is flexible" (p. 128).

Emergent paternal-involvement studies in the United States measured a variety of behavioral aspects: play activities, direct caretaking (e.g., bathing), indirect child care tasks (e.g., washing diapers), overall availability by geographical proximity, involvement in decision-making regarding child care, affective involvement (e.g., cuddling), and taking sole responsibility for child care during some portion of the week (Cronenwett, 1982). The current methdological trend of collecting data directly from the fathers, either by interview or by observation, is a departure from earlier paternal-involvement studies where typically the researcher asked the mother for a report (Pedersen & Robson, 1969).

Cronenwett (1982) compared questionnaire and interview techniques and found that questionnaires were more likely to elicit egalitarian responses about paternal domestic roles and were less likely to reveal any problems which new parents face. Other methodological critiques of fathers' participation question the sensitivity of measuring the degree and extent of involvement (McKee, 1982).

Formation Function

The father's contribution to the formation of the child's character and personality is termed "formation function." Traditionally, where the mother does not work outside the home, this may also include the responsibility of introducing the child to the outside world. Fathers are seen as playing an important role in socializing the child in qualitatively different ways than the mother (Abelin, 1975; Lamb, 1975).

Wartime conditions in England during World War II provided the backdrop for studying infants without the benefit of intimate family formation influences. Research on these infants (Freud, 1944) documented the psychological and developmental traumas possible even in the presence of excellent physical caregiving.

From a more specific father-absent sample, Anderson (1968) reported that fatherless boys were more likely to become delinquent, that boys who became delinquent despite having fathers were more likely to have fathers who were either unusually passive or excessively chiding and punitive, and that fatherless boys were less likely to become delinquent if a surrogate father existed in their lives. Others, however, (Herzog & Sudia, 1972) questioned the assumption of singling out "father's absence" as necessarily the culprit variable to predict problems with school achievement, juvenile delinquency, or masculine identity.

Later Life Cycle Function.   Throughout the life cycle, power-deference relations between father and child change over time. Cross-culturally, if the father and child relate on equal terms, it is universally thought of as a weak power position for the father and the highest possible power position for the child. Cross-culturally, the father is rarely submissive to the child (Stephens, 1963).

A father's granting his son emancipation occurs gradually and is a matter of degree. In most societies, fathers do not grant full emancipation until their deaths. If a child's emancipation is delayed even beyond the death of the father, it is due to "two widespread social conditions: (1) deference customs, which in many societies are due to elder male kin as long as they live; and (2) the extended family" (Stephens, 1963, p. 393).

According to Roberts and Zuengler (1985), a father encounters two major issues at mid-life: launching children, and adjusting to role change. Fathers who were more closely involved with their children in earlier years are more likely to encounter conflict in the child-launching process. Fathers who were less involved with children are more likely to feel that they have missed valuable experiences, after children depart.

Concepts, Issues, and Patterns Related to Fathering

Variation in Human Male Parental Involvement

Abraham, Christopherson, and Kuehl (1984), in a comparison of Anglo and Navajo childrearing behaviors, identified that in both cultures, childrearing is considered to be more of a maternal than a paternal role. However, within the Anglo culture, parental role differentiation is greater. This was demonstrated by asking children which of their parents were more responsible for 14 parenting behaviors. For the Navajo children, mothers were perceived to be more responsible on only five of these behaviors, (as opposed to the 11 for Anglos).

In a cross-cultural analysis of previously published ethnographic records of 186 pre- and postindustrial societies, researchers concluded that "fathers around the world are not (statistically) significantly less warm toward their children than are mothers: neither are fathers more or less hostile, neglecting, or controlling than are mothers on the average" (Rohner & Rohner, 1981, p. 257).

In a subsequently questioned study of five industrialized countries[2] that revealed little difference in male involvement, Mackey and Day (1979) compared the frequency in which men in five countries appeared in public with a child or children during two time intervals: one when men could not be with children according to cultural norms (e.g., at work); the other was a time interval designated as optional time with children (e.g., weekends, holdays, and evenings). The incident of adult–male/child dyads roughly doubled in the United States, Ireland, and Japan in the time intervals when cultural norms permitted men to be present. Cultural norms discourage men from appearing in public with children during the hours men usually work, such as from 9 to 5, Monday through Friday. This result suggests that men in those countries would spend more time with children were they not precluded by conflicting cultural demands, such as work. Man/child dyads increased only about one-third in

Mexico and actually decreased in Spain; however, the difference was made up by a corresponding increase in man/woman/child triads and larger groups in those two countries. Mackey and Day conclude that there is little difference among the five countries in father involvement by the public appearance measure, nor in the interaction, touching, or proximity score, which they included in their study.

Based on the study cited above and a subsequent study (Mackey, 1985) one might agree that American children are not particularly deprived of nurturing behaviors from the father figure. However, as Levine (1988) pointed out, Mackey's methodology was "significantly flawed" for two reasons: first, because Mackey "never knew how many of his man-child dyads were father-child dyads," and second, because "proximity in public places during daylight hours" is a "superficial" indicator which leaves no room "to examine the behaviors that most people would think of as fathering, and he never really gets close enough to look at the dimensions of parenthood that lead others to urge that men should be doing more" (p. 554). Although it is understandable that the studies required a highly generalized indicator (proximity) for an examination of widely divergent cultures, the weakness of Mackey's generalized indicator dramatizes the difficulty in identifying universal behaviors of fathering involvement. More studies of specific behaviors in fathering involvement (cross-cultural and within cultures) are needed.

Father Differentiation in Care of Boys and Girls

Studies have examined paternal/maternal differential treatment on variables related to punishment/control, nurturance/affection, and achievement expectations (Maccoby, 1966). Patterns in parent–child interactions—on attachment, preferences, or behavior—emerged from one of three analytical approaches differentiating (1) father interactions from that of mothers with all children, not distinguishing the children by gender; (2) male children from female children, without differentiating the parents by gender; and (3) both parents and children by gender.

The evidence is clear that gender makes a difference in how adults relate to children as parents (Greenberg, 1978; Lamb, 1976, 1977a, 1977b, 1977c; Langlois & Downs, 1980; Lewis, 1972; Manion, 1977; Moss, 1967; Rohner & Rohner, 1981), as teachers, (Serbin,

O'Leary, Kent, & Tonick, 1973), and as health professionals in the hospital—even in the newborn nursery where the diaper hid the only distinguishing feature (Sternglanz, 1975). Cross-culturally, fathers differentiated between their male and female children in highly variable ways (Mackey, 1985; Rohner & Rohner, 1981). However, fathers merely conform to societal patterns of differential treatment—where the entire group usually gives male children more physical punishment, more negative feedback, and more positive feedback (praise and encouragement) than female children. The evidence is insufficient to generalize that fathers are unique in differentiating their interactions by gender of the child.

Many parents deny that they differentiate their involvement, discipline, or expectations by gender of the child. Parents in one study reported they wanted both their sons and daughters to be equally neat, helpful around the house, able to control their anger, considerate, able to control their crying, competitive, and able to defend themselves. However, when parents were asked "In what ways do you think boys and girls are different?" their responses indicated stereotypical expectations: They felt boys were naturally more active, competitive, aggressive, noisy, and messy; and that girls were naturally more gentle, neat, quiet, helpful, courteous, and so forth. Because the parents believed that boys and girls were naturally different, it is difficult to accept the claim of undifferentiated approaches to parenting (Maccoby & Jacklin, 1974).

Balance of Work and Parental Roles

According to Henderson (1980), although researchers have studied the effect of fathering on children, they have paid inadequate attention to the effect of fathering on fathers. Heath (1978) designed a longitudinal study to remedy this factor. Studying professional men from college age to their early 30s, Heath investigated what influence fathering had on the maturing process of men. Although given 20 opportunities to do so, 29% of the men selected no fathering activities as determinants of their maturity, and another 29% selected only one, for a combined total of 58%. They reported their wives and occupations more pervasively in their responses. Their wives corroborated these findings by reporting that while at home the fathers acted as if their minds were elsewhere. Heath concluded that parental competence is not central to a professional man's identity in the United States, at least in the early years of marriage and career.

Vaillant's monumental work confirms these findings. In his 35-year longitudinal study, Vaillant (1977) interviewed a small cohort of healthy men, following their maturational growth. All men faced stress and conflict at one time or another—many times from work and parenting responsibilities. But the most successful adaptations stemmed from the presence or absence of a maturational shift in adaptive styles, that is, the men who matured psychosocially over time were those who advanced through the Eriksonian life cycle.

In a study of employed, native English-speaking Canadian fathers, Horna and Lupri (1987), found that paternal participation in childcare activities increased when his wife also worked outside the home. However, researchers also contend since child-related activities were not listed among the five most desired activities which fathers would like to pursue more often if they had more time, these contemporary Canadian fathers probably play and spend as much leisure time with their children as they wish.

Couvade

Couvade describes the reaction of expectant fathers to the pregnancy and childbirth of their mates. Researchers have divided the phenomenon into ritual and modern couvade. Descriptions of ritual or institutional couvade are found exclusively in ethnographic reports of preindustrial cultures. Ritual couvade behaviors include special dress (Mead & Newton, 1967); a decrease in social contacts (Meigs, 1976; Read, 1952); confinement (Webster, 1942); avoidance of polluting substances (Monroe, 1980); and mock labor (Dawson, 1929). The term "modern couvade" refers to physical and emotional symptoms in men that appear during their partners' pregnancies. However, early couvade studies "did not compare their samples of expectant fathers with nonexpectant fathers in an effort to clarify the precise effect of pregnancy" (May & Perrin, 1985, p. 71).

In contrast, Clinton (1985, 1986) collected data from expectant fathers and a control group of demographically matched males. The data collection occurred at monthly intervals until 6 weeks postdelivery. Compared to nonexpectant men, expectant fathers in this repeated measures survey reported a statistically higher incidence and duration of colds during the first trimester and more unintentional weight gain during the third trimester.

Summary

Fathering behaviors are a complex constellation that combine culture, economic status, educational background, religion, and individual experiences. In this chapter, the wide range of sanctioned fathering behaviors has been examined in cross-cultural context. However, there is an important caveat related to this domain: while culture is an important component of the fatherhood constellation, it is clearly not deterministic.

Furthermore, as Bartz and Levine (1978) pointed out, discrete results from specific studies should not be broadly generalized. Specific childrearing practices which are functional and beneficial to a child's development may differ from one context to another. We must use caution in interpreting cross-cultural research so that we emerge with a relativist perspective rather than an ethnocentric bias.

Notes

1. AID fatherhood, highly organized in France, uniquely serves as a model for the specialist in the field. Delaisi de Parseval and Hurstel (1987) report that there are 20 sperm banks in France, called CECOS (Center for Study and Storage of Sperm). Since 1972, 15,000 children have been conceived and born from this method. More than 1,000 families have at least two children born through AID, and there are families with three, four, and five AID children. David (1985) reports that in the decade between 1973 and 1983, 5,000 voluntary and unpaid donors supplied the sperm.

2. The five countries included the United States (represented by Virginia), Ireland, Spain, Japan, and Mexico (represented by Coahuila). Mackey and Day selected these cultural areas for specific reasons:

> Spain and Mexico were selected as a consequence of the traditionally high value placed upon virility for men; i.e., the macho and machismo model (Pitt-Rivers, 1971; Michener, 1968; Lewis, 1960; Riggs, 1928; Brenan, 1957). Ireland was selected because of its traditionally strong family network (Arensberg, 1937; Arensberg and Kimball, 1968; Brody, 1973). Japan was selected

because of its non-Western heritage and its highly industrialized, urbanized social environment. (Hunsberger, 1972; Kawasaki, 1969; Olson, 1970)

References

Abelin, E. L. (1975). Some further observations and comments on the earliest role of the father. *International Journal of Psycho-Analysis, 56,* 293–302.

Abraham, K., Christopherson, V., & Kuehl, R. (1984). Navajo and Anglo childrearing behaviors: A cross-cultural comparison. *Journal of Comparative Family Studies, 15,* 373–388.

Anderson, R. E. (1968). Where's Dad? Paternal deprivation and delinquency. *Archives of General Psychiatry, 18,* 641–649.

Appleton, W. S. (1981). *Fathers and daughters: A father's powerful influence on a woman's life.* Garden City, NY: Doubleday.

Arensberg, C. (1937). *The Irish countryman.* Cambridge, MA: Macmillan. (Cited in Mackey & Day, 1979.)

Arensberg, C., & Kimball, S. T. (1968). *Family and community in Ireland* (2nd rev. ed.). Cambridge, MA: Harvard University Press. (Cited in Mackey & Day, 1979.)

Ayres, B. (1974). Bridge theft and raiding for wives in cross-cultural perspective. *Anthropological Quarterly, 51,* 238–252.

Barry, H., & Roberts, J. M. (1972). Infant socialization and games of change. *Ethnology, 11,* 296–308.

Bartz, K., & Levine, E. (1978). Childrearing by Black parents: A description and comparison to Anglo and Chicano parents. *Journal of Marriage and the Family, 40,* 709–720.

Bird, C. (1979). *The two-paycheck marriage: How women at work are changing life in America.* New York: Rawson, Wade.

Brenan, G. (1957). *South from Granada.* London: Hamish Hamilton. (Cited in Mackey & Day, 1979.)

Brody, H. (1973). *Inishkillane: Change and decline in the west of Ireland.* London: Penguin. (Cited in Mackey & Day, 1979.)

Broude, G. J. (1980). Extramarital sex norms in cross-cultural perspective. *Behavior Science Research, 3,* 181–218.

Broude, G. J., & Greene, S. J. (1976). Cross-cultural codes on twenty sexual attitudes and practices. *Ethnology, 15,* 409–429.

Burton, F. D. (1972). The integration of biology and behavior in the socialization of *Macaca Sylvana* in Gibralter. In F. E. Poivier (Ed.), *Primate socialization* (pp. 29–62). New York: Random House.

Chaucer, G. (1948). *The Canterbury tales* (R. M. Lumiansky, Trans.). New York: Simon & Schuster, (Original work published c. 1390.)

Clinton, J. (1985). *Couvade patterns and predictors (Final Report)*. Hyattsville, MD: Division of Nursing, U.S. Department of Health and Human Services (NTIS No. RONU00977).

Clinton, J. F. (1986). Expectant fathers at risk for couvade. *Nursing Research, 35,* 290–295.

Coltrane, S. (1988). Father-child relationships and the status of women: A cross-cultural study. *American Journal of Sociology, 93,* 1060–1095.

Cronenwett, L. R. (1982). Father participation in child care: A critical review. *Research in Nursing and Health, 5,* 63–72.

David, G. (1985). Don et utilisation du sperme [Gift and sperm use]. Proceedings of the international symposium "Genetique, procreation et droit" [Genetics, procreation and law]. Arles: Actes-Sud. (Cited in Delaisi de Parseval & Hurstel, 1987.)

Dawson, W. (1929). *The custom of couvade.* Manchester, England: Manchester University Press.

Delaisi de Parseval, G. D., & Hurstel, F. (1987). Paternity "a la Francaise." In M. E. Lamb (Ed.), *The father's role: Cross-cultural perspectives* (pp. 59–87). Hillsdale, NJ: Erlbaum.

De la Ronciere, C. (1988). Tuscan notables on the eve of the Renaissance. In G. Duby (Ed.), A. Goldhammer (Trans.), *A history of private life: Revelations of the medieval world (Vol. 2)* (pp. 157–309). Cambridge, MA: Belknap Press of Harvard University Press.

Divale, W. T., & Harris, M. (1976). Population, warfare, and the male supremacist complex. *American Anthropologist, 78,* 521–538.

Duby, G. (1988). Solitude: Eleventh to thirteenth century. In G. Duby (Ed.), A. Goldhammer (Trans.), *A history of private life: Revelations of the medieval world (Vol. 2)* (pp. 509–533). Cambridge, MA: Belknap Press of Harvard University Press.

Ember, M., & Ember, C. R. (1971). The conditions favoring matrilocal versus patrilocal residence. *American Anthropologist, 73,* 571–594.

Eshleman, J. R. (1988). *The family: An introduction.* Boston: Allyn & Bacon.

Fein, R. A. (1978). Research on fathering: Social policy and an emergent perspective. *Journal of Social Issues, 34,* 122–135.

Freud, A., & Burlingham, D. (1944). Foreword. In A. Freud & D. Burlingham (Eds.), *Infants without families: The case for and against residential nurseries* (pp. 7–9). New York: International University Press.

Frodi, A. M. (1980). Paternal-baby responsiveness and involvement. *Infant Mental Health Journal, 1,* 150–160.

Gollober, M. (1976). A comment on the need for father-infant postpartal interaction. *Journal of Obstetric and Gynecologic (JOGN) Nursing, 5,* 17–20.

Goodwin, D. W., Schulsinger, F., Moller, N., Hermansen, L., Winokur, G., & Guzo, S. B. (1974). Drinking problems in adopted and non-adopted sons of alcoholics. *Archives of General Psychiatry, 31,* 164–169.

Greenberg, S. (1978). *Right from the start: A guide to nonsexist child rearing.* Boston: Houghton & Mifflin.

Heath, D. H. (1978). What meaning and effects does fatherhood have for the maturing of professional men? *Merrill-Palmer Quarterly, 24,* 265–278.

Henderson, J. (1980). On fathering (the nature and functions of the father role): Part II. Conceptualization of fathering. *Canadian Journal of Psychiatry, 25,* 413–431.

Herzog, E., & Sudia, C. E. (1972). Families without fathers. *Childhood Education, 48,* 175–181.

Herzog, J. D. (1962). Deliberate instruction and household structure: A cross-cultural study. *Harvard Educational Review, 32,* 301–342.

Horna, J., & Lupri, E., (1987). Fathers' participation in work, family life and leisure: A Canadian experience. In C. Lewis & M. O'Brien (Eds.), *Reassessing fatherhood: New observations on fathers and the modern family* (pp. 54–73). Beverly Hills, CA: Sage.

Howells, J. G. (1971). Fathering. In J. G. Howells (Ed.), *Modern perspectives in child psychiatry.* New York: Bruner/Mazel. (Cited in Fein, 1978.)

Hunsberger, W. S. (1972). *Japan: New industrial giant.* South Orange, NJ: American Asian Educational Exchange. (Cited in Mackey & Day, 1979.)

Jackson, S. (1987). Great Britain. In M. E. Lamb (Ed.), *The father's role: Cross-cultural perspectives* (pp. 29–57). Hillsdale, NJ: Erlbaum.

Katsh, B. S. (1981). Fathers and infants: Reported caregiving and interaction. *Journal of Family Issues, 2,* 275–296.

Kawasaki, I. (1969). *Japan unmasked.* Rutland, VT: Charles E. Tuttle.

Kitahara, M. (1975). Significance of the father for the son's masculine identity. *Behavioral Science Research, 10,* 1–17.

Lamb, M. E. (1975). Fathers: Forgotten contributors to child development. *Human Development, 18,* 245–266.

Lamb, M. E. (1976). Twelve-month-olds and their parents: Interaction in a laboratory playroom. *Developmental Psychology, 12,* 237–244.

Lamb, M. E. (1977a). The development of mother-infant and father-infant attachments in the second year of life. *Developmental Psychology, 13,* 637–648.

Lamb, M. E. (1977b). The development of parental preferences in the first two years of life. *Sex Roles, 3,* 495–497.

Lamb, M. E. (1977c). Father-infant and mother-infant interaction in the first year of life. *Child Development, 48,* 167–181.

Land, H. (1986). Women and children last: The reform of social security. In M. Brenton & C. Ungerson (Eds.), *Yearbook of social policy 1985–86*. London: Routledge & Kegan Paul. (Cited in Jackson, 1987.)

Langlois, J. H., & Downs, A. C. (1980). Mothers, fathers, and peers as socialization agents of sex-typed play behaviors in young children. *Child Development, 51*, 1237–1247.

Levine, J. A. (1976). *Who will raise the children?: New options for fathers (and mothers)*. Philadelphia: J. B. Lippincott.

Levine, J. A. (1988). Book reviews. [Review of *Fathering behaviors: The dynamics of the man-child bond.*] *Journal of Marriage and the Family, 50*, 553–555.

Levinson, D., & Malone, M. J. (1980). *Toward explaining human culture: A critical review of the findings of worldwide cross-cultural research*. New Haven, CT: HRAF Press.

Lewis, M. (1972). State as an infant-environment interaction: An analysis of mother-infant interaction as a function of sex. *Merrill-Palmer Quarterly of Behavior and Development, 18*, 95–121.

Lewis, M., & Feiring, C. (1978). The child's social world. In R. M. Lerner & S. B. Graham (Eds.), *Child influences on marital and family interaction: A life-span perspective* (pp. 47–69). New York: Academic Press.

Lewis, O. (1960). *Tepoztlan*. New York: Holt, Rinehart, & Winston.

Lynn, D. B. (1974). *The father: His role in child development*. Monterey, CA: Brooks/Cole.

Maccoby, E. E. (Ed.). (1966). *The development of sex differences*. Stanford: Stanford University Press.

Maccoby, E. E., & Jacklin, C. N. (1974). *The psychology of sex differences*. Stanford, CA: Stanford University Press.

Mackey, W. C. (1985). *Fathering behaviors: The dynamics of the man-child bond*. New York: Plenum.

Mackey, W. C., & Day, R. D. (1979). Some indicators of fathering behaviors in the United States: A crosscultural examination of adult male–child interaction. *Journal of Marriage and the Family, 41*, 287–299.

Manion, J. (1977). A study of fathers and infant caretaking. *Birth and the Family Journal, 4*, 174–179.

May, K. A. (1978). Active involvement of expectant fathers in pregnancy: Some further considerations. *Journal of Obstetric, Gynecologic and Neonatal (JOGN) Nursing, 7*(2), 7–12.

May, K. A., & Perrin, S. P. (1985). Prelude: Pregnancy and birth. In S. M. H. Hanson & F. W. Bozett (Eds.), *Dimensions of fatherhood* (pp. 64–91). Beverly Hills, CA: Sage.

McAdoo, J. (1986). A Black perspective on the father's role in child development. *Men's changing roles in the family*. Haworth Press.

McKee, L. (1982). Fathers' participation in infant care: A critique. In

L. McKee & M. O'Brien (Eds.), *The father figure* (pp. 120–138). London: Tavistock.

McNall, L. K. (1976). Concerns of expectant fathers. In L. K. McNall & J. Galleener (Eds.), *Current practice in ob-gyn nursing* (pp. 161–178). St. Louis, MO: Mosby.

Mead, M., & Newton, N. (1967). Cultural patterning of perinatal behavior. In S. Richardson & A. Guttmacher (Eds.), *Childbearing—its social and psychological aspects* (pp. 142–244). Baltimore: Williams/Wilkins.

Meigs, A. S. (1976). Male pregnancy and the reduction of sexual opposition in a New Guinea Highlands society. *Ethnology, 15*, 393–407.

Michener, J. A. (1968). *Iberia*. New York: Random.

Mitchell, G., & Brandt, E. M. (1972). Paternal behavior in primates. In F. E. Poirier (Ed.), *Primate socialization* (pp. 173–206). New York: Random House.

Monroe, R. L. (1980). Male transvestism and the couvade: A psycho-cultural analysis. *Ethos, 8*, 49–59.

Moss, H. A. (1967). Sex, age, and state as determinants of mother–infant interaction. *Merrill-Palmer Quarterly of Behavior and Development, 13*, 19–36.

Munroe, R. L., Whiting, J. W. M., & Hally, D. J. (1973). Institutionalized male transvestism and sex distinctions. *American Anthropologist, 71*, 87–91.

Olson, L. (1970). *Japan in postwar Asia*. New York: Praeger.

Passingham, R. E., (1984). *The human primate*. San Francisco: Freeman.

Pedersen, F. A., & Robson, K. S. (1969). Father participation in infancy. *American Journal of Orthopsychiatry, 39*, 466–472.

Pitt-Rivers, J. A. (1971). *The people of the Sierra*. Chicago: University of Chicago Press. (Cited in Mackey & Day, 1979.)

Pleck, J. H. (1979). Men's family work: Three perspectives and some new data. *The Family Coordinator, 28*, 481–488.

Poirier, F. E. (1972). *Primate socialization*. New York: Random House.

Radin, N. (1981). Childrearing fathers in intact families, I: Some antecedents and consequences. *Merrill-Palmer Quarterly, 27*, 489–514.

Read, K. E. (1952). Nama cult of central highlands of New Guinea. *Southwestern Journal of Anthropology, 10*, 1–43.

Reisman, P. (1983). On the irrelevance of child rearing practices for the formation of personality. *Culture, Medicine and Society, 7*, 103–130.

Riggs, A. S. (1928). *The Spanish pageant*. Indianapolis, IN: Bobbs Merrill.

Roberts, C. L., & Zuengler, K. L. (1985). The postparental transition and beyond. In S. M. H. Hanson, & F. W. Bozett (Eds.), *Dimensions of fatherhood* (pp. 196–216). Beverly Hills, CA: Sage.

Rohner, R. P., & Rohner, E. C. (1981). Parental acceptance-rejection and parental control: Cross-cultural codes. *Ethnology, 20*, 245–257.

Rosenblatt, P. C., & Hillabrant, W. J. (1972). Divorce for childlessness and the regulation of adultery. *The Journal of Sex Research, 8*, 117–127.

Russell, G. (1987). Fatherhood in Australia. In M. E. Lamb (Ed.), *The father's role: Cross-cultural perspectives* (pp. 333–358). Hillsdale, NJ: Erlbaum.

Schlegel, A. (1972). *Male dominance and female autonomy: Domestic authority in matrilineal societies.* New Haven, CT: HRAF Press.

Schneider, D. M. (1968). *American kinship: A cultural account.* Englewood Cliffs, NJ: Prentice-Hall.

Serbin, L. A., O'Leary, K. D., Kent, R. N., & Tonick, I. J. (1973). A comparison of teacher response to the preacademic and problem behavior of boys and girls. *Child Development, 44*, 796–804.

Simonds, P. E. (1974). *The social primates.* New York: Harper and Row.

Stephens, W. N. (1963). *The family in cross-cultural perspective.* New York: Holt, Rinehart & Winston.

Sternglanz, S. (1975). Studies beyond the nuclear family—The newborn nursery. [Abstract] *Society for Research in Child Development.* (Cited in Greenberg, 1978.)

Trivers, R. L. (1972). Parental investment and sexual selection. In B. Campbell (Ed.), *Sexual selection and the descent of man: 1871–1971* (pp. 136–179). Chicago: Aldine.

Vaillant, G. E. (1977). *Adaptation to life.* Boston: Little, Brown.

Veyne, P. (1987). The Roman empire. In P. Veyne (Ed.), A. Goldhammer (Trans.), *A history of private life: From pagan Rome to Byzantium (Vol. 1)* (pp. 5–233). Cambridge, MA: Belknap Press of Harvard University Press.

Webster, H. (1942). *Taboo: A sociological study.* Stanford: Stanford University Press.

West, M. M., & Konner, M. J. (1976). The role of the father: An anthropological perspective. In M. E. Lamb (Ed.), *The role of the father in child development* (pp. 185–217). New York: Wiley.

Whiting, J. W., Kluckhohn, R., & Anthony, A. (1958). The function of male initiation ceremonies at puberty. In. E. E. Maccoby, T. M. Newcomb & E. L. Hartley (Eds.), *Readings in social psychology* (3rd Ed.) (pp. 359–370). New York: Holt, Rinehart, Winston.

Winnicott, D. W. (1965). *The maturational processes and the facilitating environment: Studies in the theory of emotional development.* New York: International Universities Press.

Yablonsky, L. (1982). *Fathers and sons.* New York: Simon & Schuster.

2

Fatherhood in Historical Perspective: The Role of Social Change

Peter N. Stearns

Historical knowledge about fatherhood in Western society, and in the United States, has developed considerably over the past 10 years, in response both to new interest in fathers in our own time and to immense strides in the study of changing family life. This essay, focused on the evolution of fatherhood in West-European and American society since about 1600, outlines the current state of our knowledge and its implications for other disciplinary approaches toward fathers' roles. It also suggests some leading agenda items for further consideration. This task entails exploration of some characteristic tensions in traditional patterns of Western fatherhood, where some strikingly contradictory images emerge; paternal impact has been complex for a long time. It also involves a grasp of basic changes brought by industrialization a century and a half ago, when new problems emerged that bedevil fathers still; and it focuses on another period of adaptation efforts in more recent decades, seen against both of the earlier (traditional and industrial) patterns.

The need for knowledge of the history of fatherhood should be obvious, if only because so many recent pleas and critiques have argued against a real or imagined past. In one formulation, fatherhood has long been cursed by certain limitations (too much stiffness, undue harshness) and for some time at least has suffered further from sheer lack of attention, as fathers, understandably or not, turned from active involvement and failed to do their fair share. Thus a sense develops of some longstanding (though rarely precisely delineated) traditions that need attention, and also a more recent transition that reduced fatherhood from a previously superior state. A few analysts (Pleck & Sawyer, 1974) go on to argue a much newer (and most would admit, rather tentative) additional transition, toward a new-style androgynous fathering—another twist in what is still a historical view.

It is beginning to be possible to offer a more nuanced approach to fatherhood's history than that suggested by generalized blasts against traditions or delighted surprise at some contemporary turnabout. It is true that much is still unknown. Several fine essays have sketched certain broad contours of the subject, both for the modern era (properly defined as the last century and a half or so) and for more traditional phases of the Western past (Demos, 1986; Rotundo, 1985). The vast surge of family history, as a major theme in the study of previous societies and processes of social change, has produced a host of specific findings, as spinoffs from an interest in family structure, emotions, children, or women's roles. In the main, however, historians concerned with family have been conditioned by the same evaluative criteria that until recently skewed other kinds of family research, in tending to see fathers as outsiders to the central family processes, economic men more than integral actors. The result is a knowledge of bits and pieces of the motivations and impact of fathers in key historical periods, along with somewhat better understanding of assigned roles, plus a set of good questions not yet fully resolved. We know enough about the past to guard against some of the simplest efforts to contrast the present, and we know also what caused some of the newer constraints against which fathers still struggle. But this is a historical field still developing, full of exciting prospects.

One point is sure: Even if our history is less clear or detailed than it should be, we do know some of the cultural traditions in which fatherhood has long operated in our society and we can pinpoint a number of key changes that help us understand past and present alike. It is also becoming apparent that we can assess paternal conditions now and in the future better if we pay closer attention to how they became what they are—in other words, to their history.

Traditional Context

It is logical to begin with the centuries before industrialization, roughly between 1500 to 1800, when a history of change dominated our larger understanding of Western family functions and relationships. This beginning point immediately raises one of the central questions that has not yet been fully addressed: Was there a distinctive tradition of fatherhood in Western society, before whatever modern clutter supervened?

The easy part of this question takes us to what is known about fathers' involvement with children, particularly sons, and how this contrasts with more modern roles. From a contemporary standpoint, the most obvious approach to premodern fathering suggests how simple and rewarding it must have been. Demos (1986) recently explored the contrast between current frustrations and colonial American satisfactions. Ordinary farmers and artisans, working in the home or close to it, interacted regularly with their offspring. Boys were sent to the fields to begin occasional labor quite young, by age five, which added to interaction some sense of shared production and training. It was easy, certainly, for fathers to find in their children— again, particularly boys—a sense of generational continuity, for in most instances they and their sons alike would expect that both property and skills would be passed on. In a minority of cases, the sons of farmers or peasants would be sent to the city to take up different careers, or in cases of overlarge broods would simply take off because prospects were so poor at home. Generally, however, fathers would find replicas of themselves in their sons, and this gave a wider purpose to life and work. At some points, naming practices that passed on paternal or other male-ancestral names both confirmed and reflected this kind of link (Smith, 1985).

Fathers also interacted with children even apart from work. They may not have played with children too formally—we know too little about fathers and leisure save that most children's recreation linked broad age groups across families, at the community level. Fathers were certainly responsible for much religious guidance. In Protestant homes this meant considerable Bible reading as well as earnest father–child conversation. The practice of paternal reading lasted well into the 19th century in many groups.

The interactions between fathers and children were not simply economic or religious during the premodern centuries. Emotional bonds could be strong as well. A study of fathers during the German Reformation, though based mainly on statements of ideals rather than knowledge of actual practice among ordinary families, urged a recognition of the loving, even gentle concern that fathers could bear for their children (Ozment, 1983). Diaries from 17th to 18th century Britain and America frequently reported fathers' delight in the birth of a child. They also reported real anguish at a child's illness and the frequent cases of infant death. Premodern people found it rather natural to be sad—men wept with relative ease—and certainly this sadness was often tapped by the fates of children. Somewhat ironically, many premodern fathers had little sense of what they might do to protect their offspring; accidents occurred that more modern parents would find readily preventable, but such was the lack of belief in the possibility of control that many premodern fathers could only bemoan the fate of a child who died in a fall down the stairs or into an unprotected well. (Stearns, 1988). The sense of attachment, nevertheless, shines through. Recently some historians (Pollock, 1984), have argued that premodern fathers (and mothers) were no different in their loving contacts with children than their modern counterparts. While this idea is exaggerated, it is also true that there was much less paternal cruelty and disdain, before the rise of more conscientious modern standards, than some authorities have claimed.

Fathering may have been particularly devoted in colonial America. Demos (1986) finds no cases of child abuse in 17th or 18th century Massachusetts—a part of his argument that fatherhood has deteriorated with modernization. An earlier study pointed to the effort New England families made to banish angry exchanges from family life, even when relationships with others in the neighborhood might prove surprisingly sour by our standards (Demos, 1970). There was a deliberate effort to build emotional security within the family amid a more acrimonious community life. Similarly, Greven (1972) detailed the ways in which colonial fathers might arrange unusually smooth transmissions of property to their sons, thus facilitating what by European standards were relatively early marriages and attendant economic independence. Abundant land encouraged smooth father–son relations, for an older parent could peel off part of the property without necessarily jeopardizing his own economic security. There were also good reasons for parental care in dealing with children. Frontier land provided an option for children who might rebel against parental harshness. Though relatively few colo-

nial sons (particularly in much-studied New England) actually pulled
up stakes, concern about children abandoning the home may well
have colored American parenthood, creating a strand of worry that
has lasted to the present day. This worry was not so virulent in more
settled societies. The labor of children, certainly, was vital to colonial
households, in an economy perenially short of hands; this was one
reason colonial families were unusually large, but it might also impel
solicitous fathering. Emotionally, also, colonial families seem to have
encouraged unusual intensity (again by early modern European standards) because of the disruption of large community bonds and the
sheer strangeness of the new land. Fathers and children alike, thus,
may have depended on each other as points of reference.

   There are a number of questions unanswered amid the findings
about concerned fatherhood in early modern society. Little is known
about fathers' relationships with young children, save in references
to worries about illness, or about the ways prosaic childrearing tasks
were parcelled between two parents. Rotundo (1985) sketches the
most likely scenario, in arguing that although colonial fathers often
showed keen interest in infants and toddlers, they left the practical
care and the really intimate bonds to mothers. Fathers took over
more definite authority only when children reached an age (probably
around three) when they could understand what parents told them,
at which point the paternal tutorial role developed. Fathers were
certainly eager, when a wife died, to find a replacement, in part
because of a desire to find a primary steward for the children. It is
also worth noting that widowers raising children alone, save for the
active help of older siblings, remained an important minority phenomenon into the 20th century. Interactions with daughters also
have yet to be explored, save again for diary references to interest
and attachment. Still, for all the gaps, a sense of the importance of
active, even loving fatherhood shines through in much of the recent
work on early modern family history. Revealingly, when colonial
sons wrote home, from school or apprenticeship, they wrote their
fathers, asking only to be remembered to their mothers. Had there
been football teams and television, "Hi, Dad" would have flourished,
in contrast to the obligatory "Hi, Mom's" of our own day.

   Yet there remains another side that reminds us of some distinctive needs and standards. Premodern Western society was firmly
patriarchal; indeed, various historians have argued that the patriarchal qualities increased in the 16th and 17th centuries (Stone, 1980).

Christianity held up a model of a stern, judgmental God, the Father, and while this view had been qualified during the Middle Ages by increasing emphasis on Christ and Mary as interceder, the linkage between authority and fatherhood was never shaken. The linkage may actually have grown firmer, at least in Northern Europe, as a function of the religious changes that led to and were furthered by the Reformation. Certainly Protestants heavily emphasized the themes of control and judgment as part of God's paternity. Erikson (1962) suggested that a paternal dominance helped prod Martin Luther to emphasize strict control in his view of the Godhead. Changes in Western family and economic life by the 16th century, led to stress on nuclear family units built around the economic prowess of the husband-father and on the property controlled by this father. This established a material base for the reliance on patriarchal firmness in the direction of children; in that a child's ultimate livelihood depended directly on a father's willingness to give or bequeath land.

Patriarchy meant, in practice, an abundant willingness to intervene in children's lives. Fathers played a great role in arranging or forbidding marriages, guiding choices of training, and in cases of dispute, they assumed control over children from their wives. Patriarchy, Western-style, also meant firm discipline. Fathers administered frequent physical punishment. By the 17th century, sensitive men reported some concern about controlling their tempers, in the interest of proper humility, but these injunctions were rarely explicitly directed to behaviors concerning children. Beatings and authority frequently went hand in hand. American Indians were appalled at the routine physical harshness of white-settler parents, particularly fathers (Erikson, 1964). Even if outright child abuse (however defined) was rare, as Demos (1970) claims for colonial New England, many fathers had abundant outlets for considerable nastiness.

In some cases the stress of physical punishment involved more than the enforcement of authority. Some premodern fathers vented no small amount of venom on their offsprings. For example, King Henry IV of France, early in the 17th century, insisted on daily whippings of his son, the future Louis XIII, on grounds that he had been treated similarly and the results were good. He also randomly deprived the child of cherished toys. A pattern of intergenerational anger may have been at work in cases like this, in which a harshly treated boy saved up a rage he could not safely express against his attackers, subsequently taking it out on his own offspring (Hunt, 1970; DeMause, 1974). Harsh fathers were not, to be sure, necessarily consistent, sometimes alternating the explicitly punitive mood with periods of indulgence in which a young child might be treated virtually as a toy. Henry IV, once again, frequently dandled his boy on his knee in front of company, playing amusedly with his genitals. (While this may also have been abusive, it was not so regarded, being held at the time as a direct alternative to discipline.)

The tensions implicit in harsh patriarchy showed up in later father–child interactions. Many families, in colonial America as in Western Europe, sent teenage children to work as servants for other households, often binding them to rigid contracts and virtually assuring stern treatment. There was solid economic motivation for this practice; overlarge broods could be sustained when parcelled out to childless households where labor was needed. But it is possible also that the practice of sending children away was designed to minimize tensions, particularly between sons and fathers, at an age when discipline might otherwise be challenged. Certainly there is abundant indication of conflict between young-adult sons and their fathers. A few cases of dispute between adult daughters and fathers have also surfaced, particularly in quarrels over marriage arrangements. Aging fathers frequently had to write out careful contracts with their sons, lest they themselves be mistreated by their sons as their physical capacities waned. Indeed, as in 18th century France, older fathers constituted the largest category of murder victims, at the hands of family members (Fischer, 1977; Stearns, 1977). Again, economics underlay these tensions in part. Sons could not reach full economic adulthood or marry until their fathers turned over some or all of the family property, which virtually assured some ill-feeling. This proved true by the 18th century in land-blessed America, as the best property in the settled areas began to run short (Greven, 1972). Some emotion entered in as well, as adult sons took out on older parents some of the frustrations that had not been safely expressed when patriarchy was in full vigor. Certainly more than one son greeted illness or death of father with relief or indifference, sometimes not even mentioning the event in an otherwise detailed account, at other times expressing pleasure that independence had arrived at last.

Western fatherhood was thus Janus-faced, and it is hard to capture in a single formula. It involved concern, even affection, but also stern authority and frequent tension. This combination had several consequences. One, obvious enough but important to assert against facile stereotypes, is that individual fathers varied widely, because they could stress one or the other aspect of the general context of fatherhood. Variation may have been greater than random, because of conflicting poles of affectionate concern and patriarchal discipline. Some distinct subgroups might develop around various definitions of the tension. Greven (1977) described for 18th century America, three approaches to parenthood based on religious-psychological affiliations (in which fathers took an important though not total role). In the first approach, the evangelical tradition, harsh discipline produced internal stresses that were manifested in intolerance to outsiders. In the second or moderate tradition, carefully restrained parental emotions, doused with more liberal if gentle affection, aimed at producing personal restraint. The third approach, particularly current among the Southern planter groups, yielded unusual self-approval.

Personal and group variation, however, should not obscure the generalizations on the overall complexity of fatherhood ideals, and also some effort toward explaining the complexity itself. Many cultural traditions may yield complex paternal models; work is needed in comparative history, which is virtually nonexistent, to claim with any certainty that the tensions sketched for the West are really distinctive. Yet, for a combination of cultural and structural reasons, Western traditions may have been unique.

Western Christian beliefs, in the first place, virtually built in some tension in manhood ideals, and therefore in paternal behavior especially toward sons. God the Father and Christ the merciful interceder might be mirrored in fluctuating paternal impulses even within the same individual. Combined with this cultural ambivalence were the unusual needs of Western family organization. From the later Middle Ages onward—that is, well before the early modern centuries themselves—a distinctive Western-style family form had become characteristic among the masses of West Europeans, and with a few modifications it carried over to North America. The European-style family involved relatively late marriage age (late 20s for men and women in early modern Western Europe, only a bit earlier in the New World) and attendant emphasis on the independence of each nuclear unit. Some extended family contacts existed, but they were relatively weak if only because there was little overlap, given existing longevity, between an older generation and its grand-children. These features, in turn, tended at once to encourage men to emphasize their control, when they were able finally to form families, and yet to modify it in practice because of the need for careful cooperation among nuclear-family members. A father might assert his authority in principle, but in fact conciliate and care for his wife and children given daily, close interaction and mutual dependence.

Thus, a distinctive Western complexity both in ideals and practical behaviors for fathers can be suggested, which certainly answered to some unusual features of Western religion and family organization. While resultant tensions may have shown up in individual or group variations, or in some differences that may have separated colonial American fathers from their more strictly patriarchal European cousins, they may more commonly have fed an ambivalence within individual fathers themselves.

Preindustrial Change: A New Model-Father

The ambivalence of Western fatherhood helped produce change. Early modern fatherhood was not a constant; from the late 17th century onward, paternal ideals increasingly reduced the emphasis on patriarchal dominance and physical discipline. Family historians in France, Britain, and the colonial United States have stressed a growing willingness to define families as collections of partially independent individuals, as opposed to strictest hierarchy, plus a growing concern for developing emotional bonds among family members. Thus, fathers became more sensitive to children's wishes in courtship and marriage, more commonly pulling back, whatever the economic desirabilities, from a match that a cherished daughter may have found repulsive. Family manuals began to emphasize the importance of affectionate collaboration within the family and the need for men to curb their tempers in dealing with children (Stone, 1980; Flandrin, 1976; Trumbach, 1978). Contacts with babies increased in some instances; in the British aristocracy, fathers began to attend at childbirth. A growing number of fathers began to take some pride in avoiding frequent physical punishment. Discipline with this new model was designed to emphasize moral instruction and isolation rather than beatings where chastisement was required. While change came slowly, it does seem that a growing number of men at some point in the 18th or early 19th centuries tried to break away from some of the practices of their own fathers (Greven, 1973; McLaughlin, 1975).

Several factors impelled the new standards for fathers. In addition to the fact that an affectionate strand was already in place in the Western tradition, an increasingly commercialized economy reduced community closeness, prompting men to look to the family for emotional support. Here were the origins of a public–private distinction, with the family as the center of a warmer, purer alternative to the outside world of the marketplace. This would blossom more fully in the 19th century, and it definitely encouraged men to downplay authority in favor of some intimacy. More important still were religious and political ideologies—a new cultural context—that urged a new emotional balance and reduction of formal hierarchy. Not only Protestantism but some currents in Catholicism emphasized the importance and validity of family sentiments, and stressed the antithesis between love and anger in the home. Enlightenment values, in urging the educability and innate goodness of children and some fundamental human equalities, similarly worked against unadulterated patriarchy. Historians are, admittedly, still debating how much really changed in paternal behavior. They also disagree over whether the new impulses centered primarily in the upper and middle classes, later to "trickle down" to other groups, or whether lower-class people, themselves caught up in a more commercial economy, found it desirable to seek new family satisfactions and loosen some traditional controls. As wage-paying jobs became more common, for example, a father's authority over older teenagers undoubtedly declined, for the threat of withholding property became less effective. This might, for many family workers, have conjoined with new emotional and cultural impulses in ways not totally different from the patterns emerging among the more visible parents of the upper classes. At all levels, shifts in ideals undoubtedly changed more rapidly and sytematically than actual paternal behavior. Complexity by no means disappeared, even within individual fathers.

These currents of change were important, nevertheless, alongside the earlier tensions within Western paternal standards discussed earlier. A more commercial economic context and a real alteration in family culture were producing new norms and new parental needs, in advance of a fully modern family environment. These currents would continue even as additional, and in many ways profoundly disorienting, factors came into play.

The Modern Context

Two fundamental changes emerged fully in the 19th century as a result of the industrial revolution, decisively altering the practice of fathering without obliterating all traces of the traditional tensions or the 18th-century evolution. First, in a pattern launched even earlier but becoming increasingly standard during the 19th century, property declined in importance for many families, and with it the clearest bases for traditional paternal control. Growing numbers of rural families, and the vast majority of urban families, lost hold over producing property, as a result of the growing commercialization of economic life and the force of population growth. Paternal authority did not disappear, even in most proletarian families, as we will see. But the decline of the property base meant that this authority might have to be asserted more stridently, perhaps through more direct physical force. The decline of property as a paternal pillar also encouraged resentment, even some rebellion, by children, when they could see a father's insistence on authority, once unsupported by the power to assure (or withdraw) inheritance, as essentially hollow. Why obey, when father had no real power to reward?

Second, work increasingly separated from family. Factory workers were absent from home, and therefore from effective contact with young children and older girls, for 12 to 14 hours a day. While small businessmen could continue a family–work link, most middle-class occupations separated work from residence also. Even among rural families, where the home–work separation was less salient, growing numbers of transient laborers, disproportionately male, suffered a similar disruption for long periods if they had families.

These trends were not of course uniform, nor did they occur overnight except for a few particular groups such as the new factory workforce. Italian immigrants to the United States, while they could not avoid some family–work separation, were notorious for their attempts to mitigate its effects, trying to shun factory jobs and prevent daughters from entering the nonfamilial labor force. But the basic pressures were overwhelming, and they worked toward similar results in diminishing the authority and the daily involvement of fathers with their children. Other factors supplemented the new framework. Increased mandatory schooling both symbolized and furthered the diminution of fathers' roles as moral tutors and practical teachers. Tensions at work could add to the distancing between fathers and children even in leisure hours. Many fathers paused on the way home to drink, as male patterns of recreation cut into family time. Many fathers reported new problems in dealing with children after a tense day at work, often finding themselves harsher with their offspring than they intended because of work-induced strain and fatigue (Stearns, 1990). Even middle-class fathers who liked to believe themselves superior to working-class parents frequently insisted on peace and quiet when they came home, so mothers enjoined young children to respectful restraint in contrast to the noise and pranks encouraged when men were absent.

Fatherhood declined in this context, as a practical force in the lives of families and of men themselves. Yet within this framework a number of reactions developed that complicated the basic trends, sometimes exacerbating but sometimes partially countering their impact. Rather than simply claiming an unadulterated transformation, the real task of the historian of modern fatherhood is to grasp the variety of responses that change evoked, some of which built quite recognizably on earlier themes and tensions.

Responses: Bad Fathers and Triumphant Mothers

The easiest reactions to chart, and they were unquestionably important, built on the economic forces while eating still further into the paternal fabric. These reactions developed in the 19th century and extended into the 20th, thus affecting fatherhood even today.

First, the number of "bad" fathers increased, and indeed a new ability to define "bad" fathers became an important part of modern social life (Furstenberg, 1988). While abandonment of children was hardly a modern invention, it undoubtedly increased. Illegitimate birth rates began to soar throughout Western society from 1780 through much of the 19th century, rising from 2–4% to 10–12% of total births (Shorter, 1975). Although some premarital births helped lead to marriage, many did not. The opportunities many men had to move to different cities, and the stark problems of winning economic security in an economy increasingly based on market fluctuations, heightened both the possibility of and the need for transiency. Some more settled fathers were delinquent or abusive as well. The pressures of work, inadequacies of lower-class housing, and the lure of male camaraderie lead to an increase in drinking or other kinds of nonfamily involvement. The decline of community supervision, as cities replaced village environments and reduced neighborhood contacts and cohesion, removed a previous key source of enforcement of at least minimally acceptable paternal behavior. Delinquent fathers were not concentrated simply in the lowest urban classes, for business failures or other uncertainties might drive middle-class men to abandon their families. Such abandonments indeed produced the background of more than one 19th century feminist, left in childhood to exclusive maternal care by a business or professional father who never managed to get his affairs in order (McGovern, 1968). The "bad father" response to the new uncertainties of industrial, urban life—and to the new separation between men's primary sphere and the family—was by no means typical, and indeed the condemnation of bad fathers' behavior reflected more positive paternal roles' but it remained an important variant for fathers from the 19th century onward.

A more general response to the industrial context for fathering involved a deliberate reappraisal of maternal functions. From the 1840s onward the preponderance of expert literature written for parents was in fact directed almost exclusively to mothers. Much of it was explicitly titled "for mothers." The new breed of advice writers assumed that mothers had almost sole daily responsibility for children. Beyond this, in accordance with the gender imagery that arose in the 19th century and endures still today to a degree, the "experts" assumed that mothers also had the necessary inherent virtues in dealing with moralizing children—and that men largely lacked these. Moralization functions, previously a male domain, now became female, for women were by nature more moral—more naturally sexually pure, less aggressive—than men according to the standard imagery. Women could also fill more recently-defined needs, in providing love, nurturance and comfort along with exacting physical care. While some parental advice was not explicitly gender-specific, there was throughout the 19th and 20th centuries, a dearth of comment on anything that fathers as fathers could usefully do in terms of active child care or guidance (Wishy, 1968).

The literal absence of any advice literature for fathers, in a period when their roles were changing so greatly and when hortatory family manuals were so widely in demand in middle-class homes, is truly striking. The people who officially shaped family standards, men and women alike, clearly decided that there were no specific functions for fathers beyond the (admittedly demanding) task of providing for their families economically. Growing recognition of the division between work and home—a phenomenon explicitly noted in many advice manuals into the 1920s—led to abundant new responsibilities for women, but barely a wedge for fathers. Only a few modest exceptions developed even by the mid-20th century. Some comment emerged on the importance fathers could gain in providing role models for boys, but this was largely passive in tone, involving coexistence more than interaction. Standard 20th century treatments of sibling rivalry urged that fathers jump in when a new baby was born, to help provide compensatory attention to the older child. This was a temporary assignment, however, and childrearing manuals left primary responsibility for dealing with older siblings to mothers. A vast outpouring of expert advice, clothed in the latest scientific findings, thus largely shunned the father, building on but also perhaps exacerbating the work-based barriers to daily father–child interaction. Dr. Spock's first edition (1946) devoted a mere nine pages to the father's role, explicitly noting that fathers should serve but occasional functions in childcare, mainly to give mothers a periodic rest. Most specific advice sections, in this most popular of all the expert publications, were deliberately addressed to mothers alone.

Advice, to be sure, is not reality. There were other responses to the industrial context of family life which demonstrate that the absence of official new standards did not paralyze response. Unquestionably, however, the tone of the family manuals not only reflected but also created new parenting dynamics, in giving traditional paternal functions to mothers and creating a new and specifically feminine aura of mother love as a crucial (and by definition nonpaternal) ingredient in caring for children. Wider public imagery picked up this theme, as advertisements for children's products call on maternal attention alone. Dominant legal formulations quickly formalized the new division of paternal labor. Custody for children in cases of marital disruption, once a virtually unchallenged male monopoly as part of the property framework of patriarchy, now moved toward mothers. By the end of the 19th century, in Western Europe and the United States alike, custody awards were almost invariably going to mothers while few fathers even bothered to contest. The early-20th century "tender years" doctrine, which held that the interests of children under 12 were invariably served by awarding custody to mothers, simply rigidified longer-standing trends. Here clearly, was the product of the growing belief that mothers almost automatically had superior parenting skills.

Finally, there is evidence that many men internalized the same message, judging that they were incompetent in dealing at least with young children. The growing tendency to rely on female school-teachers for primary grades, while it had much to do with an ability to get by with lower salaries, reflected a widespread male belief that women had essential emotional and civilizing qualities that men lacked. Many fathers themselves, while not abandoning family responsibility, thus ceded most of the active parental terrain.

Industrial Fatherhood: More Active Responses

The central role assigned to fathers with industrialization involved breadwinning, the adequate provision for children through work and wages won outside the home. This role provided the chief criterion for measuring good fatherhood over a century-long span, for insufficient provision was a badge of male failure. This shift to a largely economic role built of course on the more traditional responsibilities of fathers in an agricultural society, but it gained new emphasis amid the uncertainties of industrialization, and as the other traditional functions of fathers tended to narrow. There is general agreement that the breadwinning role won general applause—from family experts and most actual family members—from the 19th century until after World War II. A man could feel not only responsible, but also deeply, even emotionally invested in fulfilling this role, which helps explain why the industrial context for fathering was so rarely attacked: while the fatherhood it engendered was different, it was by no means inactive. Breadwinning could measure real devotion.

Furthermore, economic provision for families could be variously interpreted, imbued with new meanings depending both on social status and paternal motivation. In the middle-class value system, urgently preached to immigrants and workers as well, a good father would not only support his children but provide the means by which they could launch themselves on successful adult careers, even exceed their fathers in achievement. Good fathers redefined what they owed their children as the American mobility ethic spread, as education became more widely valued, and as fathers and mothers alike joined in decisions to limit birth rates (a process that in the United States began as early as the 1790s), thus allowing greater attention to each individual child. By the late 19th century, fathers began providing children with allowances, paying for increasingly elaborate educations and other accoutrements, and in a host of ways indicating economically how much they valued children. As fathers' outlays demonstrated how valuable children had become, even as their direct economic contributions to the family had declined, it is easy to see how, at least in male eyes, the fathering role could be seen as demanding, active and indeed expressive (Zelizer, 1985). Because the late-20th century definition of fathering had changed, toward denigrating the provider role as cold and inadequate, contemporary Americans may fail to appreciate its century old meaning, when it served to define many a father's hopes for his children.

Furthermore, fathers could embellish the provider role with other relationships, often rather deliberately trying to modify the limitations on wider paternal functions impelled by the industrial context. Thus while interaction with young children almost inevitably declined in urban settings, many fathers actually increased their involvement in the work activities of teenagers. The preindustrial practice of sending younger teenagers away for periods of service elsewhere declined rapidly by the late 19th century, and many working-class fathers (and middle-class fathers as well, particularly before the generalization of secondary education) quickly engaged teenage sons with their work. Father–son tandems frequently operated in factories, where skilled workers were encouraged to hire their own assistants and where the resultant stabilization of the labor force pleased owners and workers alike. Obviously, there were limitations to the roles fathers could claim in training and guiding their sons economically, for among other things technological change frequently disrupts generational continuity. But the effort was common, which means the narrowing of fatherhood cannot be assumed to glibly.

Still more commonly fathers might continue to insist on key disciplinary roles, and in some families an authoritarian patriarchal tone seems to have increased again during the 19th century. The economic power attendant on the primary breadwinning role could turn in this direction, and authority claims might help fathers compensate for their loss of more intimate involvement with their families. Harsh discipline might show at various social levels, and could of course shade into outright abuse. Many fathers, however, were really trying to build on earlier patriarchal tradition, using authority to continue to shape (or attempt to shape) some moral framework for their children. Many men also blended patriarchalism with some of the newer standards in childrearing, taking pride, for example, in avoiding physical punishment while insisting on docile obedience. New concerns about instilling active sexual discipline, in urban environments filled with new temptations, added another dimension to paternal moral concerns (McLaughlin, 1975; Filene, 1986).

Another channel for asserting authority, but one which promised more innovative involvements with boys, stressed the importance of distinguishing gender characteristics among children, with fathers playing a key role in assuring that boys would grow up to be men. Gender differentiation unquestionably increased in importance in 19th century childrearing and many women joined with men in wanting to be sure, precisely because of greater female involvement in childcare, that boys developed suitably distinctive characteristics. Concern for gender differentiation increased in the later decades of the 19th century, partly because of heightened realization of the implications of the new roles assigned to men and women, which implied different personality roles to some degree. Boys, thus, had to be ready for competitive business life, possibly for military activity (a greater theme in Western Europe), in contrast to the domestic virtues to be instilled in girls. Concern grew also because of the increased importance of motherhood, commonly joined now by women's dominance in primary school teaching. Somehow, amid all this feminine attention, boys had to be made tough and assertive.

Schools could help in this process, as with burgeoning sports programs; mothers could insist that boys learn to react strongly to provocation. But fathers had an obvious role, and they could seize on the special wisdom they had for boys as a means of countering the new limitations on their other involvements as parents. Further, by setting themselves up as arbiters of manhood, they could have a lasting impact on boys themselves, even when their actual interaction was sporadic at best.

The industrial context for fatherhood thus encouraged an assertive kind of masculine guidance (Dubbert, 1979). Fathers might take it upon themselves, against the official standards of Victorian morality, to initiate their sons sexually, by a birthday visit to a local brothel. They might promote sports prowess, urging their sons on by gifts of equipment such as boxing gloves, recommended as a means of teaching boys to channel aggression without losing the aggressive impulse (Stearns & Stearns, 1986). Unquestionably, fathers deliberately differed from mothers (and from schoolteachers) in their evaluation of children's habits; studies in the 1920s showed them much more tolerant of aggressive behavior by boys, much more concerned about passivity. The distinctiveness of paternal criteria, and the mixed signals that boys might receive were significant elements in turn-of-the-century family life, and the standards urged by fathers could be more influential, even though enforced less regularly than those from other sources. Girls, too, could become touched by fathers' values, as the growing realization of the paternal role in instilling an achievement ethic may suggest.

Finally, some fathers attempted to increase their emotional involvement with children, building on the trends that had taken shape before the industrial revolution. The 19th century ideal of a tightly knit, affectionate family could draw men in toward active participation, even if wives and mothers had new standard-setting power. Men were urged to learn to restrain tempers and develop an active loving sense, and these injunctions for some fathers actually increased affective involvement (if not detailed caretaking) in childhood. Victorian fathers could and did dandle young children on their knees, displaying vigorous affection toward children (particularly daughters, a theme that deserves more attention). Many fathers, indeed, found themselves caught in interesting but not necessarily unproductive tensions between general standards of assertive manhood and the special virtues required for intimate family life (Filene,

1986). While for some men the sentimental attachment to family might be rather sterile—showing pictures of the kiddies to tavern-mates—for others it described a more active reality.

Obviously, Western fatherhood continued to be characterized by great variety and considerable complexity, as industrial society took shape in the later 19th and early 20th centuries. There was a reduction in the range and importance of paternal activities, on the average. This reduction may have been greater at the level of image, however, than in reality. Fictional accounts seized on bad fathers or harsh authoritarians—a staple, for example, in popular stories for women in the 1920s, with references to selfish fathers "chaining" daughters to obedience and service (Honey, in press). Such fiction suggested the necessity of rebellion against fathers as a condition of proper selfhood. Or fathers were made, comic-book style, into bumbling figures of fun. But many real-life fathers remained competent and involved, and some attempted to merge an undeniable impulse toward authoritarianism or manly assertiveness, with real affection (and no small economic commitment).

New work arrangements and marketplace pressures undeniably changed fathering, but they did not obliterate earlier thrusts. Fathers were not powerless in their response, and by emphasizing earlier traditions they partially answered, though diversely, the challenges of the new family context.

Change in the 20th Century

The process of adjustment continued after the early 20th century. Workplace pressures lessened to some degree from the 1920s onward, as men enjoyed greater leisure time. Leisure patterns themselves modified, away for example from reliance on neighborhood bars. Depression and war, which produced the first durable trends toward greater wage-work involvement for married women, began to reduce the centrality of fathers' breadwinning role. Finally, particularly after 1940, new childrearing standards, that urged more emotional restraint on boys in the interests of cooperative adult personalities, gradually weakened the legitimacy of aggressive male role models, particularly among suburban families (Stearns & Stearns, 1986).

For some fathers, these changes and disruptions prompted further rethinking of the roster of paternal functions. Particularly important were efforts to forge new bonds with children through recreation and play. By the early 20th century (and in individual cases, even before), many fathers defended the idea of greater leisure time primarily in family terms, and they meant at least much of what they said. Thus, shared leisure with children, used among other things to instill certain skills and values, became an important part of modern paternal life. Fathers tried to play with their offspring in settings ranging from weekend romps to the more formal practice of a family vacation, this last an explicitly modern invention designed in part to reunite father and child. Playing with children was not of course new for fathers, but playing as a means of serious contact and even explicit training unquestionably increased over the past century, as a means of allowing fathers some balance between their active family goals and work commitments.

Furthermore, there have been important signs since the 1940s of efforts by fathers to adjust their styles with children still more, and as part of this to develop new kinds of contacts with young children. Obviously, not all fathers have been involved in this effort and there have been all sorts of complications including the rising rate of marriage dissolution. Attempts by fathers to develop a friendlier style with children, deliberately to depart (at least in their own view) from the styles of their own fathers, and sometimes to reallocate disciplinary roles with mothers deserve serious attention. In some cases the modifications after 1940 seen to relate to shifts in the kind of personality fathers hope to develop in children, away from such heavy emphasis on competitive achievement and toward more coop- erative social modes. Various observers have noted (and some have lamented) a tendency of fathers to reduce certain traditional tensions with older children (Lasch, 1977), but a new interest in young chil- dren is often involved as well. This recent historical change blends into the new roles for fathers urged, since the 1970s, by experts, feminists, male-liberationists, and others, but it seems to antedate these pleas. The change thus must be explained on the basis of factors other than new ideologies alone. It stemmed initially from the desire of many fathers themselves to redefine their family role, toward greater activity through trading sterile authority for more intimacy. This desire was supported by an increase in home-based leisure time, as hours of work dropped, and also by some changes in childrearing goals that made smooth interpersonal skills preferable to some traditional masculine traits.

A playful approach toward children built in several strands of fathering that had begun to take shape earlier. It interpreted the idea of some equality and comradeship between father and child, that had surfaced in the familial changes of the 18th century, as against strictest patriarchal tradition. It recognized the primacy of mothers, and indeed held out increasing authority as mothers became chief disciplinary arbiters and guides, against the lingering patriarchal impulses of the 19th century. Yet playfulness with children did constitute an effort to engage in parenting more actively, to counter some of the isolation imposed by the breadwinner focus (and to compensate for the declining value attached to this focus). Some fathers, at least, continued to respond creatively to new contexts (Parke & Stearns, 1988).

The variety of actual fathering roles in precontemporary American history, the powerful movement to emphasize men's family involvement and to define it in emotional terms, and the more recent but not brand-new shift in some fathers' styles feed into some of the expert reassessments of fathers' actual and potential impact on child development today. Also, the more negative aspects of the modern historical framework help explain some of the ongoing limitations that have been discovered in contemporary fatherhood. The point is, contrary to simpler uses of history in this area, the modern history of fathering is complex, not unidirectional, and this complexity helps explain some of the crosscurrents revealed in current research on paternal impacts.

It is essential to recognize that variety and tension continue in Western fatherhood patterns, and the impulses toward new activity have been seriously counterbalanced by further retreats from paternal involvement. The rate of abandonment by fathers obviously escalated in the 1960s, particularly among teenaged and divorced fathers. Even in two parent families, there is some evidence of a decline in the amount of time average fathers spend with their children (Lamb, 1982). Most authorities agree that parental authority generally has deteriorated since World War II, as children increasingly respond to other voices including those of peers. Contacts between fathers and teenagers, particularly, have suffered as part of this pattern. Relatively few fathers have taken advantage of new opportunities for rebalancing their roles. In countries like Sweden that provide for paternal leave, work continues to hold primacy, and even fathers initially willing to experiment with heavy involvement tend to revert within two years.

Furthermore contemporary fathers themselves hold deeply ambivalent attitudes about their own parental goals. Overall, according to poll data since the 1950s, fathers and mothers alike have found decreasing pleasure in parenting; less than half as many fathers in 1976, for example, found children providing a major goal in life, compared to their counterparts in 1957 (Veroff, 1981). Breadwinner responsibilities have declined, but they have not been fully replaced; a concept of children as fun thus has remained roughly stable since mid-century. Men and women alike, as they define family satisfaction, look increasingly to relationships with spouses, not with children, often now seen as an interference with family purposes and outside interests alike.

Conclusion

The history of modern fatherhood in Western society, though still sketchy, yields general conclusions as well as many particulars. First, diversity and tension have long marked the Western paternal tradition. The past is not as simple, nor as simply delightful, as some visions hold. Second, there have been important changes in direction produced by basic shifts in economic setting and accompanying alterations in family culture and male ideals. These have produced important innovations in fatherly behavior, as in attempts (however criticized in recent times) to link fatherhood with the development of manhood suitable for modern life, or the significant strand of creative playfulness that has emerged more recently. There is, nevertheless, a general tendency, linked to the development of modern society, toward reducing the paternal role and paternal satisfactions. While the tendency is rooted in home–work separations generated by the industrial revolution, it may by the 20th century have taken on something of a life of its own, as fathers, mothers, experts, even children tend to assume limited paternal involvement. Attempts to assume a magic transformation of contemporary fatherhood to match the decreasing maternal commitment of many working mothers simply do not match reality. Small wonder that many sober authorities urge the need to introduce much more formal encouragement, a new set of causal factors, if the directions of modern fathering are really to be altered among the population at large (Furstenberg, 1988). The factors to be combated, some of them dating well back in American history, are serious and pervasive.

Third, and finally, however, it remains vital to recognize the various stimuli to which fathers have responded in modern Western history, lest society fall victim to an oversimple, and perhaps overgloomy, modernist determinism. The most pressing context for fatherhood over the past century has been the change in work–family relationship, a structural stimulus of unusual importance. Various fathers, however, have adapted within this fundamental framework, under the impulse of key cultural and emotional standards. Ideas of redefining relationships with children toward providing greater gender guidance, or toward achieving greater comradeship and intimacy combine new strategies with some strong flavors of the past. Prior definitions of fatherhood yield slowly and incompletely, even to dramatic new forces, which means that history itself, along with material structure and cultural context, becomes a causal force. An 18th century father would not recognize the distance contemporary men face between work and home, or the importance of sports in father–child relations, or the parental leadership granted to mothers or indeed the number of bad fathers. An 18th century father would, however, recognize certain contemporary tensions, such as a balance between seeking and giving love, on the one hand, and defining proper authority, and he might feel kinship to present-day fathers who sense some tension between responses they regard as male and special restraints required for proper family life. Fatherhood, though modernized to its cost, maintains some continuities that help explain diversity and that can provide some basis for creative response.

References

DeMause, L. (Ed.). (1974). *The history of childhood*. New York: Harper.

Demos, J. (1970). *Little commonwealth: Family life in Plymouth Colony*. New York: Oxford University Press.

Demos, J. (1986). *Past, present, and personal: The family and the life course in American history*. New York: Oxford University Press.

Dubbert, J. L. (1979). *A man's place: Masculinity in transition*. Englewood Cliffs, NJ: Prentice Hall.

Erickson, E. (1962). *Young man Luther*. New York: Norton.

Erickson, E. (1964). *Childhood and society*. New York: Norton.

Filene, P. (1986). *Him-her-self: Sex roles in modern American*. Baltimore: Johns Hopkins.

Fischer, D. H. (1977). *Growing old in America*. New York: Oxford University Press.

Flandrin, J. (1976). *Families in former times*. Cambridge, England: Cambridge University Press.

Furstenberg, F. F. (1988). Good dads/bad dads: Two faces of fatherhood. In A. Cherlin (Ed.), *The changing American family and public policy*. Washington: Urban Institute Press.

Greven, P. J., Jr. (1972). *Four generations: Population, land, and family in colonial Andover, Massachusetts*. Ithaca: Cornell University Press.

Greven, P. J., Jr. (Ed.). (1973). *Childrearing concepts, 1628-1861*. Itasca, IL: Peacock Press.

Greven, P. J., Jr. (1977). *The Protestant temperament: Patterns of childrearing, religious experience and the self in early America*. New York: Knopf.

Honey, M. (in press). Feminism and women's imagination after the vote: Periodical fiction of the 1920's. *Journal of Social History*.

Hunt, D. (1970). *Parents and children in history: The psychology of family life in early modern France*. New York: Basic Books.

Lamb, M. E. (Ed.). (1987). *The father's role: Cross cultural perspectives*. Hillsdale, NJ: Lawrence Erlbaum.

Lasch, C. (1977). *Haven in a heartless world: The family besieged*. New York: Basic Books.

McGovern, J. (1968). Anna Howard Shaw: New approaches to feminism. *Journal of Social History*, 3, 135-163.

McLaughlin, W. G. (1975). Evangelical childrearing in the age of Jackson. *Journal of Social History*, 9, 20-39.

Ozment, S. (1983). *When fathers ruled: Family life in reformation Europe*. Cambridge: Harvard University Press.

Parke, R. D., & Stearns, P. N. (in press). Fathers and childrearing. *Journal of Family History*.

Pleck, J., & Sawyer, J. (1974). *Men and masculinity*. Englewood Cliffs, NJ: Prentice Hall.

Pollock, L. (1984). *Forgotten children: Parent-child relations from 1500 to 1900*. New York: Cambridge University Press.

Rotundo, E. A. (1985). American fatherhood: A historical perspective. *American Behavioral Scientist*, 29, 7-25.

Shorter, E. (1975). *The making of the modern family*. New York: Basic Books.

Smith, D. S. (1985). Child-naming practices, kinship ties, and change in family attitudes in Hingham, Massachusetts, 1641 to 1850. *Journal of Social History*, 18, 541–566.

Stearns, C. Z. (1988). 'Lord, let me walk humbly': Anger and sadness in England and America, 1570–1750. In C. Stearns & P. Stearns (Eds.), *Emotion and social change*. New York: Holmes and Meier.

Stearns, C. Z., & Stearns, P. N. (1986). *Anger: The struggle for emotional control in America's history*. Chicago: University of Chicago Press.

Stearns, P. N. (1977). *Old age in European society*. New York: Holmes and Meier.

Stearns, P. N. (1990). *Be a man! Males in modern society*. New York: Holmes and Meier.

Stone, L. (1980). *Family, sex and marriage: Fifteen hundred to eighteen hundred*. New York: Harper & Row.

Trumbach, R. (1978). *The rise of the egalitarian family: Aristocratic kinship and domestic relations in 18th century England*. New York: Academic Press.

Veroff, J., Douvan, E., & Kulka, R. A. (1981). *The inner American: A self-portrait from 1957–1976*. New York: Basic Books.

Wishy, B. (1968). *Child and the republic: The dawn of modern American child nurture*. Philadelphia: University of Pennsylvania Press.

Zelizer, V. (1985). *Pricing the priceless child*. New York: Basic Books.

3
Ethnicity and Fatherhood

Alfredo Mirandé

Over the past decade or so, as evidenced by the proliferation of books and articles on the topic, there has been growing interest in the impact of the father role on the family. Despite increased concern with fatherhood, cultural variations in the father role have been virtually ignored. Especially neglected have been interethnic variations in fatherhood. Research has generally focused on dominant societal patterns, neglecting ethnic effects on the father role. This chapter addresses the broad issue of how ethnicity influences the way fathers perceive and enact their familial roles. Specifically, differences and similarities in the father role in African American, Latinos, Asian American, and Native American cultures will be critically examined and discussed.

At the outset, it is important to note several limitations of the chapter. First, it is not intended to be exhaustive. The focus, instead, is on how ethnicity affects the father role in four particular groups. The groups—Blacks, Hispanics, Asian Americans, and Native Americans were selected because they are recognized as the major racial/ethnic minorities in the United States. An additional limitation is that the groups in question are incredibly diverse. The term "Latino,"

Partial funding for this chapter was provided by a grant from the Research Committee of the Academic Senate of the University of California, Riverside.

for example, encompasses many different nationalities, cultures, and racial groups. While Latinos are predominately mestizo or Indian, it should be noted that there are also White, Black, and Asian Latinos. "Asian American" similarly incorporates many nations, cultures, and language groups. Such internal diversity makes it extremely difficult to generalize. Without stereotyping the groups or minimizing their internal diversity, this chapter seeks to identify common cultural features that distinguish racial/ethnic groups from the dominant pattern and to isolate how cultural forces impact on the father role.

Role of the Father in African-American Culture

If there is a persistent image of the African-American father, it is that of an invisible figure who is either absent from the home or peripheral to the day-to-day functioning of the family. This image has been reinforced by dominant societal stereotypes and a wealth of academic literature that depicts the Black family as an unstable unit that was radically altered by the institution of slavery. The eminent sociologist, Frazier, noted in *The Negro in the United States*, that African family patterns were virtually destroyed by slavery. According to Frazier (1949), the few isolated incidents of cultural survivals "only indicate how completely the African social organization was wiped out by slavery" (p. 11). Rejecting the idea that the prevalence of common law marriages and illegitimacy, and the important role of the woman in the family represented continuity of a diluted form of the polygynous African family, Frazier argued that "the latter are regulated by custom and tradition while the former lack the sanction of traditions and customs" (pp. 12–13). According to Frazier, such mating patterns and family forms, rather than being cultural expressions, were essentially a response to economic and social conditions under slavery.

> The important position of the mother in the Negro family in the United States has developed out of the exigencies of life in the new environment. In the absence of institutional controls, the relationship between mother and child has become the essential social bond in the family and the woman's economic position has developed in her those qualities which are associated with a "matriarchal" organization. (p. 14)

In *The Negro Family in the United States*, Frazier (1948) observed that women continued to occupy a central role in the family in the period following reconstruction. African-American women, for example, asserted themselves during the election of 1868 in Mississippi (p. 102). These women, after all, were forced to be self-reliant and self-sufficient during slavery.

> As a rule, the Negro woman as wife or mother was the mistress of her cabin, and, save for the interference of master or overseer, her wishes in regard to mating and family matters were paramount. Neither economic necessity nor tradition had instilled in her the spirit of subordination to masculine authority.

As the male acquired power and property, however, the African-American family developed a patriarchal form of social organization similar to the Anglo-American family. Emancipation necessitated new economic arrangements and increased the authority of the male in the family and led to the economic subordination of the woman. A former slave who had been able to acquire a "one-horse" farm and hire two men to work for him, for example, noted that "I felt as a king whose supreme commands were 'law' and 'gospel' to my subjects" (p. 127).

The prevailing view of the slave family held by Frazier (1948, 1949) and others was that marriages were not sanctioned under slavery so fathers did not play a significant role in the socialization of children. This view has been challenged recently by historians who held that the family system was in fact recognized and encouraged by many slave owners (McAdoo, 1988). Blassingame (1979) reports that plantation owners often permitted the slave family to remain intact and that fathers played a significant role in the family. Fathers hunted and trapped small animals and retained their authority in the family, and were sometimes viewed as strict disciplinarians (Genovese, 1976).

The past decade or so has witnessed the emergence of a significant body of literature focusing on the role of the African-American male in the family. This literature does not support the traditional conception of the family as a pathological unit where the father is either absent or uninvolved with his wife and children. While African-American women undoubtedly play a significant role in the family, men are far from superfluous. Perhaps what most distinguishes the emerging scholarship is its emphasis on the unity, stability, and adaptability of the African-American family. Earlier studies were based on a pathological model which stressed the negative features of family life. McAdoo (1981) offers the following critique of the traditional literature:

> Social scientists have generally studied the structure of the most economically deficient, socially vulnerable, problematic Black family and inferred negative interaction patterns from that structural viewpoint. These vulnerable Black families have usually been compared to economically stable white middle-income families. (p. 115)

Research focusing on intact, economically stable families has begun to paint a very different picture of the contemporary African-American family and the role of the father within that unit. This research suggests that fathers play an essential role in the family (Daniel, 1975; McAdoo, 1988; Staples, 1988). A study of adolescent male socialization among African-American and White middle-class families in Chicago, for example, found that Black fathers were very involved in the rearing of their sons, and that generally African-American parents were developing well adjusted, motivated sons (Allen, 1981). Interestingly, wives rated the involvement of their husbands in child care and child-rearing somewhat higher than did their White counterparts. While the mother occupies a central role in the family, African-American fathers were found to take an active part in the socialization process and to retain warm interpersonal relations with their sons.

Sexual and racial comparisons revealed differences in parental roles, but these differences did not support the pathological view of the African-American father role. The negative conception of male family roles, according to Allen (1981, p. 111), resulted from the tendency of researchers to approach the African-American family as a deviation from the White norm. The African-American family should be viewed as a distinct cultural form that has been shaped by unique social, historical, economic, and political forces, rather than as a deficient White family.

An observational study of 40 middle-class African-American fathers and their preschool children carried out by McAdoo (1981) also failed to support the deficient view. The predominant verbal interaction type found in this study was nurturance, as almost two-thirds of the men demonstrated behavior toward their children that could be identified as warm, loving, supportive, and sensitive to the child's needs. Only 25% of the respondents exhibited behavior that was classified as restrictive, verbally controlling, and threatening (McAdoo, 1981). Patterns of nonverbal interaction were less clear. However, questions relative to child-rearing attitudes suggested that African-American fathers were actively involved in the socialization of children. They were similar to fathers in other studies, in that most (seventy percent) reported that they and their spouses were equally involved in making decisions relative to child-rearing (p. 125). While the fathers in the study saw themselves as "strict," their interaction patterns indicated that they were "authoritative," rather than "authoritarian" in that they were firm with children, made their expectations clear, explained behavior that would be punished, and were warm and nurturant (p. 128).

Other studies supported the view that the African-American family generally represents an authoritative parental pattern. In one of the few interethnic comparisons of childrearing roles, Bartz and Levine (1978) found that compared to Chicano and Anglo-American parents living in the same working-class neighborhood, Black parents expected earlier autonomy, were highly controlling and supportive, valued strictness, did not allow "wasted time," and encouraged equalitarian family roles (p. 709). Significantly, few differences by gender were uncovered, suggesting that ethnic group differences are more salient than are gender differences within ethnic groups. Black mothers expressed more equalitarianism in their relationships with children than Black fathers, as Black fathers demanded more unquestioning responses from their children. Black mothers scored highest on egalitarianism, whereas Black fathers were intermediate between Anglo-American and Chicano fathers. Both Black fathers and mothers were more controlling than their Anglo-American or Chicano counterparts. In short, these findings suggested that (1) interethnic differences in childrearing were evident even when socioeconomic status was controlled, (2) Black parents were more authoritative than Anglo-American or Chicano parents and provided an environment which was strict, encouraging early assumption of responsibility, and was nurturant and rewarding, and (3) despite gender differences in parental roles, African-American parents were more similar than dissimilar.

A descriptive study of the father role found that 135 African-American fathers in their sample generally perceived the experience of fatherhood positively (Hyde & Texidor, 1988). While 99.3% of the men saw child care as a responsibility to be shared by mother and father, some 40% viewed the mother as having a more important role in this area. The majority of the fathers felt that activities such as diapering (58%), feeding (61%), bathing (58%), and dressing (57%) should be shared. Significantly, fathers were more likely to have performed the task than to say that it "should" be shared, suggesting that while societal norms may dictate that these are primarily female responsibilities, the majority of men perform them (1988). Almost all of the respondents (99%) believe that child care tasks should be shared by both parents and the vast majority (more than 80%) were involved in various childrearing tasks such as rule setting, teaching morals, and disciplining children (1988). Seventy-three percent believed that direct contact with their children is needed everyday and 90% would like to spend more time with their children. Significantly, 87% felt that "their children had needs that only they, as fathers, could meet" (1988, p. 74). Seventy-one percent also believed that their own fathers provided good examples as fathers (1988).

In sum, recent research focusing of fatherhood in the African-American family did not support the traditional view of the father as an absent or insignificant figure. On the contrary, fathers played an integral role in the family and, rather than being absent or permissive, typically assumed an authoritative role.

Role of the Father in Latino Culture

The prevailing image of the role of men in the Latino family stands in sharp contrast to the image of African-American men. Whereas the Black male has traditionally been viewed as absent and as relatively weak, the Latino male has been depicted as a dominant, authoritarian figure. Ironically, the strong so-called Black matriarch has its counterpart in the macho patriarch who is said to have ruled the family with an iron hand. Although these images of Black and Latino families may appear disparate at first, upon closer examination they are more similar than dissimilar. Because family researchers have typically used the Anglo-American family as the benchmark against which other family forms are measured, more often than not, African-American and Latino families have been found wanting. Rather than seeing them families as adaptive and viable units that are responsive to different structural, political, and historical conditions, these families were considered deficient or maladaptive Anglo-American families.

While there has been a long-standing interest in the role of the male within the African-American family, there has been very little systematic research into the role of the male in the Latino family. This is surprising given that machismo and the so-called "cult of masculinity" have been assumed to be central components of Latino culture. Much has been written and said about Latino men, but such generalizations have typically been based on impressionistic or anecdotal evidence (Mirandé, 1988). In this literature, the Latino family is seen as "an authoritarian, patriarchal unit where the macho (i.e., male) is lord and master of the household and the woman is a quiet, submissive, servile figure." However, just as the traditional view of the role of the African-American male as an absent or nonexistent figure has been called into question by recent literature, so has the image of the Latino father as a cold and distant authority been challenged by recent research. Consequently, two very different and conflicting images of Latino fathers have emerged—traditional and emergent.

The traditional view of Latino men has been articulated by a number of ethnographers in Mexico and the United States. Lewis (1960, 1961), for example, carried out ethnographic field work in both rural and urban settings in Mexico. Lewis (1960) noted that the ideal Mexican cultural pattern in Tepoztlán, a village south of Mexico City, was for the father to make all major decisions and to be master of the household. Fathers were also said to avoid intimacy in the family and to maintain respect by instilling fear in other family members. Wife beating, although less common than in the past, was still prevalent, and may be provoked by minor incidents such as not having a meal ready on time or talking back to a husband in front of his friends (1960). Severe punishment of children was also common. Although mothers punished more often, fathers administered more severe punishment.

In a study carried out later in four communities in South Texas, ranging from a simple folk-village to an urban center, Madsen (1973) similarly maintained that machismo is a value that ranks second in importance in Mexican culture only to devotion to family. The so-called "cult" of machismo is such that men were believed to have an incessant preoccupation with sex and extramarital affairs. Like a fighting rooster, a "real macho" was said to be "proud, self-reliant, and virile" (p. 22). Whereas Black women, like machos, have been viewed as strong and independent, Latino women traditionally have been seen as docile, submissive, and dependent. This view was supported by Madsen (1973), who observed that the cult of machismo dictated that men prove themselves smarter, stronger, and otherwise superior to women. According to Madsen, "where he is strong, she is weak. Where he is aggressive, she is submissive. While he is condescending toward her, she is respectful toward him" (p. 22).

Although the Mexican-American man may have been affectionate with very small children, his relationship with children was said to become more distant as they entered puberty (Madsen, 1973). The father was seen as a stern disciplinarian who kept family members in line and was respected and feared, but certainly not loved.

Another ethnographic study of a Texas barrio (Rubel, 1966) concluded that respect for elders and male dominance are the two key organizing principles in Mexican culture so that the ideal is that "the older order the younger, and the men the women." Once again, fathers were to be feared and respected. Children were often reluctant to laugh or tell jokes in front of the father. Even as adults, children did not tell jokes or smoke in front of the father for fear of being disrespectful.

In a more recent study, Sánchez-Ayéndez (1988) similarly observed that in Puerto Rican culture, "From early childhood, individuals are socialized to a double standard about gender and an interaction pattern of male dominance." The woman's world centered primarily around household duties and children, whereas the man's world centered around the world outside the home. Hence, women were seen as belonging in the home, and men as belonging on the street. Women were viewed as subordinate to men. The concept of machismo was "associated with the need to prove virility by the conquest of women, sexual aggressiveness, dominance over women, and a belligerent attitude when confronted by male peers" (p. 178). Sánchez-Ayéndez believed that despite changes in gender roles which have brought about more sharing in decision-making and greater autonomy for women, they were still seen as being primarily responsible for the domestic realm and subordinate to men.

Recent research has suggested, however, that the Latino families may be less authoritarian and the power of the male less absolute than we have been led to believe. This emergent literature includes a number of studies of conjugal decision-making and action-taking which reported that decisions were usually shared by husbands and wives (Hawkes & Taylor, 1975; Ybarra, 1977, 1982; Baca Zinn, 1975).

A study of 32 sets of Chicano parents and 123 children in a large Southwestern city carried out by Zapata and Jaramillo (1981) failed to support the view that the *la familia* is rigidly structured along age and gender lines. Although the findings were not conclusive, children generally saw females as more socially cooperative, and alliances within the family were viewed as being gender-based. Parents, however, seem to apportion family responsibilities equally among male and female children. Whereas children distinguished among sibling roles and alliances, "neither parents nor children clearly nominate either parent as responsible for 'managing' the household" (p. 286).

Studies have also begun to challenge the traditional view of the Latino father as a cold and distant figure. A study based on 88 interviews from households in southwest Detroit, concluded that fathers occupied a more important role in the family than is usually believed (Luzod & Arce, 1979). Latino fathers were seen as "being important to their children" and as providing "significant positive influences" on the development of children.

Counter to the image of Mexican fathers as distant and aloof, Rubel (1966) found in his ethnographic study that men were observed to be very warm and affectionate in relating to young children.

> Without exception, direct observations note the warmth and affection exhibited by fathers with their young sons and daughters. . . . In several instances the field notes comment that the father was, in fact, far more gentle with his children than was their mother. (p. 66)

This view is supported by a study of 78 parent–child dyads among Mexican families. Bronstein (1984, 1988) found fathers to be a great deal more playful and companionable with children than mothers. Fathers played an important and distinct role which ran counter to the traditional image of the Mexican family.

Although there is no measure of the hours per day each father in the present sample spent at home, most did seem to spend most of their non-working hours and their days off there or in recreational pursuits with their families. Furthermore, when they were with their children, many of the fathers seemed genuinely involved with them, in friendly, nonauthoritarian interaction. (1984, p. 1000)

A cross-ethnic comparison of the father role among middle-class respondents suggests that Mexican American and Anglo-American parental roles may be more similar than dissimilar (Mejia, 1975). Relative to the treatment of children, Anglo-American mothers appeared most permissive and Chicano mothers most restrictive, while Anglo-American fathers and Chicano fathers did not differ in permissiveness (p. 96). Although both Anglo-American and Chicano fathers identified responsibility as an important component of the father role, Chicanos stressed providing for the needs of the family and basic necessities like food and shelter (p. 115). Overall, however, "Mexican Americans did not adhere to published conceptions of authoritarianism-traditionalism, extended family or the submissive wife concept as noted in the literature" (p. 179).

Findings from several studies suggest that gender roles among Latinos are not only less rigid than is commonly believed but that men increasingly are adjusting to drastic alterations in the traditional role of the male. A study of Latino men (Chavez, 1984) who found themselves in a situation in which the female was defined as the principle breadwinner, for example, found that most men were able to adjust to their status as house husbands. These men were sometimes teased or referred to as *chavalas* (girls) by friends because they did not occupy a dominant role, but they generally accepted their role and maintained a positive masculine self concept. Interestingly, although women became the principle breadwinners and men assumed a greater share of the burden, women continued to perform the majority of household chores such as cooking, doing the laundry, and caring for children. Men also defined their status as house husbands as a temporary one brought about by economic necessity.

Another study by Nieto (1983) focused on Hispanic single custodial fathers, a topic that heretofore had been completely neglected. Data were obtained from 200 questionnaire responses and 50 personal interviews in four cities in Texas, interviews with five custodial fathers in a large Mexican city, and the clinical experience of the author. While Latino men were generally socialized to assume an instrumental, rather than an expressive role, the culture placed a heavy emphasis on familism. Hence, once the role of single custodial parent was assumed by the man, "the full resources of the Hispanic family will be mobilized in its support" (p. 19). Although many of the men reported that their fathers were aloof, distant and lacked warmth, they were determined not to duplicate this type of relationship with their own children.

From this review of recent literature on fatherhood in Latino culture it is clear that, like African-American fathers, Latino fathers did not conform to traditional portrayals found in the literature. Rather than being cold and distant figures, Latino fathers often appeared to be warm, nurturing, and companionable.

Role of the Father in Asian Culture

Despite obvious differences between Latino culture and Asian culture, there have been striking similarities in social science portrayals of the family and gender roles within each group. First, both Asian and Hispanic families have been viewed essentially as rigidly graded along age and gender lines. The belief that "the older order the younger, and the men the women," seems even more applicable to traditional Asian culture than it does to traditional Latino culture. The father was depicted as the dominant figure; the mother as quiet, submissive, and self-sacrificing. Chinese women in fact, were to be subordinate not only to their husbands but to their husbands' parents. The second similarity is that Latinos and Asians were both said to be familistic and to place a heavy emphasis on familial relations, particularly the extended family. The needs of the individual, thus, were often subordinated to those of the collective. A final point of commonality is that there has been almost no research that has systematically examined the role of the father in the family, and, consequently, numerous myths and stereotypes have been perpetuated regarding both groups.

Before discussing the contemporary Asian American family, it is important to note once again that because Asian Americans are a diverse group it is neither possible, nor desirable, to attempt to identify a "typical" Asian American family. Instead, an attempt will be made to identify certain cultural values that appear to be shared by various Asian groups, and which have impacted on the role of the father in the family. If there is a dominant theme in the literature, perhaps it is that the Asian American family was in flux and that there had been a dynamic tension between traditional values and the demands made on families in contemporary United States society.

Chinese Americans

The prototype of the Asian American family was the traditional Chinese family. Briefly, the family in ancient China was patriarchal, family centered, and male dominated. The definition of the father role in Chinese culture was based on Confucian ethical principles (Ho, 1987). As head of the household, the male was said to exercise almost complete control not only over his wife and children but over all of the descendants of his offspring and their spouses. According to Lee (1953), the family emphasized (1) the father–son relationship, (2) family pride, (3) the large family, (4) ancestor worship, and (5) common familial ownership of property. The traditional Chinese family was patrilocal and patrilineal in that married couples were expected to live with the parents of the husband, and property and land were passed on through the male line (Wong, 1988). Finally, ancestor worship was an important component of the traditional Chinese family. A man could attain immortality only if the family line was continued. Thus, as in Latino culture, a premium was placed on siring male children who would carry on the family line so that one of the greatest misfortunes that could befall a man was to die without having any male heirs (Wong, 1988).

The patriarchal family system, however, was an ideal pattern that was attained primarily by the wealthy members of the gentry-scholar class (1972). While peasants may have identified with the pattern and sought to emulate the life style of the elite classes, it was difficult for them to maintain large households. The ideal that six generations would live under the same roof and that property would only be divided after several generations was not really within the reach of most members of the peasant class. There is reason to believe, in fact, that the average household size in ancient China was not very large. A census taken in the year 2 A.D. reported the average size of a household as only 4.87 persons (Ping-ti Ho, 1965).

While the authority of the Chinese family was maintained both by tradition and law, familial power ultimately was tied to its control over economic resources. The family controlled not only the distribution of property and wealth, but the means of obtaining a livelihood (Lee, 1953). Occupational skills and crafts were passed on from father to son.

Although the father was the ultimate source of power and authority, the mother had considerable influence. Authority was vested in both parents and in more senior direct patrilineal descendants, not simply in the father. Ultimately, "the basic legal and ethical principle regulating the traditional Chinese family was based not so much on sexes as on senior–junior relationships" (Ho, 1965). Filial piety, or a reverence and respect for one's elders, was, therefore, a very important value in Chinese culture (Wong, 1988).

If one is to understand the contemporary Chinese American family it is essential to recognize that the traditional family had to adapt and modify to changing economic, cultural, and demographic conditions. Especially important was the fact that the early period of immigration (1850–1920) was characterized by the migration not of entire families but of single men, or married men who left their families behind. While men viewed their stay in the United States as a temporary status and planned on returning to China, many were forced to stay. The early Chinese family, thus, was a "mutilated" or "split household" (Wong, 1988). In 1890, for example, there were 103,607 Chinese men and 3,868 Chinese women, or a sex ratio of 2,679 men for every 100 women (1988). In 1920, there were approximately 700 men for every 100 women. Even as late as 1950, the sex ratio was 190 to 100. Prior to 1920 it is therefore difficult to talk about the Chinese American family as a normal functioning unit. Racism also impacted on the family, as anti-Chinese sentiment was so intense that it led to passage of the Chinese Exclusion Act in 1882, thereby halting Chinese immigration to the United States.

Japanese Americans

Japanese labor supplanted Chinese labor as most Japanese immigrated between 1890 and 1930. The first Japanese to immigrate went to Hawaii in 1885 (Kitano, 1988). Although these early immigrants were predominantly single men who came as contract laborers and expected to return to Japan, by 1920 there were over 109,000 Japanese in Hawaii. Immigration to the mainland started in the 1890s. Like their Chinese counterparts, these early immigrants experienced intense racism and prejudice, and were limited mostly to low-paying unskilled jobs.

The Japanese were familistic and individuals were expected to submerge their needs to those of the collective. The family structure was hierarchal "with the husband at the top and preferences for male heirs, appropriate role behavior dependent on age, status, and sex, and the importance of obligation, duty, and loyalty" (1988, p. 260). The family system was organized around the concept of the *ie*, which was represented as family, household, or house. Confucian political principles were based on the precept that stable families were the cornerstone of a stable society (1988). Because the *ie* continued over time, the needs and goals of the individual were subordinate to those of the collective. While most of the early immigrants were men, there is evidence which suggested that the Japanese family in this early period was less fragmented than the Chinese family, as many of the persons who immigrated after the Gentleman's Agreement of 1909 were relatives and spouses.

The concept of generation is critical to an understanding of the Japanese American family. The *Issei*, or first generation, followed the traditional model of the family, which was characterized by male dominance, a rigid division of labor, priority of filial relations over the marital bond, and emotional restraint. For the *Issei*, marriage was a relationship that brought together two very different but complementary gender domains—"inside" and "outside." "By far the commonest way in which the Issei described the responsibilities, activities, and concerns of spouses was to say that wives took care of things 'inside' the house, home, or family, and husbands took care of things 'outside' it" (Yanagisako, 1985, p. 97). Although the two spheres were separate and complementary, they were certainly not equal, for the female sphere was encompassed and governed by the male sphere. Because the male participated both outside and within the family, he was accorded more power and considered the head of the family.

The children of the *Issei*, on the other hand, attempted to create a balance between the rigid Japanese marriage system and the more egalitarian marital ideal. The *Nisei* gave priority to the conjugal relationship over the parent–child relation. Although they retained the notion of male and female domains, these domains were considered complementary and relatively equal.

The grandchildren of the first generation, *Sansei*, are the most assimilated to American society, and their family patterns and conjugal division of labor most closely approximate the American pattern. For the *Sansei*, love became the primary motive for marriage, and there was not a sharp division of labor, although men still tended to be viewed as being primarily responsible for the external sphere (Kitano, 1988).

Korean and Southeast Asian Americans

Although there was a great deal of internal diversity among Asian American groups, the family system of the more recent Asian immigrants was very similar to the Chinese. The Vietnamese, for example, emphasized the needs of the collective over those of the individual and Vietnamese culture was patriarchal, patrilineal, and male dominated (Van Tran, 1988). According to Pyong Gap Min (1988), the impact of Chinese culture on Korea is even more apparent, as Chinese culture spread southward first to Korea and, then, Japan. Hence, it is impossible to understand the Korean family without first understanding the traditional Chinese family and Chinese Confucianism.

Whereas Asian women traditionally were expected to stay at home and to care for children, low wages and harsh economic conditions have forced many of these recent immigrants into the labor force. The majority of Korean women in the United States, for example, have participated in the labor force (Gap Min, 1988), and such participation appears to have increased their relative power and authority in the family. Korean immigrant husbands still exercised more power than their American counterparts, but there is also evidence which suggests that the Korean American family has moved towards a more egalitarian pattern (Hong, 1982). Vietnamese women similarly are participating increasingly in the labor force and, as a result, are gaining power and influence in the family (Van Tran, 1988).

As Asian women have increased their labor force participation and their power in the family, the traditional male role has likewise been altered. The father may still be the dominant figure in the family, but his power and authority is not absolute. A study of recent Vietnamese immigrants carried out by Kibria (1986), for example, concluded that while traditional conceptions of gender persisted, "women played a highly crucial and influential role in the coping and adaptive process" (p. 380). Although Asian women are actively involved in the labor force, they are still primarily responsible for domestic duties. Asian American men appear to play a minimal role in rearing children, particularly infants (Suzuki, 1985). According to Shwalb, Imaizumi, and Nakazawa (1987), the Japanese father exercised a relatively weak role in the family which varied according to the child's developmental level. Only his economic power remained firm. Fathers spent a limited amount of time with children, but they appeared to be indulgent in dealing with them, since most of the discipline was relegated to the wife.

> However, when the children reach school age they are no longer indulged and begin to assume duties and responsibilities in the household. They also are subjected to stricter discipline and taught in various ways that their actions will reflect not only on themselves but on the entire family. (p. 114)

As children got older, the father assumed a greater role in disciplining and began to spend more time with children, especially males. Chinese fathers, similarly, were said to maintain authority and respect within the family by keeping a certain amount of emotional distance from other family members (Wong, 1988).

In summary, this brief overview of the literature suggests that while traditional Asian culture, particularly Confucian principles have had a significant impact on Asian Americans, Asian Americans have modified and adapted these traditional values to meet the exigencies of contemporary society. The scarcity of Asian women in the United States and the need for both spouses to work outside the household, for example, have weakened traditional patriarchal values and increased their status and power in the household.

Role of the Father in Native American Culture

Of all of the groups under study, none has been more neglected than the Native American. There is very little research on Native American families, and even less on the role of the father within the family.

Such neglect is pervasive. A recent family text that focuses on "diversity" in families of the United States, particularly ethnic and cultural variations, for example, does not have a single reference to Native American families (Baca Zinn & Eitzen, 1987).

One of the most prevalent myths regarding Native Americans is that they represent a single monolithic group. There are currently 1.5 million Native Americans in the United States, comprising 280 tribal groups and 161 different linguistic groups (Staples, 1988). In reality, terms such as "American Indian" and "Native American" encompass a variety of cultures, nationality groups, languages, and family systems. It is, thus, very difficult to generalize about such groups.

An additional factor that has worked to limit research on Native American families is that traditionally the study of Native Americans has not been defined as the purview of sociologists. In the academic division of labor, it was the anthropologists who studied "simpler," less developed societies. Thus, numerous generalizations concerning the Native American family are derived from older, culturally myopic ethnographic studies that were based on a negative or deficient model of Native American culture and family life. The Native American family was viewed as a deficient White family. Whereas the White family was a "modern," independent, isolated nuclear family, the Native American family was assumed to contain the opposite characteristics. Because the Native American family was not modern, it was believed to approximate family forms found in "simpler," "primitive" societies.

John (1988) isolated twin themes found in Native American studies. The first theme was that extended families are the norm; the second, that changes that have occurred within the Native American family are the direct result of acculturation to the dominant culture (1988). The Native American family has, thus, been depicted as an extended family system that integrates several generations into a cohesive whole. As with the Asian family, elders, according to this view, are to be venerated and respected. Elders, particularly males, are expected to exercise considerable power and authority in the family.

The evidence relative to male authority and gender role differences in the Native American family is mixed. Strodtbeck (1951), for example, found that Navajo women exercised greater power in decision-making in the family than White Texan or Mormon women. There is also considerable evidence which suggests that Native Americans arrive at decisions in the family utilizing much less verbal interaction than non-Native Americans (John, 1988). Price (1981) found that Indian women are largely concerned with emotional, expressive concerns and men with instrumental ones. Aginsky and Aginsky (1947), on the other hand, report a complete role reversal among the Pomo from a male-dominated culture to a woman-dominated culture.

While no Indian group can be considered "typical," the Navajo experience provides an interesting example of how traditional gender roles have been altered by contact with the dominant society. In traditional Navajo society women exercised a role that was equal to, if not greater than, that of men. Women assumed a prominent role in the subsistence economy as their duties included taking care of the hogan, weaving blankets, and making clothes, pottery, and baskets (Hamamsy, 1957). Navajo society was matrilineal and matrilocal so that the sheep were usually owned by women and inheritance was passed on through the female line. Women were responsible for the care and maintenance of children, but they also made many of the financial decisions in the home. Many of the teaching and disciplinary functions normally carried out by the father were assumed by the wife's brothers. Female participation in activities outside of the home in ceremonial or political events, however, was limited.

Interestingly, contact with White culture had the effect of diminishing the power of women in the home. Under allotment, land policy was altered so that only married men were considered eligible for land ownership (Blanchard, 1975). The move from a subsistence to a wage market economy gave men added economic power and further reduced the influence of women (Rapoport, 1954). Navajo women were able to find jobs outside the home, but they were generally not paid as well as men doing the same work (Blanchard, 1975). As the society moved from a matrilocal to a neolocal residential pattern, "the father became increasingly important within the family, and the mother lost much of her influence and security, no longer being able to rely on the immediate support of her own family" (1975). With increasing assimilation to White culture, the young began to reject traditional Indian ways and to question parental authority (1975).

John Red Horse (1988) rejects the notion that there is a single uniform "Indian family," suggesting, instead, that Native American family systems range on a continuum that includes traditional, neo-traditional, transitional, biocultural, acculturated, and panrenaissance family types. The traditional family system was derived from the village structure that was common among tribal groups. Such groups were small, ranging from 200 to 350 residents, and prevailing values revolved around village and kinship structures. The community was generally isolated from outside influences, and kin relations were dominant. All residents of a village were members of an extended kin system. Because villages were viewed as sacred societies, "life events and kin relationships were interpreted according to sacred law" (1988, p. 92). As in Asian society, elders were respected and revered for their wisdom, and their authority was sacred.

Neotraditional families are found among groups like the Ya-quis, who were converted to Christianity in mass but retained most of their traditional practices and beliefs. Transitional families, on the other hand, resulted from forced geographic relocation and separa-tion from extended kin systems. Parents usually retained their native language and it was the preferred language in the home, but English became the dominant language with the second generation and in the community at large. The extended kin system was fractured and modified to fit the new surroundings. Among bicultural families the nuclear household became the norm, although a strong Native American identity was retained through fictive extended kin struc-tures. Acculturated Native American families were assimilated into the dominant society and reflected dominant values and behavior. They retained nuclear households outside of a distinct Native Ameri-can community, and most of their primary social relations were with non-Native Americans. Finally, panrenaissance families sought to revitalize traditional Native American cultural values and religions.

The contemporary Native American family cannot be under-stood without looking at governmental policies which have sought directly and indirectly to destroy or radically alter Native American culture. The program of systematic removal of Native American children from their families was initiated by the United States gov-ernment in the early 1800s and continues to the present day (Blan-chard & Unger, 1977). The disruption of families was justified on the grounds that it would Christianize, educate, and otherwise "civilize" Native American children. Prior to passage of the Indian Child Welfare Act in 1978, some 25–35% of all Native American children were forcibly removed from their families and placed in foster homes, put up for adoption or relocated to institutions (1977). Few of these children were removed for reasons of physical or emotional abuse, but rather because of "social deprivation" (Byler, 1977). The removal of Native American children from their natural homes was generally effected without regard to due process and without granting parents the opportunity to be represented by counsel (Byler, 1977). This legislation sought to correct this problem by establishing minimum standards for the removal of Indian children and giving Native American tribes jurisdiction over child welfare matters (Cross, 1986).

Ironically, in traditional Native American society, children were protected, loved, and nurtured, not only by parents but by siblings, aunts, uncles, cousins, grandparents, and other extended kin (London & Devore, 1988). Native American family networks, moreover, were much more extensive than traditional extended family units in Western society. In the European model, extended relations are bounded by the household unit, whereas Native American kin networks are structurally open and extend to the village (Red Horse, Feit, Lewis, & Decker, 1978). European extended families consist of three generations under one household; Native American networks include several households "representing significant relatives along both vertical and horizontal lines" (1978).

Children were valued in Native American society, and most social activities incorporated them. Adults would seldom strike children (London & Devore, 1988) or yell at them. The extended kin network was such that childrearing was shared by a number of adults (Cross, 1986). This system provided safeguards and protection for children, since parents did not have absolute, or even necessarily primary, authority over children.

> Community opinion governed parent's behavior with regard to child rearing, and parents who did not meet community expectations were often ridiculed into compliance. In some tribes, the role of disciplinarian was assigned to a specific tribal member or even a mythological figure, removing the burden for physical discipline from parents and placing it on a "wise one" or on "powers far greater" than any one member of the community or family. (Cross, 1986, p. 284)

While little has been written about the father role per se, it is clear that in traditional Native American society, ultimate power and authority was vested neither in the father nor the mother, but in the community as a whole.

Several forces have worked to diminish the impact of Native American values and traditions. As Native Americans moved from reservations to cities, it became increasingly difficult to maintain the traditional Native American way of life. Since the majority of Native Americans today live in urban areas, they are separated from extended kin networks (London & Devore, 1988). Government policies have further eroded the impact of the extended family as the government has sought to detribalize and to assimilate Native Americans (London & Devore, 1988). These government policies, in short, have led to the virtual destruction of Native American families (Unger, 1977).

Clinical Implications

Although much of the literature reviewed in this chapter is based on empirical research rather than clinical experience, the findings of such studies have important implications for practitioners and family therapists. If there is an underlying theme, perhaps it is that ethnic minority families in the United States are incredibly diverse. There are substantial cultural differences in fatherhood not only between racial/ethnic minorities, on the one hand, and the dominant White society, on the other, but among them as well. An additional complication is that each racial-ethnic group is itself internally diverse. Although there are some parallels between Asian American and Hispanic conceptions of fatherhood, in many instances, racial/ethnic minorities are as different from one another as they are from the dominant society. If family therapy is to be effective, it is essential "that the therapist raise relevant contextual questions, avoid errors of assessment due to ethnocentric or stereotypic views, and set up appropriate treatment goals and culturally consonant interventions" (Jaes Falicov, 1982, p. 134). Therapists must realize that terms such as "Latino" or "Asian American" are convenient labels used to represent culturally distinct groups. One cannot assume, for example, that treatment goals or intervention strategies designed for rural *mexicanos* are somehow appropriate for New Mexican *hispanos*, or third- or fourth-generation urban California Chicanos. Neither can one assume that treatment strategies used with urban, middle-class professional African-American families will be effective with rural, poor, working-class Black families. There is a saying in Spanish that practitioners should always heed in dealing with minority clients— *juntos, pero no revueltos* ("united, but not mixed up"). The saying is equally applicable to the other racial/ethnic groups discussed here. Treatment goals and strategies developed with one Native American group cannot be applied uncritically to another group. In the case of child welfare practice, for example, "because there are a wide variety of child-rearing standards and styles that depend on tribal identity, degree of assimilation, and other factors, Indian child welfare programs are currently developing foster care standards to fit local community standards" (Cross, 1986).

Practitioners and family therapists should also be cognizant of the nuance and complexity of minority cultures. Asian and Latino cultures are similar in that they draw an important distinction between public and private domains. It is, therefore, important to penetrate beyond "public" reality. Kitano has observed that "Asian Americans by and large do not communicate their needs in the same way as White Americans; the more subtle, non-verbal levels of communication are misunderstood if not ignored completely, both by government in designing certain social welfare services and by those actually providing the services" (1978, p. 10). It is, therefore, essential that therapists be sensitive and aware of these more indirect nonverbal levels of communication.

One of the most disturbing myths surrounding Asian Americans is that they are not in need of family therapy or counseling. Although depicted as the "successful" minority and as inscrutable, there is evidence which suggests that they are undergoing considerable stress as a result of forces such as immigration, acculturation, and racism. While clearly in need of mental health services, they tend to underutilize such services (Ryan, 1985).

Latino cultural norms similarly often refer to "public" norms regarding how things "ought" to be, but there may be a sharp contrast between the way things really are and the way they "should" be (Falicov, 1982). For example, while the norm that the father is *el jefe de la casa* (the head of the household) and that he should be honored and respected is widely accepted, there is a substantial body of literature which indicates that the Chicano family is, in fact, mother-centered and that decision making in the family is more egalitarian than we have been led to believe (Mirande, 1988). Baca

Zinn (1975) has noted that the ideology of patriarchy can persist and exert an influence despite the presence of egalitarian decision making. It is, therefore, crucial to distinguish between male dominance as a cultural norm and male dominance as a behavioral reality (Mirandé, 1988).

The evidence reviewed here, on the other hand, suggests that the Black family may be less matriarchal and that Black fathers exercise more power and authority in the family than is popularly believed. It may well be that the conception of the Black family as matriarchal and the father as absent or insignificant reflects more of a public than a private reality.

Conclusion

The first conclusion that is evident from this review is that the traditional social science literature on ethnic families and the father role is significant perhaps more for what it tells us about social scientists than for what it tells us about ethnic differences in fatherhood. The most persistent theme in the traditional social science literature on racial/ethnic families, it is that such families are somehow deviant or defective Anglo-American families. Because dominant societal standards were used as the benchmark against which other family forms were measured, minority families, not surprisingly, were often found wanting. The Anglocentric ideal was that the family should be democratic and egalitarian with each member contributing equally. Television depicted the American family as an idyllic unit in families like "Ozzie and Harriet" and "The Cunninghams." But the American father was perhaps best epitomized by Robert Young in the program "Father Knows Best"; an easy going, kind, wise, and thoughtful figure who served more as a good friend or counselor to his children than as a strict disciplinarian. Although contemporary programs like the "Cosby Show" ostensibly depict "Black families," the dominant model of the family employed is still the Anglo-American familial ideal.

Ethnic minority families did not fit this mold. Hispanic families and Asian American families, for example, were perceived as rigidly structured along age and gender lines. The Latino and Asian American father was authoritarian, patriarchal, in other words, "un-American." Rather than being a friend or a benevolent figure, he was a dictator who was to be respected and feared, but certainly not loved. African-American fathers and Native American fathers also did not fit the ideal, but for very different reasons. The prevailing view of African-American and, to a lesser extent, Native American fathers was that they were either absent or relatively uninvolved with the family. Because African-American families and Native American families were perceived to be matriarchal or mother-centered, they too did not fit the model of the ideal Anglo-American family.

Recently, such traditional and stereotypical depictions of ethnic minority families have been called into question. Revisionist scholars have noted not only that ethnic minority families are incredibly diverse but that there is not a single monolithic African-American, Latino, Asian, or Native American family. There are substantial regional, income, educational, urban–rural, and generational variations within each group, for example. Unfortunately, all too often poor, unstable first-generation minority families have been compared with middle or upper-middle class, stable Anglo-American families.

Recent research suggests that Black fathers, especially middle-class fathers, often are very much involved and play an integral role in the family. Black parenting roles, in fact, appear to be authoritative, rather than authoritarian or permissive. Latino fathers also play a distinct and unique role in the family, but it is not always the role of strict disciplinarian that is found in the literature. Latino and Asian fathers appear to be warm, affectionate, and nurturing, expecially with very young children.

One of the reasons that ethnic minority families have been so widely misunderstood is that, in the past, researchers and practitioners often lacked a true understanding or appreciation of the subtlety and complexity of minority cultures (London & Devore, 1988). Latino and Asian cultures, for example, distinguish between "external" and "internal" roles and between public and private domains. To the outside world, the man was presented as "head" of the family, but this did not necessarily mean that he was Lord and Master or that the woman had no power in the family. To the contrary, several researchers have suggested that patriarchal norms notwithstanding, Latino and Asian American women exercise considerable influence within the domestic sphere (Baca Zinn, 1975; Kibria, 1986). At the same time that children were expected to honor and respect the father, he was permitted considerable latitude to be warm and affectionate with them. Native American cultures, similarly, emphasize gestures and nonverbal communication, and spend less time talking before arriving at a decision. To the untrained observer, the behavior of Native American families could easily be misinterpreted or misunderstood.

In the past, the prevailing model used to analyze minority families was one that stressed modernization (Baca Zinn, 1982; John, 1988). This model held that whereas the Anglo-American family is a modern, nuclear, egalitarian unit, minority families are traditional, extended, and authoritarian. Changes that occur within minority families are, thus, viewed as resulting from contact with the dominant culture. Minority families were seen as clinging to traditional values and norms. With the exception of the African-American family, which was erroneously assumed to have been destroyed by slavery, extended families were considered the norm as several generations lived under one roof and were integrated into a cohesive whole. Yet, such families were also seen as problematic because they were rigidly structured along age and gender lines. Contact with the dominant culture, however, would inevitably lead to assimilation and rejection of traditional values. According to this model, then, the emergence of isolated, independent, egalitarian, nuclear families was the result of a natural evolutionary process. Families that did not fit this model were necessarily deficient.

Social scientists who adhered to the traditional model have also been obtuse in not recognizing that contemporary minority cultures and families are not static entities. To the contrary, minority families have always had to change and adapt to different economic, political, and social forces. For example, Confucian values and world views undoubtedly impacted on contemporary Asian American families, but the traditional Chinese family could not be imported in mass to the American continent. Racism as well as economic, political, and demographic forces simply precluded the institutionalization of the traditional Asian family in the United States. Traditional patriarchal values notwithstanding, Asian women in the United States were typically forced to work outside the home. Since Asian men assumed the least desirable, poorest paying jobs, and they did not own property, it was next to impossible to maintain the traditional patriarchal family where many generations lived under one roof and property was only divided after the fifth generation. While sons were at a premium and daughters were devalued in traditional Asian culture, the unbalanced sex ratio undoubtedly served to increase the relative power of Asian women in the United States. Latino familial values and Native American values which were deeply rooted in an agrarian past have also been altered in the United States. The vast majority of Hispanics and more than half of all Native Americans today reside in urban areas.

In short, traditional conceptions of racial/ethnic minority families must be discarded in favor of theoretical and clinical approaches that take into account contemporary exigencies faced by such families. This is not to suggest that minority families are not culturally distinct, but rather that traditional values are not static and have been shaped and modified to fit social and economic conditions. The task facing future researchers is to determine how such cultural forces have shaped the performance of the father role in contemporary society.

Acknowledgment

I would like to thank Patricia Portillo for her assistance in the preparation of this manuscript.

References

Aginsky, B. W., & Aginsky, E. G. (1947). A resultant of intercultural relations. *Social Forces, 26,* 84–87.

Allen, W. R. (1981). Moms, dads, and boys: Race and sex differences in the socialization of male children. In L. E. Gary (Ed.), *Black Men* (pp. 99–114). Beverly Hills: Sage.

Baca Zinn, M. (1975). Chicanas: Power and control in the domestic sphere. *De Colores, 2,* 19–31.

Baca Zinn, M. (1982). Chicano man and masculinity. *The Journal of Ethnic Studies, 10,* 29–44.

Baca Zinn, M., & Eitzen, D. S. (1987). *Diversity in American families.* New York: Harper & Row.

Bartz, K. W., & Levine, E. S. (1978). Childrearing by black parents: A description and comparison to Anglo and Chicano parents. *Journal of Marriage and the Family, 40,* 709–719.

Blanchard, K. (1975). Changing sex roles and protestantism among the

Navajo women in Ramah. *Journal of the Scientific Study of Religion, 14*, 43–50.

Blanchard, E. L., & Unger, S. (1977). Destruction of American-Indian families. *Social Casework, 58*, 312–314.

Blassingame, J. W. (1979). *The slave community: Plantation life in the antebellum south*. New York: Oxford University Press.

Bronstein, P. (1984). Differences in mothers' and fathers' behaviors toward children: A cross-cultural comparison. *Developmental Psychology, 20*, 995–1003.

Bronstein, P. (1988). Father–child interaction: Implications for gender–role socialization. In P. Bronstein & C. P. Cowan (Eds.), *Fatherhood today: Men's changing role in the family* (pp. 107–124). New York: Wiley.

Byler, W. (1977). Removing children—The destruction of American Indian families. *Civil Rights Digest, 9*, 19–27.

Chavez, V. (1984). Hispanic househusbands. Unpublished manuscript.

Cross, T. L. (1986). Drawing on cultural tradition in Indian child welfare practice. *Social Casework, 67*, 283–289.

Daniel, T. E. (1975). A definition of fatherhood as expressed by black fathers. Unpublished doctoral dissertation, University of Pittsburgh.

Falicov, C. J. (1982). Mexican families. In M. McGoldrick, J. K. Pearce, & J. Giordano (Eds.), *Ethnicity and family therapy* (pp. 134–163). New York: Guilford Press.

Frazier, E. F. (1984). *The negro family in the United States*. Revised and abridged edition. Chicago: University of Chicago Press.

Frazier, E. F. (1949). *The negro in the United States*. New York: Macmillan.

Gap Min, P. (1988). *The Korean-American family*. In C. H. Mindel, R. W. Habenstein, & R. W. Wright, Jr. (Eds.), *Ethnic families in America: Patterns and variations* (pp. 199–229). New York: Elsevier.

Genovese, E. (1976). *Roll, Jordan, roll: The world the slaves made*. New York: Vintage.

Hamamsy, L. S. (1957). The role of women in a changing Navajo society. *American Anthropologist, 59*, 101–111.

Hawkes, G. R., & Taylor, M. (1975). Power structure in Mexican and Mexican-American farm labor families. *Journal of Marriage and the Family, 37*, 807–811.

Ho, D. Y. F. (1987). Fatherhood in Chinese culture. In M. E. Lamb (Ed.), *The Father's Role: Cross-cultural perspectives* (pp. 227–245) Hillsdale, NJ: Lawrence Erlbaum.

Hong, L. K. (1982). The Korean family in Los Angeles. In Eui-Young Yu et al. (Eds.), *Koreans in Loss Angeles* (pp. 199–132). Los Angeles: California State University.

Ho, Ping-ti. (1965). An historians view of the Chinese family system. In S. M. Farber, P. Mustacchi, & R. H. L. Wilson (Eds.), *The Family's Search for Survival*. New York: McGraw-Hill.

Hyde, B. L., & Texidor, M. S. (1988). A description of the fathering experience among Black fathers. *Journal of Black Nurses Association, 2*, 67–78.

John, R. (1988). The Native American family. In C. H. Mindel, R. W. Habenstein, & R. W. Wright, Jr. (Eds.), *Ethnic families in America: Patterns and variations* (pp. 325–363). New York: Elsevier.

Kibria, N. (1986). Patterns of adaptation and survival among Vietnamese in an urban setting: A study of family and gender. Unpublished doctoral dissertation, University of Pennsylvania.

Kitano, H. (1978). Asian American families. In *Summary and recommendations, conference on Pacific and Asian American families and Hew-related issues*. Sponsored by divisions of Asian American Affairs, HEW, National Institute of Education, HEW (pp. 10–11). Washington, DC: U.S. Government Printing Office.

Kitano, H. H. L. (1988). The Japanese American family. In C. H. Mindel, R. W. Habenstein, & R. W. Wright, Jr. (Eds.), *Ethnic families in America: Patterns and variations* (pp. 258–275). New York: Elsevier.

Lee, Shu-Ching. (1953). China's traditional family: Its characteristics and disintegration. *American Sociological Review, 18*, 272–280.

Lewis, O. (1960). *Tepoztlán*. New York: Holt, Rinehart & Winston.

Lewis, O. (1961). *The children of Sanchez*. New York: Random House.

London, H., & Devore, W. (1988). Layers of understanding counseling ethnic minority families. *Family Relations, 37*, 310–314.

Luzod, J. A., & Arce, C. H. (1979 December). An exploration of the father role in the Chicano family. Paper presented at the National Symposium on the Mexican American Child, Santa Barbara, CA.

Madsen, W. (1973). *The Mexican-American of South Texas*. New York: Holt, Rinehart & Winston.

McAdoo, J. L. (1981). Black father and child interaction. In L. E. Gary (Ed.), *Black Men* (pp. 115–130). Beverly Hills: Sage.

McAdoo, J. L. (1988). Changing perspectives on the role of the Black father. In P. Bronstein & C. P. Cowan (Eds.), *Fatherhood today: Men's changing role in the family* (pp. 79–92). New York: Wiley.

Mejia, D. P. (1975). Cross-ethnic father roles: Perceptions of middle class Anglo-American and Mexican-American parents. Unpublished doctoral dissertation. University of California, Irvine.

Mirandé, A. (1988). Chicano fathers: Traditional perceptions and current realities. In P. Bronstein & C. P. Cowan (Eds.), *Fatherhood today: Men's changing role in the family* (pp. 93–106). New York: Wiley.

Nieto, D. S. (1983). Hispanic fathers: The growing phenomenon of single fathers keeping their children. *National Hispanic Journal, 1*, 15–19.

Price, J. A. (1981). North American Indian families. In C. H. Mindel & R. W. Habenstein (Eds.), *Ethnic families in America: Patterns and variations* (pp. 245–270). New York: Elsevier.

Rapoport, R. N. (1954). Changing Navaho religious values. *Peabody Museum Papers, 41*(2).

Red Horse, John (1988). Cultural evolution of American Indian families. In C. Jacobs & D. C. Bowles (Eds.), *Ethnicity and race: Critical concepts in social work* (pp. 86–102). Silver Spring, MD: National Association of Social Workers.

Red Horse, J. G., Feit, M., Lewis, R., & Decker, J. (1978). Family behavior of urban American Indians. *Social Casework, 59*, 67–72.

Rubel, A. J. (1966). *Across the tracks: Mexican-Americans in a Texas city.* Austin: University of Texas Press.

Ryan, A. S. (1985). Cultural factors in casework with Chinese-Americans. *Social Casework, 66*, 333–340.

Sánchez-Ayéndez, M. (1988). The Puerto Rican American family. In C. H. Mindel, R. W. Habenstein, & R. W. Wright, Jr. (Eds.), *Ethnic families in America: Patterns and variations* (pp. 173–195). New York: Elsevier.

Shwalb, D. W., Imaizumi, N., & Nakazawa, J. (1987). The modern Japanese father: Roles and problems in a changing society. In M. E. Lamb (Ed.), *The Father's Role: Cross-cultural perspectives* (pp. 247–269). Hillsdale, NJ: Lawrence Erlbaum.

Staples, R. (1988). The black American family. In C. H. Mindel, R. W. Habenstein, & R. W. Wright, Jr. (Eds.), *Ethnic families in America: Patterns and variations* (pp. 173–195). New York: Elsevier.

Strodtbeck, F. L. (1951). Husband-wife interaction over revealed differences. *American Sociological Review, 16*, 468–473.

Suzuki, B. H. (1985). Asian-American families. In J. H. Henslin (Ed.), *Marriage and family in a changing society* (pp. 104–119). New York: Macmillan.

Unger, S. (1977). *The Destruction of American Indian families.* New York: Association of American Indian Affairs.

Van Tran, Thanh (1988). The Vietnamese American family. In C. H. Mindel, R. W. Habenstein, & R. W. Wright, Jr. (Eds.), *Ethnic families in America: Patterns and variations* (pp. 276–299). New York: Elsevier.

Wong, M. G. (1988). The Chinese American family. In C. H. Mindel, R. W. Habenstein, & R. W. Wright, Jr. (Eds.), *Ethnic families in America: Patterns and variations* (pp. 230–257). New York: Elsevier.

Yanagisako, S. J. (1985). *Transforming the past: Tradition and kinship among Japanese Americans.* Stanford, CA: Stanford University Press.

Ybarra, L. (1977). Conjugal role relationships in the Chicano family. Unpublished doctoral dissertation, University of California, Berkeley.

Ybarra, L. (1982). When wives work: The impact on the Chicano family. *Journal of Marriage and the Family, 44,* 169–178.

Zapata, J. T., & Jaramillo, P. T. (1981). The Mexican American family: An Adlerian perspective. *Hispanic Journal of Behavioral Sciences, 3,* 275–290.

4

Changes in Legal Views of Parenthood: Implications for Fathers in Minority Cultures

Lynda Henley Walters
Steven F. Chapman

Little is known about the particular effects of family law on fathers in subcultures within the United States. However, as rights of fathers have changed over time, it is possible that fathers within minority cultural groups have been and are being affected by laws differently than fathers in the majority culture. Indeed, Norgren and Nanda (1988) have concluded that "American courts . . . have responded inconsistently to the claims of culturally diverse groups in our society" (p. 231). Furthermore, they suggested that when courts have tried to accommodate cultural practices that challenge or contradict main stream values, "they have done so by describing the most narrow, culturally specific parameters within which the behavior would be sanctioned" (Norgren & Nanda, 1988, p. 234).

Legal change both reflects and promotes social change (Friedman, 1977; Nagel, 1970; Thomas, 1979). With changes in the ways parental roles are viewed and growth in the size and visibility of minority cultural groups, fathers in groups whose socialization practices and values differ from the mainstream can expect to find the legal system less understandable and less sympathetic to their needs.

The purpose of this chapter is twofold: to review issues that affect all fathers and to identify questions that must be answered in order to gain insight into the peculiar effects of laws in cultures that vary from the mainstream. This chapter contains the following sections: a review of shifts in judicial preference for mothers and fathers with movement toward gender neutrality (see Walters & Elam, 1985, for additional review of law and fatherhood); a review of current status of law and legal interpretations on custody, support, and paternity; a review of cultural expectations of Blacks, Hispanics, and Asian Americans. Within each cultural review section, questions for research are raised.

Legal Change Toward Gender Neutrality

Legal rights of fathers and mothers in their children have changed over time in part as a function of preference for one gender over the other. At the turn of the 19th century, it was thought that fathers bore the responsibilities for and rights in children. This presumption had been long standing and was supported by compelling economic reasons (cf. *King v. de Manneville*, 1804). Children belonged to fathers, and mothers stood little, if any, chance of securing custody in the event of a divorce.

During the 19th century, the presumption in favor of fathers began to change. It was preceded by changes in sex roles and in the beliefs held by society at large. The importance of psychological family bonds was recognized along with the need for economic security. Mothers were assigned the responsibility for creating an environment conducive to the well-being of all family members. Nurturance and education of children, considered basic to the emotional health of the family, were duties assigned to mothers. It became the father's responsibility to represent the family in the outside world, to protect the family, and to provide for its financial security (*Bradwell v. Illinois*, 1873). Fathers were still heads of households, but the rights of parents in their children had shifted. This subtle but significant change in the legal response to families was supported by popular and professional thinking about the roles of men and women in the family (Bettelheim, 1956; Bowlby, 1951; Freud, 1949; *Jenkins v. Jenkins*, 1921).

The preference for fathers as caretakers of children had shifted to a preference for mothers. However, it is the intensity of the new presumption that is most important for understanding the impact of the change. For example, the preference for mothers led one judge to assert, "[t]here is but a twilight zone between a mother's love and the atmosphere of heaven" (*Tuter v. Tuter*, 1938, p. 205).

Rationales for preference for mothers as custodians of children have progressed from motherhood as instinct, to the tender years doctrine, to the standard of best interests of the child. *Tender-years* was a direct outgrowth of the belief that young children belong with their instinctively nurturant mothers (cf. *Bruce v. Bruce*, 1930). It was not until the latter half of the 20th century that the tender-years doctrine was seen for what it was. In *State ex rel Watts v. Watts* (1973) it was acknowledged as a blanket judicial finding of fact that mothers are always better suited to care for young children. Ultimately, the presumption required a father to *prove* that his wife was not better suited to care for the child(ren) than he was. The *Watts* court rejected the tender-years presumption and, using the best interest standard, awarded custody to the father. However, even with a precedent for gender (or parent) neutral application of "best interest," mothers have continued to be favored when best interest is considered from a tender-years perspective (Jones, 1977–78).

In contrast to the early shift from preference for fathers to preference for mothers, preference for mothers has not been followed by a return to preference for fathers. Instead, the trend is toward preference for shared parenting (Folberg, 1984; Folberg & Graham, 1979; Freed & Walker, 1988; *Mayer v. Mayer*, 1977; Weyrauch & Katz, 1983). This is a much more complex situation that is exacerbated by a tension between beliefs about the roles of men and women. Although shared parenting does not necessarily imply gender neutrality, it does involve modification of traditional beliefs about parenting behaviors and the roles of men and women. Some of the barriers to modification of traditional beliefs are reviewed by Martin (1986).

Underlying the tug-of-war between males and females, there is social change in favor of gender neutrality. However, there is little historical precedent for gender neutrality, either in societies or within an individual's life experiences. Gender neutrality is not intuitively logical; the simple appearance of males and females makes us think of differences, and differences are difficult to reconcile with neutrality. Both our social and legal histories suggest that males and females should be considered differently, and our casual observations confirm this broadly accepted belief.

In other words, we have progressed in social change toward gender neutrality to a point that is more complex than prior times. This change affects assumptions in nearly every sphere of life, and response in one sphere influences response in another. Glendon (1975) considered the social change to be so far advanced that the legal system had come to reflect it. She referred to it as a profound "change in the ideology expressed in the law" (p. 3).

As a principle, gender neutrality has significant implications for family law, especially when laws are applied in minority cultures where progress toward neutrality is slower. Evidence in the law for growing neutrality is presented for custody, support, and even paternity. However, the introduction to the next section serves as a reminder of the halting nature of social change.

Fathers and Law

> Fathers have not been granted full parental status in our society. Nurturance has most often been associated with femininity. Indeed, it is usually called 'mothering' rather than 'parenting' because of the mistaken assumption that fathers simply do not parent. (Biller & Meredith, 1975, p. 106)

Corroborating Biller and Meredith, McCant (1987) asserted that the decrease in discrimination against fathers that results from movement toward gender neutrality is an illusion. He cited empirical studies and other literature, indicating that although we have evidence that fathers can nurture, there are still powerful cultural assumptions that fathers are providers and mothers are parents. He reviewed evidence from the 1970's and 1980's that fathers are disenfranchised as parents by family law courts.

There is little argument that many courts continue to protect women and prefer them as parents. However, in both statutory reform and appellate court decisions, the cumbersome progress toward gender neutrality is more evident.

Custody

Social change is not linear; it is not possible to track a change and see gradual movement toward current beliefs without also seeing evidence of regression at some levels of analysis and short term random change (Bengston, Furlong, & Laufer, 1974; Katz, 1974; Treiman & Terrell, 1975). Thus, a review of changes chronicling a move toward gender neutrality in custody decisions is not without its confusing moments. For example, even though most of our domestic relations laws are based on English common law, there is no simple linear trend from considering children the property of their fathers to considering children as individuals with rights who have two parents charged with their care. It is possible to find evidence of the consideration of children as property of their fathers, but in this country, custody decisions have tended to be influenced by the facts of the case rather than prescribed by rights (Foster & Freed, 1978; Weitzman & Dixon, 1979). Thus, even in early decisions, the preference for fathers as parents was tempered by circumstances.

Perhaps the most compelling evidence for unbridled gender preference is in the maternal preference that was pervasive in custody decisions beginning in the early 20th century. This preference followed social changes during the 19th century in which women became the revered nurturers of family relationships, particularly children (*Broussard v. Broussard*, 1975; Jones, 1977–78; Thomas, 1979). More mothers were able to stay home with their children because more fathers were working outside the home and making enough money to support their families. In addition, psychological theories about the differing needs of children at different ages became common during this period. These changes supported the growing belief in the importance of maternal care. In addition, during the 19th century, women had gained in legal status with enfranchisement and right to own property, giving them greater visibility as competent adults. Social forces converged to give women a decided advantage as the parent of choice in the custody of children.

Maternal preference has given way to the best interest standard, a test first used in 1881 by a judge in Kansas. In this case, custody was not given to the father but to the grandmother; however, the rationale was the best interest of the child—the welfare of the child was judged to be more important than the natural right of the father.

It was almost one century later, 1971, when the equal protection clause of the fourteenth amendment was applied in a decision about rights and responsibilities of husbands and wives as a gender issue (*Reed v. Reed*, 1971). Application of the fourteenth amendment to family relationships provides a constitutional protection for individuals in families that represents a significant departure from thinking about families in earlier years. In the *Reed* decision, the Supreme Court began using the heightened intermediate scrutiny test for classification based on gender. The level of scrutiny required by the fourteenth amendment equal protection clause is increased when it can be proven that persons are placed in a category in order to discriminate against them ("Developments in the Law," 1980; *Village of Arlington Heights*, 1977). (Intermediate scrutiny requires that classification, such as gender, be regarded with greater suspicion than some classifications, but not as great as race, which requires strict scrutiny, the most stringent level of scrutiny.) An earlier application of the fourteenth amendment to parenthood issues is found in *Stanley v. Illinois* (1972). In *Stanley*, the Court analyzed the claims of an unwed father under the due process provision of the fourteenth amendment and ultimately held that the Illinois statute violated the equal protection clause of the amendment. This is the landmark case for the protection of rights of unwed fathers.

It would be misleading to conclude that fathers and mothers receive equal treatment in custody decisions—or any other family matter. However, significant changes are being made in state laws to promote the best interests of children, and nearly all reflect the social goal of equal protection and equal responsibility for mothers and fathers.

For example, by 1980, 13 states had specifically "de-sexed" custody laws; 37 had enacted laws that specifically rejected the tender-years doctrine. In 1984, Foster & Freed reported that "tender years" had either been rejected or relegated to tie-breaker in most states. By 1982, 28 states had passed statutes *supporting* joint custody; by 1985, 35 had passed such statutes. Many state statutes establish a presumption that joint custody, though not necessarily joint physical custody, is in the best interest of children. In addition, gender neutral guidelines for custody decisions had been written into statutes in many states by 1985. These new guidelines include indicators of psychological and physical well-being of children (Foster & Freed, 1981, 1982; Freed & Foster, 1984; Freed & Walker, 1985).

However, even with these changes in state laws, empirical evidence on actual custody awards serves as a reminder of the rate and unevenness of social change (cf., McCant, 1987; Weitzman & Dixon, 1979).

Support

Under common law, husbands acquired the property of their wives, but also had the absolute responsibility for support of the wife during and in the event of termination of marriage. As women gained rights, including the right to their own property and a presumption in their favor for child custody, men continued to bear the full burden for support. The responsibility to support included wife and children whether the marriage remained intact or not (Weyrauch & Katz, 1983).

By 1978, influenced by appellate decisions based on the 14th amendment or state equal rights amendments, 32 states had laws that placed the responsibility for support of children on both parents (Ellman, Kurtz, & Stanton, 1986; Foster & Freed, 1978). In fact, the burden of support was likely to fall on mothers because even when responsibility was assigned to fathers, those who did not provide support were ignored. According to Krause (1983) federal involvement in child support enforcement is due to failure of states to accept responsibility for enforcing support which is time consuming and costly. Clearly, federal long-arm statutes have been designed with the intent of collecting delinquent payments from errant fathers.

Viewed only from the perspective of those who cope with the nonpayment of child support, the problem is with fathers. Enforcement experience more often involves the pursuit of fathers than mothers. Thus, we have two trends between which there is substantial tension: the trend toward gender neutrality of child support and the trend toward more efficient pursuit of fathers who do not pay.

However, there is another side to the picture. According to McCant (1987), it is a rare exception when a father is not legally required to pay child support. When investigating his belief, McCant was told that less than 1% of child support orders in one country were given to women. At the same time, mothers may deny fathers access to the child. The legal structure for recovering child support payments is much more efficient than the structure for enforcing visitation and shared custody orders. McCant cited the assignments of personnel in the office of the District Attorney in San Diego County as evidence of inequity in the enforcement of divorce orders: 102 employees were charged with the enforcement of payment of child support and prosecution of offending fathers, and two employees were charged with assisting fathers whose visitation rights were being violated.

The importance of the ability of a mother to deny visitation is well illustrated in *Lehr v. Robertson* (1983). In this case, the biological father of an illegitimate child wanted to establish his paternity and develop a relationship with his child. Even though the mother had hidden the child from him so that he could not establish a relationship, the court held in favor of psychological parenthood, and in this case, allowed the mother's current husband to adopt the child without any notification of the proceeding to the biological father. There are technical grounds for this ruling, but more importantly, it provides evidence for the need for states to insure fathers an opportunity to develop and maintain relationships with their children (cf., Barnes, 1986; Haynie, 1986; Wheeler, 1987).

Although many local courts do not require that mothers provide financial support, when support actions reach appellate courts, the likelihood of enforcing support from mothers increases. For example, in *Meyer* (1983), both parents had increases in income and both had adequate homes; the court did not award child support payments by the father to the mother because the mother was equally able to support. On appeal this decision was upheld. In *Vandiver* (1986), the mother was ordered to pay child support for a child in his father's custody who was 17 years old and retarded; the award was to continue for as long as the son was unable to care for himself. In both *Polite* (1987) and *Hunn* (1986), New York and South Carolina reaffirmed that child support payments are to be based on the needs of the child (or costs of support) and the parties' ability to pay.

As a rule, when a support decision is appealed, the issue at appeal is something other than *which* parent should pay. When the issue is who will be required to support, appellate courts are consistently reminding lower courts that the responsibility rests in both parents.

The trend toward equal responsibility to support seems to be influenced by several factors. One is that, in general, men have access to better-paying jobs than women. Women are still more likely than men to have stayed home to care for children or had jobs that allowed them to concentrate more effectively on home and children during nonworking hours. This situation perpetuates the traditional assumption that fathers bear the responsibility for support.

However, the number of women who hold better-paying jobs than their spouses is increasing, and there are even a few instances of men who choose to take care of the home and children rather than being gainfully employed outside the home. In one case, a father described himself as being like a mother (Clary, 1982), perpetuating the myth that mothers are the natural nurturers while at the same time demonstrating that as a father he was a competent nurturer and, thus, family roles should not be gender bound.

Paternity and Rights of Unwed Fathers

The Supreme Court has vacillated on the importance of biological versus psychological parenthood (Haynie, 1986). Nowhere is this more evident than in case law on unwed fathers. In the past, nearly every action to establish paternity was motivated by a desire to have the father assume responsibility for support of a child. In fact, in some states, there is no legal avenue for a father to bring an action to establish paternity of a child born to a mother who is married at the time of the child's birth. Technically, action can always be brought to establish paternity of an *illegitimate* child, but not necessarily for a legitimate child, a child born in wedlock. For example, in *P.B.C.* (1985), a putative father asked that mother and child be required to submit to a human leukocyte antigen (HLA) test to establish his paternity. Because the mother had been married to another man at the time of the child's conception (but divorced at the time of the birth), the child was considered technically legitimate. At the appellate level, the court extended the presumption of legitimacy from married-at-time-of-birth to married-at-time-of-conception. The putative father was not allowed to rebut the presumption of legitimacy in order to establish paternity.

From an historical perspective, the question of paternity is relatively new. Because beliefs about parental rights and responsibilities have always been based in part on economic considerations and because there were no conclusive tests to establish paternity, it was assumed that the husband of a woman bearing a child was the father of the child. This assumption removed the stigma of illegitimacy from children and relieved the state from support responsibility.

However, in recent years, tests have been developed that exclude men from paternity and establish the fact that a specific man is the father of a given child (HLA test). Because of the substantial burden to support, few men have used the test to establish paternity, and many have avoided the test in an effort to escape the responsibility to support.

For those fathers who have wished to establish paternity, and particularly if they have pursued custody, courts have relied most heavily on psychological parenthood. Those fathers who have obtained custody have been able to document their involvement with the child ranging from economic support to time spent in care of the child. To date, biological parenthood has only been applied in cases dealing with *families* rather than *one parent*. For example, in a recent landmark case (*Smith*, 1977), procedures for removing children from foster family custody in favor of biological parents were found to be constitutionally adequate. A family with at least one biological parent is preferred over a single biological parent.

The trend toward gender neutrality is something of a double-edged sword. Because it is a trend toward favoring neither males nor females, either can be disadvantaged. In a minority culture where the general system of values, beliefs, and practices are significantly different from the mainstream culture, and where rights and responsibilities of parents may follow gender lines, it can be expected to be particularly difficult for fathers to understand and protect their rights.

Minority Cultures and Social Change

Ours is a pluralistic culture with a legal system that is designed to insure that individuals from different ethnic, religious, and racial backgrounds are guaranteed equal protection and opportunity. However, little is known about the effect of family law in the United States on fathers from ethnic minority groups. Are the effects in minority groups different from the effects in the mainstream white culture; and, if so, are the differences a function of cultural variations, class differences, racial identity, or discrimination?

A basic knowledge of values, beliefs and practices common within ethnic minority families is necessary in order to understand the challenges presented to fathers by the legal and social welfare systems. A comprehensive survey of ethnic minorities in the United States is beyond the scope of this chapter. However, we do provide a brief review of salient aspects of larger ethnic groups: Asian Americans, Black Americans, and Hispanic Americans. These categories were chosen because the Statistical Abstract of the United States refers to ethnic minority groups under the labels Black, Hispanic, and Other (including 7.1 million Asian Americans). It should be remembered that these groups are by no means homogeneous. Each group varies within itself in terms of language, customs, history, and culture. This is not to say that there are no generalizations that can be made about the families in these groups. Indeed, valid generalizations carry with them important implications and raise questions for research, some of which are suggested in the following review.

Asian American Families

Asian Americans are one of the fastest-growing ethnic minorities in the United States, increasing from 5.2 million in 1980 to 7.1 million in 1985, a growth rate of 37.5%, compared to the national growth rate of 5.4%. Although a moderate projection for the U.S. population in the year 2000 shows a decline to 198 million, the Asian American population is expected to increase to 9.5 million. For the year 2080, Asian Americans will constitute 23.4 million of a declining U.S. population of 176 million (U.S. Bureau of the Census, 1987).

The Asian American Family Tradition.   The extended family or household unit, which may be a part of a larger community unit, is the most salient social structure for Asian Americans. The attitude of most Asian Americans toward family could be characterized as traditional. Asian Americans are socialized to subordinate themselves to the group, in contrast to the prevailing cultural values of independence and autonomy of mainstream Americans. Group identity naturally becomes a strong motivator for conformity in this group. For example, divorce is discouraged not because of religious beliefs, but largely by diffuse social pressure: "What would people think?" (Harrison, Serafica, & McAdoo, 1984; Huang, 1981). To gain insight into the effects of legal assumptions and laws within the Asian American family tradition, questions for future research might include:

1. Will Asian American couples seek legal divorce, or will they use some other culturally acceptable way of dealing with an irretrievably broken marriage?
2. Can a divorced father expect support from his Asian American community?
3. What is the rate of single fatherhood among Asian Americans? Does it vary by class, income, the extent of acculturation (length of time in the United States, and/or number of generations since immigration)?

Family Structure: Status and Roles in Asian American Families. Status and roles within most Asian American families are prescribed by age, gender and "seniority," with a strong authoritarian patriarchy (Kitano & Kikimura, 1981). Filial piety is valued and encouraged. Male children are especially valued, because they insure the continuity of the male lineage within the family. Southeast Asian women traditionally are subordinated to men, expected to serve father, husband and sons, with no legal or economic rights or right to divorce or remarry (Huang, 1981). In view of status and roles within the Asian-American family, questions for further research might include:

4. What is the relation between strength of role expectations and pursuit of custody among Asian American fathers?
5. Will Asian American fathers who are involved in a divorce proceeding wish to have custody of their children?
   a. Will Asian American fathers prefer to have custody of their male children rather than their female children?
   b. In the Asian American community, are children considered the property of the father or of the father's family?
6. Will Asian American fathers' childrearing attitudes and knowledge facilitate a father custody arrangement?
7. Will Asian American fathers be willing to share custody with their former wives?
8. If fathers are willing to share custody, will they expect their wives to subordinate their wishes for the child(ren) to the wishes of the father?
9. In the event the mother is granted custody, will Asian American fathers be more or less likely than other men to support their children financially?

10. In the event the mother is granted custody, will Asian American fathers be likely to visit their children regularly?

Parenting Practices. Parenting practices include the use of diffuse social pressure in the socialization of children. Harrison, Serafica, and McAdoo (1984) noted four major goals of socialization in Asian American families: group consciousness, deference to authority, dependence, and commitment to reciprocal aid. Partly because of the patriarchal power structure, and partly due to discrimination by the cultural majority, Asian Americans teach their children what the Japanese refer to as *Enryo,* a norm for the way inferiors are to defer to superiors (Kitano & Kikimura, 1981). Out of deference, embarrassment, or ambiguity, Asian Americans may seem noncommittal and hesitant to speak out or be assertive. They are socialized to keep differences between themselves and others from becoming too salient in order to avoid conflict, thus the lack of direct statements of honest and true feelings. Invisibility is also highly valued, because lifestyles and behaviors which might draw attention to or embarrass the community are discouraged (Huang, 1981). Thus, their interaction with the legal system or social welfare system is limited, and their use of outside professionals is reluctant (Kumabe, Nishida, & Hepworth, 1985). Research questions raised by this view of Asian American socialization goals, values, and practices are:

11. Will Asian American fathers accept or reject the directness of the language in custody decrees?
12. Will the community in which an Asian American father lives reject him if he brings outside attention to the community in his pursuit of custody?
13. If an Asian American father pursues custody of his child, will his extended family support him?
14. How will single Asian American fathers provide for care of their children during the hours when they are not with them?
     a. Will they turn major responsibility for childrearing over to parents or other extended family members?
     b. What are their attitudes toward and use of non-family-based day care?
15. Will putative Asian American fathers seek legal confirmation of paternity?

Factors Unique to Asian American Families: Cultural Transition.   The process of acculturation and assimilation is traumatic for both recent immigrants and well-established Asian Americans. Significant differences have been reported in childrearing attitudes between first, second, and third generations of immigrant Asian Americans (Harrison, Serafica, & McAdoo, 1984). Even though Southeast Asian women, especially those from Vietnam, had already begun the transition from traditional women's roles to entry into the work force and demands for more egalitarian relationships, many Asian American women are only now assuming an antisubmission, anti-arranged-marriage attitude (Spero, 1985). Where before there were discrete sex roles, now there is an intermixing of such roles (Kitano & Kikimura, 1981). Divorce among Asian Americans is relatively infrequent, however, it does occur, and increasingly as third and fourth generation immigrant children adapt to mainstream American culture and rebel against the values of the older generation (Huang, 1981; Kitano & Kikimura, 1981). In view of the transitions in roles within the Asian American family, future research should include the following questions:

16. If an Asian American mother has a better paying job than the father at the time of a divorce, how will the father be affected by a court decree that says he is less responsible than his former wife for economic support of his children?
   a. How will be father's family and community respond to him if a court declares that he is not responsible for economic support of his children?

In spite of being stereotyped as the "ideal minority," Asian Americans are experiencing serious social problems. For example, problems of violence in the home and delinquent youth are being reported (Huang, 1981; Spero, 1985). In other words, the ideal minority is developing problems that are found in the majority. Perhaps the old stereotypes are no longer useful. Research on the stereotypes that surround the Asian American family could include the following:

17. What is the influence of cultural stereotypes about Asian Americans on the attitudes and behaviors of lawyers and judges in litigations of family disputes?

Black American Families

Whereas cultural mythology errs in an overly optimistic view of the Asian American family, it errs in an overly pessimistic view of the Black American family. As noted by Staples (1988), almost all research on Black family life is problem-oriented, concentrated on the lower-income strata, and ignores stable poor and middle-class families. Research on the Black family has been biased toward the lower class family, measured by white middle class norms, and defined as "pathological" when it deviated from them (Moynihan, 1965).

Blacks make up about 12% of the American population—29 million people (U.S. Bureau of the Census, 1987). Of the total population, 31% of Blacks live below the poverty level (U.S. Bureau of the Census, 1988). Acording to Landry (1987), by 1982, 26% of Black males were considered middle class (compared to 46% of white males) and over 50% of Black females were considered middle class (compared to 69% of white females).

The Black American Family Tradition.   The family is considered the greatest source of life satisfaction for Black people in America (Gary, Beatty, Berry, & Price, 1983). Black families may be characterized by their extended nature, multiple parenting and informal adoption practices, child-centeredness, flexible role definitions, and a network of relationships with other families within the community (Nobles, 1978). The importance of extended family relationships among blacks has been recognized as a mechanism that not only supplies satisfaction and emotional support, but material resources, child care, and other forms of mutual assistance (Hill & Shackleford, 1986; Wright, Watts, Saleeby, & Lecca, 1983).

Extended families are composed of a core group of adults made up of generational groupings and include children, grandchildren, and occasionally various individuals who sojourn with the family in response to a variety of needs. There is a common geographic base, often the home of one of the "founders" of the family, which facilitates frequent visitation, a network of interdependency, and serves as the emotional center of the family (Wright et al., 1983). Possible questions for research on the network of aid within the black extended family include:

1. To what extent do extended family resources influence the decision a Black couple makes to divorce or separate?
2. Are extended family resources as available to single Black fathers as they are to single Black mothers?

Family Structure: Status and Roles Within the Black American Family. The Black American family has been characterized as a tangle of pathology. It is thought to have a strong matriarchy and weak, ineffectual men whose devastated self image compounds their inability to find and maintain employment; however, most of these characteristics have been debunked as cultural myths (Staples, 1971, 1976). According to Staples (1988), Black families are increasingly structured along class lines. Eshleman (1985) suggested three distinct patterns for Black families: matriarchal or matricentric families; egalitarian, two-parent families; and patriarchal affluent families. These patterns are not restricted to the nuclear family alone, nor is any particular family pattern necessarily "pathological,"though they are linked to socioeconomic status. Each pattern has its own characteristic relationships, childrearing practices, and values.

The matriarchal-matricentric family is usually a single-parent family in which about one-half of all Black children are reared. This family type is beset with the many problems that are found in families with low income, poor education, etc. (Eshleman, 1985). Some include fathers who cannot support a family or who cannot exercise the authority of partenthood (Eshleman, 1985). These families have been thought to socialize their children to be of little bother to parents and to mature and achieve independence earlier than other children (Staples, 1971).

Egalitarian, two-parent families are primarily middle-class couples with or without children, who prefer an egalitarian relationship (Eshleman, 1985; McAdoo, 1981). These parents attempt to prepare their children for survival in a racist environment, which involves teaching flexibility in coping, while buffering negative messages which might damage their self-esteem (Peters, 1981).

The patriarchal affluent family reflects a strong tendency for the husband to be perceived as the dominant partner. It is closest to the traditional family with strict patterns of socialization and social control similar to those of the higher socioeconomic levels of the mainstream white culture. In view of the change in the role of the

Black father relative to socioeconomic status the following questions arise:

3. Will middle class Black fathers who are involved in a divorce proceeding seek custody of their children?
    a. If they believe that they cannot compete for custody, is it because of a cultural bias, a fatalistic attitude, or a realistic expectation based on experience?
4. If Black fathers are interested in sharing custody, will they expect to provide more of the support for the child or will they expect their wives to assume the more stereotypical provider role with the children?

It is well documented that Blacks have a higher tendency to divorce, partially due to the effects of lower socioeconomic status (Fine & Schwebel, 1988; Staples, 1981). Isaacs and Leon (1988) investigated the effect of race on visitation by fathers and found that race was not directly related to the frequency of visitation by Black fathers even though the majority of Black fathers (60%, compared to 26% of White fathers) visited their children one time per month or less, and 23% of Black fathers (compared to 8% of White fathers) never visited their children at all. Isaacs and Leon reported that Black couples were less likely to have a regular plan for visitation after divorce, were more likely to be separated by large distances, and were less likely to discuss the children after the divorce. In addition, Black women were more likely to move in with their parents following separation. These variables were related to low frequency of visitation regardless of race or socioeconomic status. In view of these findings further research questions arise:

5. Are Black fathers more likely to move back to the geographical region in which his extended family is located after divorce?
6. Will a Black father who has joint custody and is required to stay in the same region as his former wife be more likely to violate the decree by moving with the children to the region in which is extended family is located?

Blacks also have a higher rate of adolescent childbearing. Franklin (1988) noted that nearly half of Black first births are to women

under the age of 20, and these early childbearers are more likely to
establish single-parent, female-headed hoseholds. Black, adolescent
males are more likely to have children out of wedlock and to live
apart from them than are white males; Black women 15 to 19 years
old have four times as many out-of-wedlock births than their white
counterparts (National Center for Health Statistics, 1981, 1984).

In view of the higher tendency of adolescent Black males to have
children out of wedlock:

7. Do Black men who become fathers during their teen years
    hold different views of the roles and responsibilities of
    fatherhood than Black men who become fathers during
    their adult years?
8. Is the likelihood of seeking to establish paternity a function
    of economic well-being or age of Black fathers?
9. Will Black fathers differ in their attitudes toward custody of
    their legitimate and illegitimate children?
    a. Will the support from family and community vary ac-
        cording to the legitimacy of children?

Parenting Practices.   Black fathers have been noted more for
their absence than for their presence in the family setting. However,
it has been reported that the provider role is perceived as the most
important by middle-class Black fathers (Cazenave, 1979). Middle-
class Black men tend to view themselves as important to their
children and resent being stereotyped as absent or incompetent.
They consider themselves effective, active participants in the care
and upbringing of their children (Harrison, 1981). Price-Bonham
and Skeen (1979) found that middle-class Black fathers tend to be
more expressive and affectionate with their children than their
White counterparts. Cazenave (1979) found that middle-class Black
fathers were more inclined to participate in childcare than were their
own fathers, indicating that roles were still shifting toward more
egalitarian, expressive, and involved relationships. The role and
behavior of the Black father clearly differs by class.

Several researchers have reported that middle class Black fathers do not differ from White fathers in their use of discipline
methods. Black fathers have been found to view themselves as
authoritarian, but flexible, preferring not to ignore a child as a
method of discipline (Price-Bonham & Skeen, 1979). Black parents

inculcate personal uniqueness, obedience, and gender-neutral approaches to household tasks, especially the nurturance of younger children (Peters, 1981). They also stress and encourage education and achievement for their children.

The following are important questions for futher research on parenting issues:

10. As Black families enter the middle class, will Black patterns of fathering be similar to middle class White fathering patterns, or will they be unique to Black American families?
    a. Will the desire of Black fathers to share parenting of a child with a former spouse change as they move into the middle class?
    b. Will Black fathers whose former wives earn more be more likely to share parenting than Black fathers who earn more than the former spouse?
11. Are Black fathers who are expressive and affectionate with their children also strongly attached to their children?
12. Will Black fathers who are expressive and affectionate with their children want to assume more responsibility for them through joint or sole custody?
13. Will the childrearing attitudes and knowledge of Black fathers facilitate a father-custody arrangement?

Factors Unique to Black Families: Fosterage.   Another important aspect of the family is an informal or consensual type of adoption, referred to as *fosterage* (Hill & Shackleford, 1986; Stack, 1974). Fosterage occurs when the natural parents of a child are unable, for whatever reason, to rear that child. They may give the child to a family or individual within their extended family (usually a grandparent, sometimes a friend) with the understanding that while they are not abdicating their rights as natural parents, they expect that child will be reared responsibly. Fosterage circumvents the normal judicial and social welfare institutions, and it assures that in spite of the present difficulty in the immediate family, the child will be nurtured within a familial context. In view of the practice of fosterage among Black families:

14. Are maternal or paternal parents more likely to be resources for fosterage?

15. If the child(ren) is in a familial fosterage setting, will the
     father be more likely to stay in touch with the child than if
     the child is (a) in a nonfamilial fosterage or (b) in the
     mother's custody?

Understanding of Black American family life and the problems
which Black families must cope has been hampered by myths, cultural near-sightedness, and racism. Although there is awareness of
racial discrimination toward Blacks, entry into middle class status has
been slowed by the effects of prejudice (Landry, 1987).

In view of the cultural mythology surrounding Black American
family life:

16. Will stereotypes about Black matriarchy and weak, ineffec-
     tual Black fathers have a direct effect on the custody, child
     support, or paternity decisions made by courts?
17. What is the influence of cultural stereotypes about Black
     Americans on the attitudes and behaviors of lawyers and
     judges in the litigation of family disputes?

Hispanic American Families

In addition to great diversity in countries of origin and racial identity,
the social history of Hispanic groups in the United States contributes
to the complexity of forces that have shaped the Hispanic American
family. As is the case with Black families, stereotypes and mythology
have affected attitudes and scholarship concerning Hispanic families.

Growing from 14.6 million in 1980 to 17.8 million in 1985 (a
growth rate of 22%), the Hispanic segment of American population
is diverse in origin and race (62% Mexican American, 13% Puerto
Rican, and 25% other countries) (U.S. Bureau of the Census, 1987).
It may also be much larger if illegal alien estimates are correct,
perhaps 10+ million more than official census reports. With a high
rate of fertility (25.2 per 1,000 in 1985) and immigration, the Hispanic population is expected to reach 25.2 million (9.4% of the total
population of the U.S.) by the year 2000, and 60 million (19% of the
total population of the U.S.) by the year 2080 (U.S. Bureau of the
Census, 1986). Hispanic families tend to be large, with the average
size of a Mexican American family at 4.2, compared with that of the
total population of 3.0 (Alvirez, Bean, & Williams, 1981).

The Hispanic American Family Tradition. Generally, observers note four features of the idealized family, common in all Hispanic groups, that greatly influence roles and status within the family (Alvirez et al., 1981; Fitzpatrick, 1981; Queen, Habenstein, & Williams, 1985). The first is an important tradition within Hispanic American families. Labeled *familism*, it is a deeply held loyalty to all family members, including extended family. The family is the source of social, economic and emotional support, as well as the center of obligation. In view of this Hispanic American family tradition:

1. If couples seek legal divorce rather than resorting to some other culturally acceptable way of dealing with an irretrievably broken marriage, will the extended family provide psychological, social, and/or financial support for single fathers?
2. If an Hispanic American father pursues custody of his child(ren), will his extended family support him?
   a. If not, will it be because care and nuturance of children is unacceptable for men in the Hispanic American culture?
   b. What effect, if any, will socioeconomic status have on extended family support to single Hispanic American fathers?

Family Structure: Status and Roles in Hispanic American Families. The second feature of the idealized family is a structural issue. Hispanic American families exhibit an extended or modified extended structure or network that encompasses nuclear families. Family status formerly, and now to a lesser degree, was extended in a form of ritual kinship know as *Compadrazgo*. *Compadres*—godparents—are carefully chosen for children at their baptism. *Compadres* cultivate a close, but formal, relationship with the child. In addition, they become a part of the family network, available for and accorded mutual aid in times of need. In view of Hispanic American *Compadrazgo* ritual kinship:

3. Will Hispanic fathers be willing for the compadres, or godparents, to have custody of their children rather than taking custody themselves?
   a. Will the godparents' relationship with godchildren be affected by which parent is awarded custody?

Within the extended family a third characteristic of Hispanic culture exerts considerable, though often misunderstood, influence. *Machismo*, the idea of male dominance and superiority, has been as much maligned as the source of a "tangle of pathology" for Hispanics as "Black matriarchy" has been for Black families (Wright et al., 1983, p. 136). Presumably, *machismo* represents a need to compensate for feelings of inferiority. It is often expressed through brutal dominance and subordination of women. However, it is more than simply the evidence of compensatory need. It also has to do with a cluster of "masculine" values including courage, honor, responsibility toward the family, and respect for others (Fitzpatrick, 1981). In view of this aspect of Hispanic American culture:

4. Will fathers whose attitudes reflect high machismo wish to have custody of their children?
5. Is machismo more highly associated with the acceptance or avoidance of responsibility to support a child and former wife?
6. Will unwed Hispanic American fathers seek to establish paternity because of their need to demonstrate masculinity and virility?
7. Will fathers who seek custody express less machismo and greater psychological well-being?
8. Will middle class fathers be lower on machismo than lower class fathers?
9. If an Hispanic American mother has a better paying job than the father at the time of a divorce, how will the father be affected by a court decree that says he is not responsible for support of his child(ren)?

The fourth major characteristic of Hispanic families has to do with a hierarchy based on age and gender. Within the hierarchy, there are well-defined roles and functions; coupled with an aloof, authoritarian family head, the hierarchy may lend itself to an abuse of power. Stereotypically, the husband is the seat of authority and power within the family, followed by the mother, so long as the eldest son has not aged sufficiently to exercise authority over her. Children are socialized into gender-differentiated roles that materially affect the welfare of the family. Women are expected to be immersed in the bearing and rearing of children and the care of the household. In view of the hierarchical structure of the Hispanic American family:

10. Will Hispanic fathers who cannot rely on another female family member to care for children wish to have custody of their children?
11. Will Hispanic fathers be interested in sharing custody with their former wives?
    a. If fathers are willing to share custody, will they expect their wives to subordinate their wishes for the child(ren) to the wishes of the father?
12. Will fathers' childrearing attitudes and knowledge facilitate a father-custody arrangement?

Like the Black family, the Hispanic American family is differentiated increasingly by socioeconomic status in terms of characteristic relationships, childrearing practices, and values. This fact is perhaps best illustrated in the typology of families developed by Caine in 1974 and modified in 1985 by Queen and colleagues.

Culture of poverty families, the first category in this typology, are characterized by income below the poverty level, large families, inadequate child care, highly stressed parents who use authoritarian discipline methods, and a general feeling within the family of powerlessness or resignation. *Home-centered families* are charaterized by income below the poverty level as well, but feature a more orderly and managed family life. These families are more likely to inculcate middle-class values in children, stressing achievement, and using warmer, less authoritarian discipline. *Peer-group oriented families*, whose emphasis is on relationships restricted mostly to people of the same age, gender, and lifestyle, are more likely to interact with friends than with kin socially. *Community-oriented families* are focused on the nuclear family, but have community activities (mostly with kin and a few close friends) that tend to include the children and are seen as family activities, rather than adults-only activities. These families are more likely to be warm, authoritative (not authoritarian) and democratic in discipline. *Successfully mobile families*, whose income ranges above the poverty line, are more similar to White middle-class families. They are characterized by higher educational achievement and sponsorship, occupational success, delayed marriage, and focused goal orientation. Child socialization within these families is very important and is focused on competing in a white-collar world. They are more likely to be found outside the *barrios*. In view of the changes in the Hispanic family relative to socioeconomic class:

13. As Hispanic families enter the middle class, will patterns of fathering become more like middle-class, White fathering patterns?
    a. Will the interest of Hispanic fathers in sharing parenting of a child with a former spouse change as they move into the middle class?
    b. Will their shared parenting interest be associated with the economic conditions of both spouses following the divorce?
    c. Will Hispanic fathers whose former wives earn more be more likely to share parenting than Black fathers whose former wives earn more?
14. Will middle-class Hispanic fathers expect to provide more of the support for their child(ren), or will they expect their wives to assume more of a provider role with the children?

Factors Unique to Hispanic American Families: The Barrio. In the United States, over one-half of Hispanic families live in *barrios* in urban centers, including Los Angeles, Detroit, Chicago, St. Paul, St. Louis, Kansas City, Seattle, and San Francisco (Queen et al., 1985). As more Hispanics move out of the *barrios* and up the socioeconomic ladder, the social trends within their ethnic group begin to resemble those of the larger culture. The higher the socioeconomic status of a family, the more likely it is to move out of the *barrio*, have a working wife, have more egalitarian relationships, have more contact with Anglo-Americans, or experience intermarriage (Alvirez et al., 1981). In view of this trend:

15. Are any of the extended family resources available to single-parent father-headed Hispanic families who have moved out of the barrios?
    a. Will single Hispanic fathers prefer to return to live near extended family to take advange of these resources?

Factors Unique to the Hispanic American Family: The Church. Because of the Roman Catholic influence, individuals may be more likely to separate or desert rather than divorce (Queen et al., 1985). Although Hispanic divorce rates appear lower than those for Anglo-Americans, family breakdown may be underestimated due to desertion (Alvirez et al., 1981). In view of the importance of the Church to Hispanic families:

16. Is the rate of separation or desertion for Hispanics greater than in other minority cultures or the majority culture?

17. How does the Catholic process of annulment affect rates of remarriage and cohabitation among Hispanic fathers?

18. Is the Church a source of support for single Hispanic fathers?

It has been observed that patterns in Hispanic families are changing (Queen, et al., 1985). For example, there is a weakening of familism and husband's authoritarian role, Hispanic wives are entering the labor force, and children are becoming more like their peers in the larger culture through exposure to public school environments. As Hispanic American families change:

19. What will be the influence of cultural stereotypes on the attitudes and behaviors of lawyers and judges in the litigation of family disputes?

Conclusions

Since the 19th century, mothers have been considered the natural caretakers of children. That they are important to the nurturance and education of children is apparent. Inclusion of fathers in the category of "natural caretakers of children" has been slow. It requires that we question our beliefs about gender roles, beliefs that we have come to view as being grounded in the natural differences between men and women.

Beliefs about natural differences have been and continue to be used to support a preference for mothers as caretakers of children. As recently as 1973, a judge was reported to have said that "Fathers don't make good mothers" (Friedman, 1973), yet in a 1986 law review note, Martin (1986) argued that fathers should be allowed to participate in homemaking and childrearing if they wish and that they should be supported in that effort. For example, she pointed out that there are ways to modify employment practices that would support homemaking and childrearing efforts of fathers.

Still, little progress has been made toward gender neutrality in assumptions about parenting (cf., McCant, 1987; Meredith, 1985). It may be that some of the lethargy in the legal and other social systems has resulted from the inclination to think that if gender role stereotypes for parents are not appropriate, then we must think of males and females as being the same in their ability to nuture children. It is instructive to look to parenting experts for clarification on this point. For example, Lamb (1975) argued that both mothers and fathers play important, but qualitatively different, roles in the socialization of the children. This is not to say that the role played by one cannot be played by the other. The important point is that loss of either role is detrimental to the socialization process.

Lamb (1975) referred to Bronfenbrenner's view that the family should be considered a system. In a system, all roles are important, including those played by extended family members and other significant persons who become a part of the family system (e.g., *compadres* or parents in a nonrelated *fosterage* arrangement).

To understand the effects of laws on fathers in minority cultures, it will be necessary to understand the ways family systems function in minority cultures and the particular ways fathers contribute to those systems. Currently, we understand so little of family systems in minority cultures it would be nearly impossible for us to be sure whether the legal system either supports or is detrimental to fathers' contributions to parenting. Thus, if we were allowed to make only one recommendation for research on fathers and legal issues in minority cultures, it would be that the research be conducted from a systems perspective. It is in the configuration of roles that we gain our greatest insights into family functioning. In recognizing the significance of several important, qualitatively different influences in the socialization of children, it will be more possible for the legal system to be more constructive about children and parents—regardless of culture.

References

Alvirez, D., Bean, F. D., & Williams, D. (1981). The Mexican American family. In C. H. Mindel & R. W. Habenstein (Eds.), *Ethnic families in*

America: Patterns and variations (pp. 269–292). New York: Elsevier North Holland.

Barnes, S. J. (1986). Constitutional law—The law's strongest presumption collides with mankind's strongest bond: A putative father's right to establish his relationship to his child. *Western New England Law Review, 8,* 229–275.

Bengston, V. L., Furlong, M. J., & Laufer, R. S. (1974). Time, aging, and the continuity of social structure: Themes and issues in generational analysis. *Journal of Social Issues, 30,* 1–30.

Bettelheim, (1956). Fathers shouldn't try to be mothers. *Parents Magazine, 40,* 125–126.

Biller, H., & Meredith, D. (1975). *Father power.* Garden City, NY: Anchor.

Billingsley, A. (1968). *Black families in white America.* Englewood Cliffs, NJ: Prentice-Hall.

Bowlby, J. (1951). *Maternal care and mental health.* Geneva: World Health Organization.

Bradwell v. Illinois, 83 U.S. 130 (1873).

Broussard v. Broussard 320 So. 2d 236 (La. App. 1975).

Bruce v. Bruce, 141 Oklahoma, 160, 285 P. 30, 37 (1930).

Caine, T. A. (1974). *Social life in a Mexican American community.* San Francisco: R and E Research Associates.

Cazenave, N. A. (1979). Middle-income Black fathers: An analysis of the provider role. *The Family Coordinator, 28,* 583–593.

Clary, M. (1982). *Daddy's home.* New York: Seaview Books.

Developments in the law—The constitution and the family. (1980). *Harvard Law Review, 93,* 1156–1383.

Ellman, I., Kurtz, P., & Stanton, A. (1986). *Family law: Cases, text, problems.* Charlottesville, VA: The Michie Company.

Eshleman, J. R. (1985). *The family: An introduction* (5th Ed.). Boston: Allyn and Bacon.

Fine, M. A., & Schwebel, A. I. (1988). An emergent explanation of differing racial reactions to single parenthood. *Journal of Divorce, 11,* 1–15.

Fitzpatrick, J. P. (1981). The Puerto Rican Family. In C. H. Mindel & R. W. Habenstein (Eds.), *Ethnic families in America: Patterns and variations* (pp. 189–214). New York: Elsevier North Holland.

Folberg, J. (1984). Custody overview. In. J. Folberg (Ed.) *Joint custody and shared parenting* (pp. 3–10). Washington, DC: Bureau of National Affairs.

Foblerg, J., & Graham, M. (1979). Joint custody of children following divorce. *University of California, Davis, Law Review, 12,* 523–581.

Forbes, J. D. (1979). The Mexican heritage of the United States: An historical summary. In G. Henderson (Ed.), *Understanding and counseling ethnic minorities* (pp. 114–122). Springfield, IL: Charles C. Thomas.

Foster, H. H., & Freed, D. J. (1978). Life with father: 1978. *Family Law Quarterly, 11,* 320–363.

Foster, H. H., & Freed, D. J. (1981). Family law in the fifty states: An overview. *Family Law Quarterly, 24,* 229–283.

Foster, H. H., & Freed, D. J. (1982). Family law in the fifty states: An overview. *Family Law Quarterly, 26,* 289–383.

Franklin, D. L. (1988). The impact of early childrearing on developmental outcomes: The case of Black adolescent parenting. *Family Relations, 37,* 268–274.

Freed, D. J., & Foster, H. H. (1984). Family law in the fifty states: An overview. *Family Law Quarterly, 17,* 365–447.

Freed, D. J., & Walker, T. B. (1985). Family law in the fifty states: An overview. *Family Law Quarterly, 18,* 369–471.

Freed, D. J., & Walker, T. B. (1988). Family law in the fifty states: An overview. *Family Law Quarterly, 21,* 417–571.

Freud, S. (1949). *An outline of psychoanalysis.* [J. Strachey, Trans.] New York: W. W. Norton. (Original work published 1940.)

Friedman, L. M. (1977). *Law and society: An introduction.* Englewood Cliffs, NJ: Prentice-Hall.

Friedman, L. M. (1973, January 28). "Fathers don't make good mothers," said the judge. *New York Times,* Section 4, p. 12.

Gary, L., Beatty, L., Berry, G., & Price, M. (1983). *Stable Black families.* Final report, Institute for Urban Affairs and Research. Washington, DC: Howard University.

Glendon, M. A. (1975). Power and authority in the family. New legal patterns as reflections of changing ideologies. *The American Journal of Comparative Law, 23,* 1–33.

Harrison, A. (1981). Attitudes toward procreation among Black adults. In H. P. McAdoo (Ed.), *Black families* (pp. 199–208). Beverly Hills, CA: Sage.

Harrison, A., Serafica, F., & McAdoo, H. (1984). Ethnic families of color. In R. D. Parke (Ed.), *Review of child development research: Volume 7. The family* (pp. 329–371). Chicago: University of Chicago Press.

Haynie, S. M. (1986). Biological parents v. third parties: Whose right to child custody is constitutionally protected? *Georgia Law Review, 20,* 671–745.

Hill, R. B., & Shackleford, L. (1986). The Black extended family revisited. In R. Staples (Ed.), *The Black family* (pp. 194–200). Belmont, CA: Wadsworth.

Hofferth, S. L. (1985). Updating children's life course. *Journal of Marriage and the Family, 47,* 93–115.

Huang, L. J. (1981). The Chinese American family. In C. H. Mindel & R. W. Habenstein (Eds.), *Ethnic families in America: Patterns and variations* (pp. 115–141). New York: Elsevier North Holland.

Hunn v. Hunn, 289 S. C. 499, 347 S. E. 2d 108 (S. C. Ct. App. 1986).

Isaacs, M. S., & Leon, G. H. (1988). Race, marital dissolution and visitation: An examination of adaptive family strategies. *Journal of Divorce, 11*, 17–31.

Jenkins, v. Jenkins, 173 Wis. 592 (1921).

Jones, C. J. (1977–78). The tender years doctrine: Survey and analysis. *Journal of Family Law, 16*, 695–749.

Katz, D. (1974). Factors affecting social change: A social-psychological interpretation. *Journal of Social Issues, 30*, 159–180.

King v. de Manneville, 102 Eng. Rep. 1054 (K. B. 1804).

Kitano, H. H. L., & Daniels, R. (1988). *Asian Americans: Emerging minorities*. Englewood Cliffs, NJ: Prentice-Hall.

Kitano, H. H. L., & Kikimura, A. (1981). The Japanese American family. In C. H. Mindel & R. W. Habenstein (Eds.), *Ethnic families in America: Patterns and variations* (pp. 43–60). New York: Elsevier North Holland.

Krause, H. D. (1983). Reflections on child support. *Family Law Quarterly, 17*, 109–132.

Kumabe, K., Nishida, C., & Hepworth, D. H. (1985). *Bridging ethnocultural diversities in social work and health*. Honolulu: University of Hawaii School of Social Work.

Landry, B. (1987). *The new Black middle class*. Berkeley, CA: University of California Press.

Lamb, M. E. (1975). Fathers: Forgotten contributors to child development. *Human Development, 18*, 245–266.

Lehr v. Robertson, 103 S. Ct. 2985 (1983).

Logan, R. (1965). *The betrayal of the Negro*. New York: Collier.

Martin, N. (1986). Fathers and families: Expanding the familial rights of men. *Syracuse Law Review, 36*, 1265–1302.

Mayer v. Mayer, 150 N.J. Super. 556, 376 A. 2d 214 (1977).

McAdoo, J. L. (1981). Involvement of fathers in the socialization of Black children. In H. P. McAdoo (Ed.), *Black families* (pp. 225–237). Beverly Hills, CA: Sage.

McCant, J. W. (1987). The cultural contradiction of fathers as nonparents. *Family Law Quarterly, 21*, 127–143.

Meredith, D. (1985). Mom, daddy and the kids. *Psychology Today, 19*, 63–67.

Meyer v. Meyer, 663 P.2d 328 (Montana, 1983).

Moynihan, D. P. (1965). *The Negro family: The case for national action*. Washington, DC: Office of Policy Planning and Research, U.S. Department of Labor.

Nagel, S. S. (1970). Overview of law and social change. *American Behavioral Scientist, 13*, 485–491.

National Center for Health Statistics (1981). *Advance report of final natality statistics, 1981.* (Monthly Vital Statistics Report, Vol., 32, No. 9, Supplement, 1983). Washington, DC: U.S. Government Printing Office.

National Center for Health Statistics (1984). *Birth, marriages, divorces, and deaths for 1983.* (Monthly Vital Statistics Report, Vol. 32, No. 12). Washington, DC: U.S. Government Printing Office.

Nobles, W. (1978). Toward an empirical and theoretical framework for defining Black families. *Journal of Marriage and the Family, 40,* 679–688.

Norgren, J., & Nanda, S. (1988). *American cultural pluralism and law.* New York: Praeger.

Office of Refugee Resettlement. (1983). *Refugee resettlement program: Report to congress.* U.S. Department of Health and Human Services. Washington, DC: 1983, Table 1.

Orr v. Orr, 440 U.S. 268 (1979).

Peters, M. F. (1981). Parenting in Black families with young children: A historical perspective. In H. P. McAdoo (Ed.), *Black families* (pp. 211–224). Beverly Hills, CA: Sage.

Polite v. Polite, 127 A. D. 2d 465, 511 N.Y.S.2d 275 (1987).

P.B.C. v. D.H., 1985 Mass. Adv. Sh. 68, 483 N. E. 2d 1094 (1985) *cert. denied,* 106 S. Ct. 1286 (1986).

Price-Bonham, S., & Skeen, P. (1979). A comparison of Black and white fathers with implications for parent education. *The Family Coordinator, 28,* 53–59.

Queen, S. A., Habenstein, R. W., & Quandagno, J. S. (1985). *The family in various cultures.* New York: Harper and Row.

Reed v. Reed, 404 U.S. 71 (1971).

Scanzoni, J. H. (1971). *The Black family in modern society.* Boston: Allyn and Bacon.

Schaefer, R. T. (1979). *Racial and ethnic groups.* Boston: Little, Brown.

Smith v. Organization of Foster Families for Equality and Reform, 431 U.S. 8146 (1977).

Spero, A. (1985). *In America and in need: Immigrant, refugee, and entrant women.* Washington, DC: American Association of Community and Junior Colleges.

Stack, C. (1974). *All our kin: Strategies of survival in a Black community.* New York: Harper and Row.

Stanley v. Illinois, 405 U.S. 645 (1972).

Staples, R. (1971). Toward a sociology of the Black family: A theoretical and methodological assessment. *Journal of Marriage and the Family, 33,* 119–135.

Staples, R. (1976). *Introduction to Black sociology.* New York: McGraw-Hill.

Staples, R. (1981). The Black American family. In C. H. Mindel & R. W. Habenstein (Eds.), *Ethnic families in America* (pp. 217-244). New York: Elsevier North Holland.

Staples, R. (1986). Changes in Black family structure: The conflict between family ideology and structural conditions. In R. Staples (Ed.), *The Black family* (pp. 20-28). Belmont, CA: Wadsworth.

Staples, R. (1988). The emerging majority: Resources for nonwhite families in the United States. *Family Relations, 37*, 348-354.

In re State ex rel Watts v. Watts, 77 Misc. 2d 178, 350 N. Y S. 2d 285 (1973).

Thomas, G. (1979). The changing American family: Can the courts catch up? *Pepperdine Law Review, 6*, 733-749.

Treiman, D. J., & Terrell, K. (1975). Women, work, and wages—Trends in the female occupation structure. In K. C. Land & S. Spilerman (Eds.), *Social indicator models* (pp. 157-199). New York: Russell Sage.

Tuter v. Tuter, 120 SW 2d 203 (Mo. Ct. App. 1938).

U.S. Bureau of the Census. (1986). *Projections of the Hispanic population: 1983 to 2080* (Current Population Reports, Series P-25, No. 995). Washington, DC: U.S. Government Printing Office.

U.S. Bureau of the Census. (1987). *Population profile of the U.S.: 1984/85* (Current Population Reports, Series P-23, No. 150). Washington, DC: U.S. Government Printing Office.

U.S. Bureau of the Census. (1988). *Poverty in the United States: 1986.* (Current Population Reports, Series P-60, No. 160). Washington, DC: U.S. Government Printing Office.

Vandiver v. Vandiver, 491 So. 2d 251 (Ala. Civ. App. 1986).

Village of Arlington Heights v. Metropolitan Hous. Corp., 429 U.S. 252 (1977).

Walters, L. H., & Elam, A. W. (1985). The father and the law. *American Behavioral Scientist, 29*, 78-111.

Weyrauch, W. O., & Katz, S. N. (1983). *American family law in transition.* Washington, DC: Bureau of National Affairs.

Weitzman, L. J., & Dixon, R. B. (1979). Child custody awards: Legal standards and empirical patterns for child custody, support, and visitation after divorce. *University of California, Davis, Law Review, 12*, 471-521.

Wheeler, A. M. (1987). A father's right to know his child: Can it be denied simply because the mother married another man? *Loyola of Los Angeles Law Review, 20*, 705-769.

Wright, R., Jr., Watts, T. D., Saleebey, D., & Lecca, P. J. (1983). *Transcultural perspectives in human services: Organizational issues and trends.* Springfield, IL: Charles C. Thomas.

5
Social Class and Fatherhood

Rebecca J. Erickson
Viktor Gecas

In most complex societies, and certainly in our own, social class has a pervasive influence on people's lives. One's standing in the social class hierarchy affects where and how one lives; how long one lives; one's educational and occupational circumstances, and those of one's children; and a multitude of other life conditions. Because of the association of social class with differences in power, privilege, resources, and life conditions, we can expect social class to have a pervasive influence on family relations as well. Specifically, this chapter addresses the influence of social class on conceptions of fatherhood and on the attitudes and behaviors of fathers.

The Nature of Social Class

Before examining the influence of social class on fatherhood, we need to clarify the concept of social class as it will be used here. In spite of the prominence of the concept of sociological theory and research (it is arguably the most important social structural concept), there is considerable disagreement over the nature of social class and the criteria by which it should be measured. Particularly important is the distinction between the Marxian concept of "class" and the

Weberian concept of "status." "Classes" in the Marxian sense are distinguished by their relationship to the means of production, whereas "statuses," in Weber's usage, are largely based upon one's material consumption and the lifestyle it symbolizes. The stratification system in the United States has been characterized as being more suited to a system of "statuses" rather than "classes" (Gecas, 1979). This may be especially pertinent when examining the family as a class-related phenomenon:

> Critical to the traditional sociological definition of the modern family is the family's "loss" of productive functions with the Industrial Revolution, but its continued economic importance as a consumption unit. Consumption in a monetized economy requires money income so that the patterns families establish are closely tied to the financial conditions of earners, traditionally viewed in terms of the occupational prospects of husband-fathers. Consumption style and the prestige accorded to families in their community (termed *status* by Max Weber and assumed to devolve on families as a unit) are further mediated by the nature of occupations themselves and their relation to systems of production (*class* in the Marxist and Weberian senses). Whether work is manual or nonmanual, to use one common distinction, affects both class and status, as well as bringing with it a set of life chances and life experiences that shape family and consumption decisions. (Kanter, 1977, p. 7)

Kanter's observation parallels the dilemma faced by investigators of social class in relation to family life. Because most have employed indicators that reflect status levels, in the Weberian sense, we consider the concept of socioeconomic status as a more accurate classification. However, since the social class terminology is so embedded in our discussions of social stratification, we too will use "social class" in a descriptive or generic sense to refer primarily to distinctions in socioeconomic status.

Within the social class and parenting literature, there is further disagreement on what indicators should be used to measure social class. A family's social class status often relies upon the particular indicator used (e.g., occupation, education, income, or lifestyle) and/or the specific scale employed for the indicator. The determination of the family's status (which is typically treated as being synonymous with the father's status) usually occurs through an evaluation of occupational prestige, level of education, income, employment status, or a composite scale incorporating two or more of these indices. Even a cursory review of the literature on social class and socialization reveals wide variability in measurement as well as variability in research design, sampling, and data analysis (see Gecas, 1979, for a review). Such widespread heterogeneity makes comparisons across studies problematic.

A related methodological problem is the interrelationship of class, race, ethnicity and religion (see Chapters 4 and 7 for further discussion of these related topics). Some investigators (Gans, 1962; Inkeles, 1969; Hess, 1970; Kohn, 1977; Wilson, 1978) have argued that the effects of social class transcend those of other demographic characteristics, but their interaction cannot be denied.

As is true of the majority of literature pertaining to social class and socialization (Caldwell, 1964), this chapter appears to highlight the differences between classes. While this is typical of studies which focus on group comparisons, we should realize that for almost any of the socialization or family variables considered, variations (or differences) *within* class are substantially greater than variations or differences found between classes. Finally, when evaluating lower class behavior we need to keep in mind that behaviors and attitudes considered as maladaptive by White, middle-class, standards, may be quite adaptive given the conditions of lower class family life (Hess, 1970).

Given the differences in the operationalization of social class, we will first examine those studies that focus on the effects of socioeconomic status in general. Many of the studies in this section employ the Warner (1960) and Hollingshead (1958) indexes, which are the most pervasive indices combining two or more components of social class. Following this general review, social class is broken down into its main indicators of occupation, education, and income to evaluate their individual contributions to our understanding of the relationship between social class and fatherhood.

The Effects of Social Class on Fatherhood

Over the past century conceptions of fatherhood have changed both across and within social classes. Lamb (1986) summarizes the general transformation as beginning with the role of father as moral teacher and progressing through that of breadwinner, gender-role model, and finally emerging into the "new nurturant father" increasingly visible in contemporary American culture. Though these changes have known no class boundaries and have largely been linked to the Industrial Revolution, conceptions of fatherhood are also greatly affected by social class (Caldwell, 1964; Lynn, 1974). Middle-class parents are more likely to view the father's role as involving support and encouragement of their children, while those in the working class are more likely to see the paternal role as enforcing discipline and exercising control (Kohn, 1977). Kohn and others (Kohn & Carroll, 1960; Lewis & Weinraub, 1976) have also found that middle-class fathers wished to involve themselves in childrearing while working class fathers had less desire to do so, considering such involvement to be primarily the wife's responsibility

These class differences in attitudes toward paternal involvement in childrearing largely reflect class differences in conceptions of family roles. Middle-class families are more likely to emphasize role-sharing (especially as it involves parenting) and an egalitarian division of labor, whereas lower class families are more likely to favor role segregation, with the wife/mother having major responsibility for childcare and socialization (Rainwater, 1965; Eriksen, Yancey, & Eriksen, 1979; Bernstein, 1971).

In trying to determine the effect of social class on the amount of paternal interaction, Lamb, Pleck, Charnov, and Levine's (1987) conceptual distinctions among interaction, availability, and responsibility are helpful.

> *Interaction* refers to the father's direct contact with his child through caretaking and shared activities. *Availability* is a related concept concerning the father's potential availability for interaction, by virtue of being present or accessible to the child whether or not direct interaction is occurring. *Responsibility* refers to the role the father takes in ascertaining that the child is taken care of and arranging for resources to be available for baby-sitters, making appointments with the pediatrician and seeing that the child is taken to him/her, determining when the child needs new clothes, and so on. (p. 125)

Lamb et al.'s distinction between "interaction" and "availability" parallels Gecas' (1976) differentiation of child care and child socialization.[1] This distinction becomes especially important when evaluating the extent of paternal involvement. Fathers are much more likely to participate in child socialization, or interaction, than they are in "childcare" or in taking responsibility for the child (Kotelchuck, 1976; Baruch & Barnett, 1981). Some of the contradictory findings in the literature on social class and socialization are due to the failure to make these behavioral distinctions. For example, Lynn (1974) and Lewis and Weinraub (1976) state that, in general, middle-class fathers tend to be more involved in childrearing than working class fathers. However, when distinguishing among the three Lamb components, Radin and Sagi (1982) found a significant *negative* correlation between paternal availability and socioeconomic status.

In addition to the amount of paternal involvement, social class also affects the quality or nature of this involvement, particularly along the dimensions of parental support/nurturance and control/punishment. Investigators have consistently demonstrated a positive relationship between social class and parental support (Elder & Bowerman, 1963; Kohn, 1977; Thomas, Gecas, Weigert, & Rooney, 1974; Scheck & Emerick, 1976; and see Peterson & Rollins, 1987, for an extensive review). Middle-class fathers are more likely to show nurturance and affection toward their children than are lower class fathers. The findings concerning the control/punishment dimension are also quite consistent, showing that social class is positively related to the use of inductive control (e.g., reasoning with the child, explaining the reasons for the control), and negatively related to authoritarian and coercive control (Elder & Bowerman, 1963; McKinley, 1964; Erlanger, 1974). It should be noted, however, that although these findings are fairly consistent, the size of the relationships is rather modest. For example, the negative relationship between social class and use of physical punishment (one of the most consistent findings) ranges between $r = .10$ and $.20$, explaining about 4% of the variance at best.

The effects of social class on paternal involvement also vary along age and gender lines. Overall, fathers spend more time with sons than with daughters, regardless of age (Lamb, 1986). In terms of discipline patterns, Pearlin (1971) contends that while class is not unimportant, it is best considered in conjunction with gender. Pearlin concludes that gender differences are more prominent than class differences, but does find that working class sons are the most likely to be physically punished. Moreover, Bronfenbrenner's (1961) analysis specifies that gender differences are prominent only in the lower classes. Others argue that social class gender differences are better understood when seen as interacting with the child's age. For example, McGuire (1982) reports that class differences in father–child interaction appear to be minimal with infants but increase with age. Fathers, regardless of class or race, touch, talk, and spend more time with young boys (especially first born) than young girls. Lewis, Newson, and Newson (1982) report however, that by the age of seven father participation is higher in the middle classes than the working classes and remains greater for boys than girls.

Effects of Occupation

Since the earliest studies on social class and socialization (Anderson, 1936; Davis & Havighurst, 1946; Warner, 1960), occupation has been a major determinant of the socioeconomic status of men and their families (until quite recently, only the husband's occupation has been used to determine the family's class standing).

A common distinction in the research literature is between "white collar" and "blue collar" jobs, the former referring to middle class jobs and the latter to lower class jobs. But why should we expect these class-related occupations to have a bearing on parental attitudes and behavior? A number of scholars have argued that there is a functional relationship between the conditions experienced on the job and the attitudes and values that one holds, that is, values and attitudes are adaptations to work requirements (Miller & Swanson, 1958; Aberle & Naegele, 1952). The most extensive work along these lines is that of Kohn and his associates (1977, 1983). In addressing the question of how social class impinges upon individuals, Kohn has focused on conditions of work which enable or inhibit self-direction and creativity, for example degree of supervision, degree of routinization, and (especially) the substantive complexity of the work. In a series of large-scale studies, Kohn has found that these structural features of work significantly affect the development of values of self-direction/conformity and other psychological and attitudinal variables (especially intellectual flexibility). In general, the greater the freedom experienced on the job and the more complex and challenging the work, the more likely is the worker to place a high value on self-direction. On the other hand, the more constraining, routine, and simple the work, the more likely is the worker to value conformity and obedience. Expectedly, middle-class jobs are much more likely to be characterized by the former set of work conditions, whereas lower class jobs are more likely to reflect the latter. Furthermore, these work-related values become *generalized* orientations that adults have for themselves *and* for their children. Consequently, middle-class fathers are more likely to stress independence and self-direction in socializing their children, whereas lower class fathers are more likely to stress obedience (Gecas & Nye, 1974). These relationships between social class, occupational conditions, parental values, and socialization practices have received rather wide empirical support (for reviews and assessments of this research see Gecas, 1979, 1981; Kohn, 1977; Kohn & Schooler, 1983; Lee, 1982).

Despite the preponderance of research on how occupational conditions affect paternal values and behaviors, other aspects of one's job can also have an effect. Implicit within the blue-collar/white-collar and working class/middle-class distinctions is the contrast between having a "job" and having a "career." Rapoport and Rapoport (1976) define careers as those jobs that require a high degree of occupational commitment, have a "continuous developmental structure," and an "intrisically demanding character." We can assume then that careers generally require a greater time commitment from their occupants than do typical "9-to-5" jobs. Having to spend more hours involved in one's work role necessarily leaves fewer hours to spend in one's family roles. Thus, fathers who hold down "careers" may simply have less time to spend with their children than their "job"-holding counterparts. O'Brien (1982) lends support to this conclusion: middle-class or white collar men have a much higher degree of work-family conflict than blue collar men, and this conflict translates into less time spent with their families. Additionally, lower class men were found to be less engrossed in their work and less likely to bring their work home. In O'Brien's study lower class men may also have been more involved at home because a greater proportion of their wives were in the labor force (67% as compared to 35% of the middle class)—a point that will be considered more extensively later. The notion that middle-class careers hamper men's family involvement is supported by investigations summarized by Hess (1970) which used thematic apperception stories: Parents were found to play a smaller role in stories written by upper class children than were those written by working class children. Finally, Radin (1982) also found that greater paternal involvement in childrearing was associated with lower class status.

There is additional evidence that some aspects of lower class jobs may increase fathers' availability to care for children. Presser and Cain (1983) estimate that one-third of full time dual-earner couples with children have at least one spouse working other than a regular day shift (which is most likely to be a blue collar job). For 15% of these couples, there is little overlap between their schedules, and they may thus be using shift work as a solution to daycare.

Certainly not all investigators would agree that middle-class or career-oriented jobs adversely affect the amount of parental involvement. In Britain, Lewis et al. (1982) found that middle-class fathers have more time flexibility and more resources from their work to spend on family outings and activities. Working class men, on the other hand, have fewer flexible working hours, which may limit their family involvement. This observation is supported by the seminal study by Davis and Havighurst (1946) who found that, for both Black and White respondents, middle-class mothers reported that their husbands spent more time with the children than did their working class counterparts. Physically demanding jobs, more closely identified with the lower class, may also lessen father involvement (O'Brien, 1982).

Effects of Education

Even though education and occupation are strongly interrelated (i.e., those with higher education tend to have better jobs), education also has an independent influence on conceptions of the parental role, attitudes toward fathering, and the amount and type of father–child interaction. In general, education has a "liberalizing" influence on fathering. In the age of the "nurturant father" (Lamb, 1986), education has helped to broaden men's perspectives regarding appropriate roles. Now it is not only appropriate to be a breadwinner and disciplinarian but to be also a teacher, friend, and nurturer. Lamb (1982) argues that the most dramatic attitudinal changes regarding fatherhood have occurred in the middle classes. Additionally, it appears that positive outcomes from increases in paternal involvement usually result only when that increase is voluntary and consistent with the parents' attitudes and values (Lamb, Pleck, & Levine, 1985).

These attitudes and values are those correlated with higher educational achievement.

The liberalization of attitudes enhanced by education becomes especially important if Russell's (1982, 1983) results from an Australian sample can be generalized to the United States. He reported that sympathetic attitudes and values toward the fathering role often preceded increased paternal involvement. Although this is in accordance with the belief that positive consequences of paternal involvement occur only when the involvement is consistent with the father's attitudes, others (Oppenheimer, 1982) place more emphasis on changes in behavior precipitating changes in attitudes. It is still an open question, therefore, as to how much paternal behavior has actually changed as a result of changes in attitudes.

The *type* of father–child interaction also varies with class status and education. Middle-class fathers are more likely to read to their children, and take them to the library and on other trips than lower class fathers; they are also more likely to take on the teaching role with their children (Davis & Havighurst, 1946; Freeberg & Payne, 1967; Hess & Torney, 1967). Engaging in educational activities with one's children may be related to the confidence fathers have in their own educational skills: without education, and the skills which it promotes, one may not feel comfortable helping one's children in their own educational endeavors.

Effects of Income

Clearly, income matters in family relations since it has a direct affect on the quality and style of life of family members. Nowhere is the effect of income, or the lack of it, more evident than for those living in or near the poverty line.[2] However, most research on lower class parenting concentrates on mothers. This is not surprising given that in 1984 only 13% of poor children in the United States lived in male-headed households, whereas 55% lived in female-headed households (Ray & McLloyd, 1986 citing the Children's Defense Fund, 1984). Lower class fathers, if they are mentioned at all, are usually considered only in terms of their absence from the home. Consequently the majority of these families are more likely to be characterized as mother-centered (Lewis, 1966; Rainwater, 1960), with the burden of parenting falling on her shoulders.

Liebow (1967) indicated in his classic study of Black streetcorner men that some men disassociated themselves from their homes partly because they could not face the daily reminder of their inability to provide for their children. Other investigators lend support to Liebow's conclusion that men's inability to materially support their families provides a great source of male stress and contributes to their marginal position in the family (Komarovsky, 1940; Campbell, Converse & Rodgers, 1976; Voydanoff, 1983).

In most cases, paternal unemployment does undermine the father–child relationship. Regardless of social class, unemployment reduces the attractiveness of the father as a role model, particularly for sons (Ray & McLloyd, 1986). Unemployed fathers also feel less positively about their children (Sheldon & Fox, 1983, cited by Ray & McLloyd, 1986). Despite these negative overtones, and depending upon the reasons behind it, unemployment may have a positive effect on father–child relations due to the greater availability of the unemployed father for interaction (Caplovitz, 1979). For example, among husbands in 1982 who were principal caregivers while their wives worked, 24% were unemployed (Bianchi & Spain, 1986). The negative consequences of fathers' unemployment may also be some-what less for Black families (Heiss, 1975). Ray and McLloyd (1986) point out that lower class Black fathers' unemployment may result in less adverse effects largely because "family members recognize that it is due to race and class discrimination rather than enduring personal inadequacies" (p. 361).

At the other extreme of the socioeconomic scale are the upper class fathers. Though their children admire and identify with them (McKinley, 1964), and consider them valuable instructors in how to become a responsible member of the community (Hess & Torney, 1967), these fathers may also spend little time directly interacting with their children. The upper class father may wield a great deal of power (Lynn, 1974), but he may also have little actual contact with his children (Hess, 1970).

Effects of Education and Income

At first glance, it seems that education and income would affect paternal attitudes and behavior in the same direction. After all, there is a strong positive relationship between education and income. In actuality, however, they may have contrary effects. Although education is positively associated with egalitarian attitudes regarding household division of labor, Model (1981) found that as the father's income rises his *involvement* in the household falls. And yet, as the wife's education and income become more comparable to her husband's, he tends to do more work in the household. Eriksen et al. (1979) also reported a positive correlation between a wife's level of education and her husband's home participation and a negative relationship between this participation and his income level. These results lend support to the resource theory proposed by Blood and Wolfe (1960) and Scanzoni (1978): When the resources between the spouses are more disparate, the one contributing the greatest amount will be able to obtain freedom from domestic routine. As the resources become more similar, the division of labor between the spouses will also become more equal. In sum, as education increases, middle-class husbands do participate more in the care of their children. However, if this educational achievement translates into a high-paying job, the father tends to do less domestic work. Finally, the closer the spouses are in their income levels, the more equal the division of labor (Russell, 1982). It appears then that those spouses earning approximately equal salaries are the most likely to also have an egalitarian division of labor, and this is most likely to be true of lower class families:

> The majority of equal-income families were in the low-income range. Wage and education differentials are usually smaller between spouses of this group. . . . Only in three of our egalitarian households did each spouse succeed in earning $20,000 or more annually. (Model, 1981, p. 233)

The seeming contradiction in the influence of education and income can be explained by distinguishing between paternal attitudes and behavior. Education is more likely to affect attitudes; income is more likely to affect behavior. Occupation and income influence the objective circumstances of an individual. Higher paying jobs tend to demand a high level of commitment and time. A higher income, then, not only indicates a greater number of resources being brought into the relationship, but also a greater time commitment that may inhibit the availability of that parent for child care and other family responsibilities. Thus, not only are the resources contributed by the spouses more similar in the lower classes, but so is their availability for childrearing. To be sure, education does increase fathers' attitudes and motivation for being active in childrearing. However, when push comes to shove, it seems that the objective circumstances of income and work commitment will have the strongest impact on the actual behavior of fathers.

Indirect Influences of Social Class on Fatherhood

So far, most of our attention has been focused on the direct effects of social class (and its three main indicators) on fatherhood. However, because class has such a pervasive effect on family life and is found to be associated with a wide range of variables, there are also numerous indirect ways in which the influence of social class may be felt. For example, the association of social class with religious affiliation and ethnic minority identification is relevant to fatherhood. Catholics, fundamentalist Christians, and those of Eastern European and Hispanic heritage are more likely to have traditional values and orientations toward family and gender roles, which deemphasizes the father's role in childcare and socialization. These groups are also more likely to be in the lower social classes. Consequently, the association of social class with patterns of parenting is to some extent a function of the influence of these class-related subcultures.

Social class may also affect parenting indirectly through its negative effect on family size, that is, as social class increases, family size decreases. Family size is a key aspect of family structure, affecting many aspects of family and personality functioning (see Gecas, 1979, for a review). In particular, role specialization is found to increase with family size, with the roles of father and mother increasingly segregated. As the size of the family increases, order becomes more problematic, resulting in more roles and a greater emphasis on discipline and control. It is perhaps for this reason that parental, especially paternal, authoritarianism is often associated with the large family system (Bossard & Boll, 1956; Elder & Bowerman, 1963; Scheck & Emerick, 1976). Therefore, the association of paternal authoritarianism and more rigid control with lower class status may be a function, to some extent, of the class-related effects of family size.

Indirect Influences of Maternal Behavior

An understanding of the effects of social class on fathering would not be complete without including the influence that mothers have on the father–child relationship. Though we will be concentrating on the influence that mothers have on fathers, it is also true that fathers have an indirect impact on their children through their wives.

Middle-class wives expect their husbands to be as supportive of their children as they are; working class wives expect their husbands to restrain the children (Kohn & Carroll, 1960). Despite cross-class variations in attitudes toward the paternal role, the extent to which middle-class and lower class men have actually changed their behavior receives less consensual support. Maternal employment currently presents the greatest impetus for change in paternal family participation. Though investigators have focused on the consequences of maternal employment for women and children (Hoffman, 1977), some have examined the effect on the father's role.

Whether or not one finds that fathers are spending more actual time with their children—as opposed to more time in proportion to the time that mothers are spending—depends partly on the methodology used. Self-report data tend to exaggerate paternal involvement. Gilbert (1985), who used objective raters in addition to self-reports, found that 25% of the fathers had exaggerated their involvement in parenting. Investigators using "time use diaries" also tend to report a lower level of involvement than that found through questionnaire data (Lamb et al., 1987; but see Lewis & Weinraub, 1974, for an exception). However, regardless of the methodology used or the wife's employment status, all studies to date have shown that women perform more household tasks than do men (Bianchi & Spain, 1986) though men do share child rearing more often than any other task (excluding yard care and "fix-it" work).

Though married women have been an important part of the labor force for decades, only recently have investigators developed an interest in the characteristics and consequences of variations in dual-earner families. Recent attention has focused on comparisons between dual-earner (more lower class) and dual-career (more upper-middle class) families (Aldous, 1982; Pleck, 1985). There are major differences in how dual-earner and dual-career families are able to adjust to the costs associated with having both parents in the work force. Dual-career families are more able to hire outside help and services to help lighten the load (Holmstrom, 1972). Dual-earner families, because of their lower incomes, are less able to buy relief and "must juggle schedules, compromise needs, or just let things slide" (Moen, 1982, p. 17). This "juggling of schedules" in the lower classes will often necessitate greater paternal involvement in child care (Nock & Kingston, 1984; Bianchi & Spain, 1986).

The time commitment required by women's labor force participation has been found to affect the level of paternal involvement. Because fathers are more likely to look after their children when their wife works less than 25 hours per week (Eriksen et al., 1979), women may inadvertently increase their husband's participation by their choice to work part time rather than full time (Nock & Kingston, 1984). Bianchi and Spain (1982) report that

> in 1982, 10 percent of mothers who worked full time relied on the child's father as the principal caregiver while they were at work. Child care by the father was most common among women who worked part time: About 20 percent of mothers who worked part-time reported fathers as the caregivers. (p. 228)

Eriksen et al. (1979) interpret this result to mean "that when the wife works full time, the need for childcare is so great that it has to be done by outside agencies, but if she works part time, it is something that can be managed by the husband" (p. 311). Economically, the freedom to choose part time work may be more prevalent in the higher classes which seems to suggest that *middle* class men would participate in childcare more frequently. The issue of which social class fosters greater paternal availability and involvement still remains in doubt. Although greater paternal involvement in the lower classes runs counter to the values and attitudes held by lower class parents, maternal employment may necessitate the father's greater participation in child care.

Consequences of Increased Involvement

Minimal research exists concerning the effect, on the father, of increased childrearing participation. Most studies have focused on traditional fathers and their effects on child development rather than the effects on the fathers. Despite this lack of data, Russell and Radin (1983) identify five studies which report that highly participant fathers experience heightened self-esteem, self-confidence, and satisfaction with their parental role (Gronseth, 1978; Lamb et al., 1982; Lein, 1979; Sagi, 1982; Russell, 1983). However, Radin and Sagi (1982) found no relationship between the amount of satisfaction with the parental role and the extent of paternal participation. The problems of both self-selection and the biased nature of fathering samples are apparent here. It is possible that only those fathers with high levels of self-esteem take on nontraditional family roles (Russell & Radin, 1983). Additionally, Russell's (1983) study of Australian fathers reported that only 1–2% of all fathers participated in family role-reversal. Longitudinal research and representative sampling are both greatly needed to determine the direction of causality between the father's involvement in childrearing and his self-esteem and satisfaction.

Another aspect of this self-selection dilemma is the matter of choice versus necessity regarding paternal involvement in childrearing. Lamb et al. (1985) contend that increased involvement carries positive consequences only when it is chosen and is consistent with parental attitudes and values. Hence, we would expect that increasing paternal participation out of necessity, as is common in the lower classes, would have fewer positive consequences for the father than would occur in a (middle class) family in which paternal involvement is due to choice rather than necessity.

Conclusion

If this review of the literature on social class and fatherhood suggests anything, it is that there is no simple causal relationship between social class and fatherhood. Rather, what we see are various currents and sometimes cross-currents in the influence of class-related variables on aspects of fatherhood. We find that education is positively related to the development of egalitarian *attitudes* and more favorable attitudes toward paternal involvement in childrearing. However, these more favorable attitudes do not seem to translate into significant increases in actual behavior. Income, on the other hand, appears to have a more direct effect on paternal behavior, in that the higher the father's income (relative to his wife's) the lower his actual involvement in childrearing and other domestic roles. Related to this point is the influence of wife's employment status and income: Wife's employment status (and her income) may be the single most important factor affecting the degree of paternal involvement in childrearing.

In sum, it seems that the three main indicators of social class (i.e., education, income, and occupation) present us with some interesting cross-currents in their effects on paternal involvement: Father's education has a positive effect on attitudes favoring greater paternal participation; father's income has a negative effect on paternal behavior; depending upon the occupational characteristic observed, father's occupation can have either a positive or negative effect on his involvement; and mother's education, income, and employment have positive effects on paternal involvement. It is easy to see how these indicators of social class may well cancel each other out, thereby diluting and masking the overall effect of social class on fatherhood.

It is also evident here that there are a multitude of indirect ways in which social class may influence fatherhood, through its association with ethnic minorities, religious affiliations, and family size, among other things. Much of the content as well as the amount of paternal involvement affected by social class may be due to these secondary associations, within which sex role orientations tend to be more traditional. We conclude, therefore, that the influence of social class on fatherhood is pervasive, but also complex. In pursuing this relationship it is important to specify which *indicator* of social class, affects which *aspect* of fatherhood, under which *conditions*, and controlling for which *other* class-related variables. Without this level of specification we cannot hope to achieve a clear understanding of the influence of social class on fatherhood.

Policy Implications

Although fatherhood research has largely been limited to comparing the working and middle classes, social policies require a differentiation between these two groups and poverty-stricken families. Families in poverty require programs that do not discriminate against the father and focus on improving the family's living conditions. The working and middle classes, on the other hand, need policy changes in the work place and a change in corporate management's attitude toward parental involvement.

Though current policies benefitting "disadvantaged" families are written using the word "parent," their implementation seems to discriminate against the involvement of men in family life. One example is the Aid to Families with Dependent Children (AFDC) policy. In most states, a family's support payments are reduced, or even eliminated, if there is a male living in the household, whether or not he is employed. Changes in policy are needed so that poor fathers who are unemployed or do not earn enough to support their families will not have to choose between leaving their home so their family is eligible for AFDC, or remaining with their family, thereby making them ineligible (Ray & McLloyd, 1986). Gender-neutral policies are required which provide benefits to any parent who needs to stay home with his/her child. Such a program would allow the most employable parent to seek work without jeopardizing the family's social service benefits (Lamb, Russell, & Sagi, 1983).[3]

Increasing the participation of working class and middle-class fathers requires a different approach than that of lower class fathers. These men are greatly influenced by the structure of their work environment and the attitudes of their employers toward increased involvement (Gilbert, 1985). Changes in this area are required on a number of fronts: work scheduling, parental leave, and employer attitude (for a more complete discussion see Lamb & Sagi, 1983; Pleck, 1986).

The most widely discussed change in work scheduling concerns "flexitime": workers are given more flexibility about when to start and end their work day. As with all changes in the occupational sphere, cost and the effect on productivity must be taken into account. Though widespread implementation has not yet occurred, studies have found that most flexitime users do not decrease in productivity and such scheduling may even decrease absenteeism (Nollen, 1979; Winett & Neale, 1980; Lamb et al., 1983). It should be noted however that, in the one longitudinal study on this issue, the increase in paternal participation attributed to flexitime disappeared after a year (Winett & Neale, 1980). The absence of any long-term behavioral change indicates the need for other supportive factors (e.g., Lamb et al., 1987, suggest increases in motivation, parenting skills, and support from significant others) if long-term increases in fathers' participation are to occur.

Another occupationally oriented change concerns parental leave policies. Men are rarely given the variety of leave and child care options that are commonly available to women (Gilbert, 1985). The few companies that have instituted "parental leave," as opposed to maternity/maternal leave, found that men rarely used it. This seeming lack of motivation may possibly be more accurately attributed to the economic and possible career costs suffered by the families of men who take leave (Pleck, 1986).

Although more employers and corporations (as well as fathers) are becoming increasingly aware of the need for gender-neutral child care and leave-taking policies (Saltzman & Barry, 1988), there are structural constraints continuing to restrict their availability. First, few of the changes discussed above are likely to be implemented or used unless employers adopt a more gender-neutral stance regarding the parental role. As long as career-oriented men anticipate negative career consequences due to paternal leave or greater paternal involvement, they will remain hesitant to take advantage of any policies which may exist. Second, gender-based economic inequality hampers a father's freedom to choose an active paternal role. If his family suffers greater financial loss when he takes parental leave than when his wife does, economics rather than personal preference determines his level of involvement.

Finally, our hope for any social policy is not that it will come to dictate fathers' greater involvement, but rather that it will provide each family with the *option* for fathers to become more involved.

Notes

1. Gecas (1976) characterizes child socialization as "the social and psychological development of the child. It refers to those processes and activities within the family which contribute to developing the child into a competent, social, and moral person" (pp. 33-34). Childcare pertains to "the physical and psychological maintenance of the child. Activities such as keeping the child clean, fed, and warm, as well as protected from physical dangers and frightening experiences" (pp. 33-34).

2. The Census Bureau (1986) defines the poverty threshold in the United States as the minimum amount of money a family of four needs to purchase a nutritionally adequate diet, assuming they use one-third of their income for food. This roughly translates into about $11,000 per year.

3. Federal legislation is now pending that would allow for two-parent families to receive AFDC benefits though some employment or job-seeking restrictions apply.

References

Aberle, D. F., & Naegele, K. D. (1952). Middle-class fathers' occupational role and attitudes toward children. *American Journal of Orthopsychiatry, 22*, 366–378.

Aldous, J. (Ed.). (1982). *Two paychecks: Life in dual-earner families*. Beverly Hills: Sage.

Anderson, J. E. (1936). *The young child in the home*. White House Conference on Child Health and Protection. New York: Appleton-Century.

Baruch, G. K., & Barnett, R. C. (1981). Fathers' participation in the care of their preschool children. *Sex Roles, 7*, 1043–1055.

Bernstein, B. (1971). *Class, codes and control: Vol. 1. Theoretical studies toward sociology of language*. London: Routledge & Kegan Paul.

Bianchi, S. M., & Spain, D. (1986). *American women in transition*. New York: Russell Sage Foundation.

Blood, R. O., & Wolfe, D. M. (1960). *Husbands and wives*. New York: Free Press.

Bossard, J. H., & Boll, E. (1956). *The large family system*. Philadelphia: University of Pennsylvania Press.

Bronfenbrenner, U. (1961). Toward a theoretical model for the analysis of parent-child relationships is a social context. In J. Glidewell (Ed.), *Parent attitudes and child behavior* (pp. 90–109). Springfield, IL: Charles C. Thomas.

Bureau of the Census. (1986). Money income of households, families, and persons in the United States: 1984. *Current Population Reports* (Series P-60, No. 151). Washington, DC: U.S. Bureau of the Census.

Caldwell, B. M. (1964). The effects of infant care. In M. L. Hoffman and L. W. Hoffman (Eds.), *Review of child development research (Vol. 1)* (pp. 9–87). New York: Russell Sage Foundation.

Campbell, A., Converse, P., & Rodgers, W. (1976). *The quality of American life*. New York: Russell Sage Foundation.

Caplovitz, D. (1979). *Making ends meet: How families cope with inflation and recession*. Beverly Hills, CA: Sage.

Children's Defense Fund. (1984). *American children in poverty*. Washington, DC: Children's Defense Fund.

Davis, A., & Havighurst, R. J. (1946). Social class and color differences in child-rearing. *American Sociological Review, 11*, 698–710.

Elder, G. H., & Bowerman, C. E. (1963). Family structure and childrearing patterns: The effect of family size and sex composition. *American Sociological Review, 28*, 891–905.

Eriksen, J. A., Yancey, W. L., & Eriksen, E. P. (1979). The division of family roles. *Journal of Marriage and the Family, 41*, 301–313.

Erlanger, H. S. (1974). Social class and corporal punishment in child rearing: A reassessment. *American Sociological Review, 39*, 68–85.

Freeberg, N. E., & Payne, D. T. (1967). Dimensions of parental practice concerned with cognitive development in the preschool child. *Journal of Genetic Psychology, 111*, 245–261.

Gans, H. (1962). *The urban villagers*. Glencoe, IL: Free Press.

Gecas, V. (1976). The socialization and child care roles. In F. I. Nye (Ed.), *Role structure and the analysis of the family* (pp. 33–59). Beverly Hills, CA: Sage.

Gecas, V. (1979). Influences of social class on socialization. In W. R. Burr, R. Hill, F. I. Nye, & I. L. Reiss (Ed.), *Contemporary theories about the family: Vol. 1. Research-based theories* (pp. 365–404). New York: Free Press.

Gecas, V. (1981). Contexts of socialization. In M. Rosenburg & R. Turner (Eds.), *Social psychology: Sociological perspectives* (pp. 165–199). New York: Basic Books.

Gecas, V., & Nye, F. I. (1974). Sex and class differences in parent-child interaction: A test of Kohn's hypothesis. *Journal of Marriage and the Family, 36*, 742–749.

Gilbert, L. A. (1985). *Men in dual-career families: Current realities and future prospects*. Hillsdale, NJ: Lawrence Erlbaum.

Gronseth, E. (1978). Work sharing: A norweigen example. In R. Rapoport, R. N. Rapoport, & J. Bumstead (Eds.), *Working couples* (pp. 108–121). St. Lucia, Queensland: University of Queensland Press.

Heiss, J. (1975). *The case of the Black family: A sociological inquiry*. New York: Columbia University Press.

Hess, R. D. (1970). Social class and ethnic influences on socialization. In P. H. Mussen (Ed.), *Carmichael's manual of child psychology (Vol. 2)* (3rd Ed.) (pp. 457–557). New York: John Wiley & Sons.

Hess, R. D., & Torney, J. V. (1967). *The development of political attitudes in children*. Chicago: Aldine.

Hoffman, L. W. (1977). Changes in family roles, socialization and sex differences. *American Psychologist, 32*, 644-657.

Hollingshead, A. B., & Redlich, F. C. (1958). *Social class and mental illness.* New York: John Wiley & Sons.

Holmstrom, L. L. (1972). *The two-career family.* Cambridge, MA: Schenkman.

Inkeles, A. (1969). Social structure and socialization. In D. A. Goslin (Ed.), *Handbook of socialization theory and research* (pp. 615-632). Chicago: Rand McNally.

Kamerman, S. B. (1983). Fatherhood and social policy: Some insights from a comparative perspective. In M. E. Lamb & A. Sagi (Eds.), *Fatherhood and social policy* (pp. 23-37). Hillsdale, NJ: Lawrence Erlbaum.

Kanter, R. M. (1977). *Work and family in the United States: A critical review and agenda for research and policy.* New York: Russell Sage Foundation.

Kohn, M. (1977). *Class and conformity: A study in values.* Homewood, IL: Dorsey Press.

Kohn, M., & Carroll, E. E. (1960). Social class and the allocation of parental responsibilities. *Sociometry, 23*, 372-392.

Kohn, M., & Schooler, C. (1983). *Work and personality: An inquiry into the impact of social stratification.* Norwood, NJ: Ablex.

Komarovsky, M. (1940). *The unemployed man and his family.* New York: Dryden Press.

Kotelchuck, M. (1976). The infant's relationship to the father: Experimental evidence. In M. E. Lamb (Ed.), *The role of the father in child development* (pp. 329-344). New York: John Wiley & Sons.

Lamb, M. E. (Ed.). (1976). *The role of the father in child development.* New York: John Wiley & Sons.

Lamb, M. E. (1982). Maternal employment and child development: A review. In *Nontraditional families: Parenting and child development* (pp. 45-69). Hillsdale, NJ: Lawrence Erlbaum.

Lamb, M. E. (1986). *The father's role: Applied perspectives.* New York: John Wiley & Sons.

Lamb, M. E., Pleck, J. H., Charnov, E. L., & Levine, J. A. (1987). A biosocial perspective on paternal behavior and involvement. In J. B. Lancaster, J. Altmann, A. S. Rossi, & L. R. Sherrod (Eds.), *Parenting across the lifespan: Biosocial perspectives* (pp. 111-142). New York: Aldine De Gruyter.

Lamb, M. E., Pleck, J. H., & Levine, J. A. (1985). The role of the father in child development: The effects of increased paternal involvement. In B. B. Lahey & A. E. Kazdin (Eds.), *Advances in clinical child psychology (Vol. 8)* (pp. 229-266). New York: Plenum Press.

Lamb, M. E., Russell, G., & Sagi, A. (1983). Summary and recommendations for public policy. In M. E. Lamb & A. Sagi (Eds.), *Fatherhood and family policy* (pp. 247-258). Hillsdale, NJ: Lawrence Erlbaum.

Lamb, M. E., & Sagi, A. (Eds.). (1983). *Fatherhood and family policy.* Hillsdale, NJ: Lawrence Erlbaum.

Lee, G. (1982). *Family structure and interaction.* Minneapolis: University of Minnesota.

Lein, L. (1979). Male participation in home life: Impact of social supports and breadwinner responsibility on the allocation of tasks. *The Family Coordinator, 29,* 489-496.

Lewis, C., Newson, E., & Newson, J. (1982). Father participation through childhood and its relationship with career aspirations and delinquency. In N. Beail and J. McGuire (Eds.), *Fathers: Psychological perspectives* (pp. 174-193). London: Junction Books.

Lewis, M., & Weinraub, M. (1976). The father's role in the child's social network. In M. E. Lamb (Ed.), *The role of the father in child development* (pp. 157-184). New York: John Wiley & Sons.

Lewis, O. (1966). The culture of poverty. *Scientific American, 215,* 19-25.

Liebow, E. (1967). *Tally's corner.* Boston, MA: Little, Brown & Co.

Lynn, D. B. (1974). *The father: His role in child development.* Monterey, CA: Brooks/Cole.

McGuire, J. (1982). Gender-specific differences in early childhood: The impact of the father. In N. Beail and J. McGuire (Eds.), *Fathers: Psychological perspectives* (pp. 95-125). London: Junction Books.

McKinley, D. C. (1964). *Social class and family life.* New York: Free Press.

Miller, D. R., & Swanson, G. E. (1958). *The changing American parent.* New York: John Wiley & Sons.

Model, S. (1981). Housework by husbands: Determinants and implications. *Journal of Family Issues, 2,* 225-237.

Moen, P. (1982). The two-provider family: Problems and potentials. In M. E. Lamb (Ed.), *Nontraditional families: Parenting and child development* (pp. 13-43). Hillsdale, NJ: Lawrence Erlbaum.

Nock, S. L., & Kingston, P. W. (1984). The family work day. *Journal of Marriage and the Family, 46,* 333-343.

Nollen, S. D. (1979). Does flexitime improve productivity? *Harvard Business Review, 57,* 4-8.

O'Brien, M. (1982). The working father. In N. Beail and J. McGuire (Eds.), *Fathers: Psychological perspectives* (pp. 217-233). London: Junction Books.

Oppenheimer, V. K. (1982). *Work and family: A study of social demography.* New York: Academic Press.

Pearlin, L. I. (1971). *Class context and father relations: A cross-national study.* Boston, MA: Little, Brown & Co.

Peterson, G. W., & Rollins, B. C. (1987). Parent-child socialization. In M. B.

Sussman & S. K. Steinmetz (Eds.), *Handbook of marriage and the family* (pp. 471–507). New York: Plenum Press.

Pleck, J. H. (1983). Husbands' paid work and family roles: Current research issues. In H. Z. Lopata & J. H. Pleck (Eds.), *Research in the interweave of social roles: Vol. 3. Families and jobs.* Greenwich, CT: JAI Press.

Pleck, J. H. (1985). *Working wives/working husbands.* Beverly Hills: Sage.

Pleck, J. H. (1986). Employment and fatherhood: Issues and innovative policies. In M. E. Lamb (Ed.), *The father's role: Applied perspectives* (pp. 385–412). New York: John Wiley & Sons.

Presser, H. B., & Cain, V. (1983, February). Shift-work among dual-earner couples with children. *Science*, pp. 876–878.

Radin, N. (1982). Primary caregiving and role-sharing fathers. In M. E. Lamb (Ed.), *Nontraditional families: Parenting and child development* (pp. 173–204). Hillsdale, NJ: Lawrence Erlbaum.

Radin, N., & Sagi, A. (1982). Childrearing fathers in intact families, II: Israel and the U.S.A. *Merrill-Palmer Quarterly, 28,* 111–136.

Rainwater, L. (1960). *And the poor get children.* Chicago: Quadrangle Books.

Rainwater, L. (1965). *Family design.* Chicago: Aldine.

Rapoport, R., & Rapoport, R. N. (1976). *Dual-career families re-examined.* New York: Harper & Row.

Ray, S. A., & McLloyd, V. C. (1986). Fathers in hard times: The impact of unemployment and poverty on paternal and marital relations. In M. E. Lamb (Ed.), *The father's role: Applied perspectives* (pp. 339–383). New York: John Wiley & Sons.

Russell, G. (1982). Highly participant Australian fathers: Some preliminary findings. *Merrill-Palmer Quarterly, 28,* 137–156.

Russell, G. (1983). *The changing role of fathers?* St. Lucia, Australia: University of Queensland Press.

Russell, G., & Radin, N. (1983). Increased paternal participation: The fathers' perspective. In M. E. Lamb & A. Sagi (Eds.), *Fatherhood and family policy* (pp. 139–165). Hillsdale, NJ: Lawrence Erlbaum.

Sagi, A. (1982). Antecendents and consequences of various degrees of parental involvement in childrearing: The Israeli project. In M. E. Lamb (Ed.), *Nontraditional families: Parenting and child development* (pp. 205–232). Hillsdale, NJ: Lawrence Erlbaum.

Saltzman, A., & Barry, P. (1988, June). The superdad juggling act. *U.S. News & World Report*, pp. 67–70.

Scanzoni, J. (1978). *Sex roles, women's work and marital conflict.* Lexington, MA: D. C. Heath.

Scheck, D. C., & Emerick, R. (1976). The young male adolescent's perception of early childrearing behavior: The differential effects of socioeconomic status and family size. *Sociometry, 39,* 39–52.

Sheldon, A., & Fox, G. L. (1983). The impact of economic uncertainty on children's roles within the family. Paper presented at the meeting of the Society for Study of Social Problems, Detroit, MI.

Thomas, D. L., Gecas, V., Weigert, A., & Rooney, E. (1974). *Family socialization and the adolescent.* Lexington, MA: Heath.

Voydanoff, P. (1983). Unemployment and family stress. In H. Z. Lopata & J. H. Pleck (Eds.), *Research in the interweave of social roles: Vol. 3. Families and jobs* (pp. 239–250). Greenwich, CT: JAI Press.

Warner, W. L. (1960). *Social class in America.* New York: Harper & Row.

Wilson, W. J. (1978). *The declining significance of race.* Chicago: University of Chicago Press.

Winett, R. A., & Neale, M. S. (1980, November). Results of experimental study on flexitime and family life. *Monthly Labor Review,* pp. 29–32.

6
Religion and Its Impact on Fatherhood

Teresa Donati Marciano

Connections Between Religion and Fatherhood

> I walked with him down the beach and watched him in the water, swimming
> skillfully . . . and wondered who had taught him. "My father," he
> said . . . drying himself with a towel. "It's in the Gemorah. A father is
> supposed to make sure his child learns how to swim."
> *Chaim Potok, Davita's Harp* (1985, p. 324)

This opening quotation clearly links the duty of the adult Jewish man
who is a father with a specific obligation toward his child. The
implications are fascinating for what they say about religion and
fatherhood: that a religious teaching exists, which is believed, and
therefore embraced, and as a consequence obeyed. Yet each step in
those implications is, when analyzed, voluntaristic. Nothing compels
a man to acknowledge a religious teaching as either religious or, if
religious, valid; even if a teaching is acknowledged as religious, the
man may dissent from its validity or applicability in his life; he may
therefore disbelieve it, and should he happen to do what the teaching
says he should do, that is religiously incidental.

It is important to consider this voluntaristic nature of religious belief and conformity to religious teachings, because religion and its connections to any other part of our lives is more sensed than empirically demonstrated.

Objectives and Purpose

This chapter demonstrates the degree to which the impact of religion on fatherhood needs extensive study in its own right. Data currently available make interpolation and inference necessary, rather than providing direct findings on their connection. That connection, moreover, is part of a larger set of institutional and macrohistorical changes that affect families and parental roles. Thornton (1988) has described these interrelationships among family, religion, and other historical and cultural forces. For the sake of providing a summary concept, I will denote it as a need to study the "embeddedness" of religion and family in the larger fabric of culture (Marciano, 1990). Even national cultures are no longer distinctive, given the intermixing of peoples and cultural influences throughout the world. This brings with it the need for different groups and beliefs to coexist within the same national cultural setting; the mixtures and diffusions also bring protest from the "fundamentalist" or "traditionalist" elements in cultures that are inexorably changing.

Describing the recent public debates over Salman Rushdie's controversial 1988 novel, *The Satanic Verses*, Marzorati (1989) interviewed Rushdie as to why Moslems felt so affronted by the novel. Rushdie, describing the world he saw, noted how worldwide immigration has produced fragmentation of old selves, and the need to reinvent and recreate identity. Rushdie is describing an extreme case of of what is happening within all cultures that are in any way open to outside influences, and is certainly the case with culture in the United States.

That is the often-unspoken cultural basis of studies that do exist: We are pluralistic, and our beliefs are drawn from many sources besides religion. The evidence therefore points to formal religion as a case of voluntary group membership, and not one of "automatic" inheritance from one's family's religious beliefs. For that reason, the connection between religion and fatherhood will be presented as the outcome of an opportunity model: The way in which, as the boy grows into a man, his own life course as it intersects with his group memberships and historical events, shape the direction of his religious commitments and the intensity with which they are pursued.

Some Questions About Religion as a Variable in Fatherhood

Religion is often unwarrantedly treated as an independent variable. Where high correlations are found between religion and other variables, there is always a temptation to imply cause, even though correlation measures are not measures of causality. The assumption of religion as causal may also lead to wrongly-founded hypotheses, though often revealing surprising findings as a result. It is assumed, for example, that religious orthodoxies (Roman Catholic, Mormon) would inhibit the use of abortion; yet, very high numbers of Catholic and Mormon women seek and have abortions. Despite the strong emphasis on chastity in each of those faiths, premarital sex and unwanted pregnancy obviously occur in noticeable numbers. What religion may "cause," therefore, is not necessarily a reduced likelihood of abortion. Rather, the abortion findings speak more of how certain orthodoxies inhibit contraceptive preparedness, and less about how religious belief influences the decision taken in unwanted or unplanned pregnancy.

In the same way, "mechanistic" assumptions are too easily made about the connections between religious affiliation and other aspects of life. This includes assumptions about religious influences on how any male role is learned and lived. Can anyone really say that a father who is Catholic, Jewish, Mormon, or Episcopalian behaves in a given way because of his religion? How powerful, for example, is the fact of maleness (gender teaching), compared to religious teaching?

Gender and religion may confound each other as two particular, illustrative studies show. Morgan (1987) presents a good capsule overview of literature linking religion and gender-role attitudes. Her review "points to the importance of religious devoutness in consistently predicting traditional gender-role attitudes" (p. 307). This raises the question of the role played by religion in shaping, or confirming, traditional male and father roles; it also implies that religion may be a factor in resisting role changes or adaptations.

Evidence of this connection between gender role expectations and religion is found in a study by De Vaus and McAllister (1987). They begin by noting the few attempts to explain a common, well-known truth that women are more religious than men. Using Australian data, they conclude that lower female work force participation accounts for higher religious involvement. Social structural placement—in or out of the paid work force—greatly affects the choice, and even the opportunity to mingle with co-religionists, and to hear the words of sermons and worship. As women participate more in the paid labor market their religiosity may decline for reasons of time, alternative (nonreligious) satisfactions, and/or changed values. Men, particularly those in father/breadwinner roles, are already structurally placed in the labor market; the same reasons have already reduced religious effects and involvement for them. Certain kinds of gender convergence, such as work force participation, may therefore produce religious behavioral convergence. For both men and women, religion becomes more a competitor and option for the individual. In both cases also, gender is predictive only insofar as traditional roles continue to be played.

The factor of gender in value transmissions (presumably including religious values) is a major finding of a recent study by Whitbeck and Gecas (1988). This is another of the relatively few studies that separates fathers' and mothers' influence on value transmission. The values examined are categorized as "instrumental" or "terminal" values, and while none are denoted as specifically religious, some of the instrumental values which would appear to have stronger religious links are: forgiving, loving, obedient, and, responsible. Two of the terminal values that appear religiously linked are world at peace and self-respect. The sample of 82 families was drawn from churches and parochial schools, so that the religion-value link seems a valid inference here. A religiosity measure was also constructed for the sample, although specific discussions of religiosity are not included in this article but may be reported in future publications. Their findings on value congruence (or its absence) are interesting, but what is most important here is the gender linkage to value expectations. Two instances of this are:

> both mothers and fathers are more apt to attribute their values to their daughters than to their sons. (p. 836)

> The data . . . suggest different value socialization based on gender role expectations. (p. 838)

A demonstration of gender-linked parental value expectations is found in tabulated bivariate correlations between children's and parents' personal values: on the value of obedience, the correlation between fathers and boys was -0.108, while for girls it was 0.362; the correlation between mothers and boys on obedience was 0.215, and for girls 0.603 (p > 0.001). The bivariate correlations for both fathers and mothers were also far higher for girls than boys on "forgiving." Other bivariate correlations in the study also show discrepancies by sex of child, and by sex of parent. Gender is apparently the prism through which religious-types of values are filtered. This is congruent with studies showing greater parental attachment and dependency of girls compared to boys, resulting from differential socialization, and expectations, by sex (Gilligan, 1982).

The result of such differential socialization would be a greater tendency for men to reject external authority where it contradicts their personal goals or desires. Religious skepticism serves such an orientation, along with skepticism toward other sources of authoritative pronouncements. This is seen in a study of men's influence on the direction and timing of fertility, where anecdotal accounts in the raw data show an impatience with claims of family tradition or religion if the men did not want children. Where children were eventually desired, tradition and religion gained importance *after* the man's decision that this was the right time in his life to become a father, whereupon there was less patience with a wife's desire to further postpone beginning a family (Marciano, 1978; 1979).

Finally, assumptions about religious influence when studies are undertaken and hypotheses constructed, can produce some surprising outcomes. An example of this is a study reported by Brutz and Ingoldsby (1984) on modes of conflict resolution in Quaker (Society of Friends) families. The beauty of this study is not only the straightforward description of mistaken assumptions, and their cautions about the size and location of their sample, but also the fact that findings were reported separately for husbands/fathers and for wives/mothers. The authors compared national rates of family violence with rates of violence in their Quaker families sample, expecting that Quaker pacifist values would be manifested in far lower rates of family violence. While their findings did not reveal overall greater violence in Quaker families, patterns of violence differed from the national sample. They found, for example, higher numbers of reported acts of violence by fathers toward their children, than was found in the national sample. (Mothers also showed some patterns of higher-than-expected rates of violence). Among the reasons offered for this by the researchers were the fact that 78% of the respondents had converted to membership in the Friends, and therefore may have lacked the early socialization to, and interpersonal skills for, peaceful conflict resolution. Greater Quaker scrupulosity about telling the truth may also, in the researchers' view, be a reason for the disparities between national and Quaker samples. This study is a kind of cautionary tale, then, about how and why mechanistic assumptions about religion as a "cause," and here even a correlate, are often wrong.

Those interpretations, thoughtful and solid, indicate how the religious dimensions of fatherhood are neither linear (if Quaker, then pacifist), nor fixed. Religious affiliation, beliefs and family practices, are subject to changes over time as new dimensions are superimposed on old ones; there is no valid reason to assume that old beliefs are automatically replaced by new ones. Their coexistence, and action outcomes inconsistent with one or the other set of beliefs, are possible.

Perhaps it is the preoccupation with "traditional" or historical families, and perhaps more imagined than known, that leads us to assume greater "old-time" religiosity, and greater centrality of religion for each parent in the parent role. There is some evidence for this historical view, and it may indeed be the mental "benchmark" against which modern fatherhood is studied and evaluated.

Father Roles and Religion in the United States

Just as changes in ideological and economic climates have brought women into and out of the work force, and affected American views of motherhood, so men's roles have been similarly affected. We are used to the notion of "Rosie the Riveter": the women working in factories during World War II, then losing their jobs to men returning from the war, and given a new home-based definition of "femininity" (Friedan, 1963). Father roles have also changed over time; shifts from agrarian to urban living and employment, changing political and gender-role ideologies, have inevitably involved men's work and self-conceptions as well as women's.

Lamb (1987) has summarized historical studies of the "dominant motif" in the father role. He indicates that "The Moral Teacher" expectation for fathers dominated from Puritan through Colonial times and into the era of the early Republic. He writes:

> By popular consensus, fathers were primarily responsible for insuring that their children grew up with an appropriate sense of values, acquired primarily from the study of religious materials like the Bible. . . . [T]eaching literacy served as a means of advancing the father's role as moral guardian by insuring that children were academically equipped to adopt and maintain Christian ways. (p. 5)

However by the time industrialization took hold in the mid-19th century, the dominant motif became the father as "breadwinner." The good Christian father who taught his children scriptures or had them schooled in bible study did not disappear. It became secondary to the provider role, yet was incorporated into that role, for did not a proper Christian man support his family by working hard and achieving as much as he could?

These dominant father images were succeeded in turn by "the sex role model," and as of the mid-1970s, what Lamb labels "The New Nurturant Father" (1987, p. 6). Lamb's conclusion that the primary role for the modern father is one of nurturance and emotional support fits the way father roles are described in much of the current, burgeoning literature on fatherhood.

That nurturance cannot, however, be treated as synonymous with (or even related to) religiosity. Under conditions of church-state separation, heterogeneity, geographical mobility, and religious pluralism, nurturance and religion must be treated as separate dimensions of belief and action; whatever correlations that may exist between them must be discovered rather than assumed. Nurturance by fathers in a secular society can, but need not, call upon a specific set of religious teachings that are "Christian," or "Methodist," or "Moslem," or "Jewish." There are humanistic, non-church-centered beliefs in goodness or ethical behavior in the lectures of Leo Buscaglia or the philosophy of Martin Buber. Even the existence of God can easily proceed without churchly reference. We are left, then, with exploring the links between religion and fatherhood surrounded by cautions, caveats, many more doubts than assuredness over whether the two affect each other, why or why not there is effect, whether it is continuous or sporadic, and why temporal variations may exist.

Fatherhood, Male Role Patterns, and Religion

The first question about religion and fatherhood is how male role patterns and religious beliefs co-evolve. If religion can be treated in any way as causal, one must determine whether an affiliation is nominal or is more than that, and how much more. Even if a man's religious involvement is more than nominal, there is no way to know, simply from the name of his faith group, what he accepts, what he practices, and what he ignores. There is also no way to know, without asking, the degree to which any level of involvement with one faith, coexists with sets of beliefs and values derived from other faiths, and from non-faith sources. I have elsewhere demonstrated the "competitive market" quality of religious beliefs, and the fact that personal religious belief is very much a synthesis deriving from the intersections of biography and larger cultural/historical forces (Marciano, 1987). The outcomes of religious beliefs for fatherhood may therefore be less a matter of a denomination's action upon a man, than the man's consent to the denomination's teachings. This does not imply that a person is always conscious of all influences affecting behavior; far from it. The major work of therapists is precisely to raise many of those influences to consciousness where dysfunction and unhappiness exist. Lenski (1983) has demonstrated that religious beliefs and values experienced by the young in their families, become a kind of "orienting" approach to life and to the "cosmic" questions of meaning and mortality. What must therefore be emphasized is the fluidity of religious influence, the way it is affected by, and affects in turn, values held and actions taken in any role.

In terms of the father role and religion, however, data that are available on their connection are scant. Religious variables often are not even incorporated into studies, so that interpolation and inference are necessary. "Parental influence," a frequent variable in many family studies, tends to be presented in aggregate form: mothers' and fathers' influence is combined. Yet when studies are conducted that disaggregate mothers' and fathers' influence, it is clear that these are not qualitatively or quantitatively equal. Therefore a model of influence is presented, and later its clinical implications, to describe the sequences of male roles, influences on fatherhood roles as part of the larger male role sequences, and the resultant clinical benefits and necessary cautions in the religion–fatherhood connection.

Fathers, Religion, and Value Transmission: The Literature

The importance of understanding fathers' roles in the transmission of values to their children, including religious values, is already evident in the literature. Fathers play a critical role in shaping the attitudes and aspirations of their children, and particularly their daughters. Weitzman (1979), in her overview and commentary on studies of gender-role socialization, challenges traditional (and Freudian) identification theory. That theory claims that the child learns to identify through the same-gender parent. Weitzman counters with the idea that the opposite-gender parent teaches the relational values of masculinity/femininity. There is evidence in the studies she cites that high achievement in women stems from father support to a far greater extent than it does from mother support.

If this is so, what must be the influence of fathers upon children's values, including religious values? And what, in turn, has been the influence of religion upon fathers over the course of their own lives, before as well as after becoming fathers? Unfortunately, it is far easier to ask these questions than to answer them since (1) even exhaustive bibliographies tend to yield few or no studies of the religion–fatherhood connection (Hanson & Bozett, 1986); (2) studies more typically describe "parental" rather than "maternal" and "paternal" (disaggregated) patterns of influence on children's values; and (3) studies that do exist tend to show mixed, and even contradictory, results.

The fragmentation and contradictions emerge quickly in a basic bibliographic search, and a few examples are offered here as illustration. Dudley and Dudley (1986) compared father–mother–youth triads for religious value statement agreements. Value disparity between youth and parents was found on a majority of the 20-item scale, and only 27% of youth attitude variance could be predicted based upon fathers' and mothers' attitudes and that prediction involved another variable: whether the youth were baptized congregants. Another study (Hoge, Petrillo, & Smith, 1982) examined transmission of social and religious values from parents to teenage children, using Catholic, Baptist, and Methodist churches as sample sources. They found that where parents were younger, were agreed on religion, and had a good relationship with the children, the transmission of religious values was enhanced, but denomination predicted more than parents did. They concluded that cultural subgroups were more powerful value socializing agents than were nuclear families.

In both studies it would be easy to interpret whatever religious influence parents did turn out to have, as an effect of love and warmth rather than of religious teachings per se. If we are drawn to those who love and care for us, if we share many emotional gratifications with another, we are likely to be open to a wide spectrum of influences from the loving source. Thus, good parent–child relations would enhance parental religious influence simply because we have higher regard for all the beliefs of those we love and respect.

The effect of denomination/group as a more powerful agent than the nuclear family can be made from somewhat indirect evidence: Hendricks, Robinson-Brown, and Gary (1984) studied unmarried Black adolescent males, 48 of whom were fathers and 50 who were not fathers. The two groups were similar in religious orientation but differed in how they expressed their religiosity: Adolescent fathers were more open to institutionalized religion where religious presentations were received from such sources as media, outside the church/group/congregation; nonfathers were more likely to be involved in the institutionalized churches' group life. Thus, subcultural over familial influence seems supported.

The catalytic effect of religious organization on family religious effectiveness among Mormons is discussed by Thomas (1983). Discussing the highly developed social support systems of the church, with its consequences for the socialization of children (and socialization reinforcements for adults), he writes:

> There is some research showing that social institutions such as the family that attempt to exercise control in the absence of sufficient

social support systems may generate behavioral problems in the form
of rebellion, deviance . . . or the like. Conversely, institutions that are
high on the social support dimension are characterized by internaliza-
tion of values, development of social competence skills, low incidences
of nonconforming . . . behavior, and relatively high feelings of self
esteem and happiness. (p. 283)

In contrast to those studies, Acock and Bengtson (1978) found
high influence of mothers and fathers on political and religious
socialization. They found that mothers' influence is especially strong,
and that socialization theory should give greater weight to parental,
as opposed to peer, influence. From this variety of findings, and
speaking for mainstream churches only, the direct influence of parents, and of fathers in particular upon children's religious values,
seems highly variable.

Religious influence does not just disappear, however; if parents
cannot or will not assume primary religious roles in their children's
lives, churches (clergy, church hierarchies in their directives and
support, and groups within the churches focused on education of the
young) will try to compensate for the absence of religious education
in the home, ensuring adherents for the sake of that particular faith
and as a matter of duty for salvation. This has long been true even for
Roman Catholicism, where Catholic education and devout observance tends to be stereotypically assumed by non-Catholics. Johnstone (1988) cites research from 1951 showing that in-home Catholic socialization was not occurring as the Catholic church would wish,
and that practice, teaching, and observance fell far short of the
hierarchy's norm for familial-religious connection. The parochial
school was the accepted "antidote" to deficits in home religious
teaching, confirming the organizational over familial influences on
religious training of the young.

The assumption of primary church rather than family influence
is further borne out by Fichter's (1961) study of Catholic vocations
(i.e., becoming a priest, a brother, a nun, or a sister). This was
particularly evident in terms of reported family support or opposition to vocation, and reported importance of various influences upon
the young person in choosing religious life. Fichter presents data on
parental acceptance or opposition to the child's vocational decision to
enter religious life. He allows for the fact that the data cannot
account for all of the encouragement at least to try religious life, nor

for the discouragement many may have received which may have led to their never having tried a religious life, and who therefore are absent from the data (1961). He does, however, have some intriguing findings on major seminarians (i.e., men in official preparation for priesthood). He tabulated sources and incidence of opposition that the major seminarians encountered: opposition from no one, opposition from mothers, and opposition from fathers. The seminarians' answers are grouped according to the ages at which the boys/young men were accepted into their seminary.

From his table, Fichter derives the following statement about opposition encountered by each age group: that it "shows progressive maternal opposition from the youngest to the oldest category." (1961, p. 18). Father opposition frequencies, while shown, were ignored.

While Fichter's statement about maternal opposition is an accurate summary of data, he acknowledges that his focus derives from the common Catholic belief that priests are strongly influenced toward the priesthood by their mothers. It is therefore understandable that he is intrigued by the fact of progressive maternal opposition. For our purposes however, the inferences one can draw from his data on fathers and father effect on sons, are far more intriguing.

In terms of paternal support or opposition, fathers were twice as opposed as mothers to sons' entrance at 12–13 years of age; fathers were within a percentage point of mother opposition at 14–17 years of age entrance; fathers were more opposed than mothers to the entrance of 18–21-year-olds. Yet at age 22 years and older, father opposition dropped (10.3%), whereas mother opposition peaked at 15.5%.

A speculation on father opposition in these data is based in male socialization patterns and expectations: at ages 18–21, males tend to be highly sexually active, or at least desiring to be highly active, whether or not their beliefs and opportunities allow them to be so. Father memories of their own yearnings and perhaps moral struggles at those ages, may have led the fathers to oppose celibacy as a counsel of wisdom to their sons, and recognition of the inevitable struggles with denial. The decline in father opposition after age 22, compared with increased mother opposition, is also part of sex role recognition. Fichter's data were drawn from the 1950s, when legal majority was age 21, not age 18 as it is today. Once a male had reached majority, deference to his "right to live his own life" would be more forthcoming from another male, including a father, than from a female, and especially one's mother. In fact, a mother's open detachment from an adult child's decisions still today seems "unmaternal," "too disinterested" to fit the mother role, while the same detachment seems more consistent with male attitudes, including father attitudes.

Although reported opposition was a relatively small percentage of Fichter's cases, the reason why opposition was unsuccessful, and the reason the seminarians entered in the first place, remain issues here. The cases of parental opposition that did not succeed, would be accounted for by alternative supports and encouragements. Fichter does in fact report that, contrary to common Catholic belief, the greatest influence persuading them to a vocation that was reported by young seminarians, brothers, and sisters, were priests, brothers, and sisters, respectively. Mothers were reported as second most influential for all three types of vocation. Father encouragement was ranked third in influence by seminarians and brothers, and ranked fourth by sisters. To determine the actual extent that fathers exercise successful veto power on children's vocational decisions in Catholicism, however, it would be necessary to take a general sample of Catholic youth, though to do so today would be to do so in a church where membership has undergone enormous demographic and socioeconomic changes since Fichter's study.

Fatherhood, Many Cultures, Secular World

In all the studies cited thus far, the samples differ in size, in regional and temporal conditions, and in their denominational bases. This is not unusual, nor are their contributions diminished by acknowledging such limitations. It simply points to the need for specifying connections between religion and fatherhood in such terms as whether religious beliefs predate and govern fatherhood, or whether religion comes to support decisions already taken, whether both patterns operate, under what conditions, and with what effect on self and on children. (Note that effects on spouse and marital relationship would be the continuation of such investigation.)

There is also the need to recognize that not all "fatherhood" is the same, either in religious meaning or group and contextual support; additionally, there is not one single time when all men come to religious belief or fatherhood, nor do the two necessarily have simultaneous effects on the man, nor congruence between verbalized belief as expressed to a researcher, and action as expressed to his children. An excellent statement exactly expressing this effect is found in a study of fathers in Israel (Sagi, Koren, & Weinberg, 1987):

> the Israeli studies on fathers during the pre-, peri-, and postnatal stages indicate that fathers form a heterogeneous group and that paternal behavior towards infants may not necessarily be the consequence of intervention, but could result from a priori individual differences among fathers. (p. 202)

Even in a country so small compared to the United States, such a statement warns us that we cannot assume either homogeneity or monolithic cultural effects on parental roles. And these cultural realities of a modern state may, for all we know, be just as true for cultures that are tribal, isolated, or simply less developed technologically.

For all its individual variability, however, fatherhood is a social process in that it creates and recreates itself out of daily patterns of behavior in the context of larger cultural expectations. Perhaps fatherhood and religion, in the ways they converge and diverge, are our best example of how macrostructural forces affect microstructures and everyday behavior. Father norms shift from the motif of "religious teacher" to "nurturer" in a context of macro change which is generally called "secularization." This, to give a standard definition, is a condition in which religious values lose their dominance or salience and in which this-worldly values take precedence in human consciousness over other-worldly values.

Wilson (1982) gives a fine summary of secularization as a pervasive change that is not confined to churches, but that affects all social institutions. He says:

> Secularization is not only a change occurring *in* society, it is also a change *of* society in its basic organization. It is one of several concomitant processes of fundamental social change. (p. 148, emphasis in original)

Given all of this, the next step is to approach religion and fatherhood as two aspects of a man's life which are variably connected, to treat some of the connections by whatever direct data are available, and to draw upon inference or interpolation from data that do not address the connection directly.

Inferences About
Fatherhood–Religion Linkages

Shostak (1987) studied men who accompany their partners to abortion clinics. He used a sample of 1,000 men gathered from anonymous questionnaires given out at 30 clinics. He found close resemblance in the men's data to female abortion client profiles from other research. The men tended to be young (under 36 years of age), and disproportionately Roman Catholic (one-third of the sample), although 45% of the total sample were Protestant. According to Shostak: "When asked how important their religious beliefs were to them, 21% answered "very," and 47% "somewhat," while only 19% indicated "not very" or "not at all" (14%). One of the most interesting of Shostak's findings, in terms of the linkage between religion and sex role, was that a small number of the men "felt the need to experience some type of meaningful punishment, some analog for the real risk and pain being experienced elsewhere in the clinic by their sex partners" (p. 190). Although no direct correlates with this feeling and the religion of the respondent are provided, the description sounds penitential, as though some quality of mystical and physical reparation were necessary. Since the study addresses men's "'bottled up' roles and unmet needs," as the article's subtitle indicates, and because male norms of "control" and "strength" are cited in that article as well as in other sex role studies, it is possible to infer that for many men, religion may be personally important but not interpersonally salient because of the emotions that religion invites us to express, the acknowledgement of human helplessness in the face of world processes, the need to turn to an all-powerful God rather than depending only on our own resources. Then, in a situation of emotional conflict and sadness, some aspect of religious teaching—that of atonement for sin—seems to manifest itself. In terms of the male gender role and religion, then, religion seems to lack or to miss many opportunities to connect to men in terms that they can accept as continuingly valid and continuingly "manly." A "penitential" approach to the support of the male partner for the female abortion client may be one way of coping with feelings of religion's personal importance, where those religions tend to counsel against or condemn outright, premarital sex, and abortion.

Finally, a study that treats parents separately in their roles as transmitters of religious beliefs and practices by Clark, Worthington, and Danser (1988) found that:

> Accurate transmission of religious beliefs and practices is facilitated by parental agreement on religious beliefs and practices. . . . When parents differ substantially in their values, fathers usually influence their child's beliefs more than mothers do. (p. 464)

In addition, they found that fathers had a special influence on sons in transmitting religious values. It is unusual to find clear evidence of father dominance in religious transmission, and it raises questions of father absence. If divorce, separation, or death occurs, are they similar or dissimilar cases of father absence, and with what similar or variant effects on religious values of children, and especially on sons?

Given this wide variety of evidence on men, on fathers, on gender, any given father's effect upon, and ability to affect, his children seems more a sum of his life experiences and religious "opportunities" than a direct effect of his own early religious training. For that reason, an alternative model can be proposed. Such a model can conform to our understanding of socialization influences and male role sequences, which treats the acquisition and transmission of religious values more as opportunity-outcomes and choices, than as prior causal influences in fathers' lives. And, given that assumption, its clinical implications can also be examined. Choices are made at varying degrees of awareness that they are in fact choices, and all choices have costs and benefits for self and family. The following model therefore is a religious "opportunity" model, in which personality and external influences at various points in the life process co-evolve.

Religious Opportunity Model

Personality (the sum of an individual's genetic inheritance and the interactions experienced) affects and is affected by a variety of factors in culture. Because of one's social class, the time in history that a person is born, and varying life chances that are consequently available, two outcomes are: varied opportunity to see, know, or experience anything; and selectivity in perceiving and understanding those experiences and one's own life. The factors of opportunity and selectivity include family, education, peers, religion, media, experiences, travel, and occupation. The first and critical component of the model, however, is always opportunity. Typically we all grow up in some sort of family setting, but the presence of religious training in that family setting is opportunistic, rather than a "given". Travel, the kinds of peers one has over the life course, the education one receives, the media to which one is exposed (and which is understood), the occupation one comes to have—certainly these all have elements of social patterning; yet they also have undeniable elements of randomness, and "opportunity" bespeaks this random factor in all our lives.

Opportunity (exposure to life factors) influences selectivity; we tend to pay attention to, pursue, and remain involved with things and people we understand and can relate to.

Out of the personality-life factors interaction, with their opportunities and selectivity, comes a synthesis of beliefs, including religious beliefs. Synthesis is defined as the configuration of beliefs, values, and action patterns available and, as much as possible, desired. Synthesis is not static, but dynamic; it is not necessarily internally consistent, nor is its internal quality necessarily consistent with external behaviors. Internal-external dissonance may be at high or low levels, varyingly tolerated or resolved, based on group and individual supports for given patterns of belief and behavior.

The dynamic aspect of synthesis must be emphasized because its beliefs may be analogized to a river, fluid yet contained, whose components change over time in reaction to environmental changes. Therefore synthesis is evolutionary, and is co-evolutionary with sequences of male roles, both age roles and larger social roles in family and community. Opportunity and selectivity affect how infancy, childhood, adolescence, and young manhood are experienced; it affects whether the man marries, becomes a husband, and/or a father. Community roles, occupational roles, family roles (fatherhood, grandfatherhood), the experience of aging, co-evolve with beliefs. Synthesis is at any given time a temporary point of stability; and a given synthesis may be reinforced and cultivated and maintained by the individual, especially where great satisfaction and meaning are derived from it. One such synthesis may powerfully incorporate religious beliefs; another synthesis may focus on science, or the arts, or on a social identity that incorporates religion little or not at all.

The opportunity model of religion presents religious belief as an outcome, a dependent rather than an independent, variable. In this model, religious (or ethical) synthesis occurs and recurs over time not necessarily with internal consistency, but apparently with potentially high levels of "livable" dissonance. The superimposition of newer values on older ones, where they are contradictory, may serve situational purposes: In some sets of interactions and settings, one may call upon values and behaviors of one type, shifting then to conform to new interactions and settings. An example of this is found in the "boy who makes good," who returns to "the old neighborhood" to visit. Over time, old values and ways may be increasingly uncongenial; but it is also possible that the shifts between settings provide periods of respite from what may be strains in the new, and comfort in the old.

The model posits a highly variable influence of formal religion and a problematic influence of "religion" in any form. Though polls of the United States population reveal high degrees of religious feelings and experiences, and a persistently strong belief in God, these do not necessarily translate into stable or predictable patterns of specific institutional religious belief or practices. National polls show that more than half of the American population is "unchurched," not formally affiliated with any denomination. Religious "ideas and feelings" may exist outside church-related activities, or coexist with such activities and still be separate from them.

Even if one is part of a faith community, the sythesis outcome of this opportunity model offers some of these possible outcomes: a choice of affiliation (to persist in childhood affiliation, to embrace an affiliation if there had been none in childhood, or to change affiliation); the choice of disaffiliation [continuing a childhood pattern, or rejecting prior affiliations(s)]; selective conformity to religious teachings and action in or out of affiliation.

Implications For Research and Practice

At any point of the life course, the degree to which choices are conscious, or to degree to which they operate upon a life below direct consciousness, will vary as their effects will vary. Choices may be consciously made for a set of conscious reasons, that have outcomes which are not consciously planned for. The outcomes may be functional or dysfunctional for fatherhood and family life. For the purposes of this elaboration, choices will be assumed to be conscious, with outcomes that are planned at the conscious level, but with unconscious as well as conscious effects. The fact that any of these may be genogramic, that is, that they may manifest generational continuity of (dys)functional patterns in a family, is another stipulation of these implications. In research and practice, therefore, attention must be paid to "which religion"—if any—and how it is exercised. Choice of affiliation including the conditions under which choices are made, and family power hierarchies supported by religion, are examples of implications for reaearch and practice.

Choice of Affiliation

If religion is not assumed to be an independent variable in all cases, entry into a faith (embracing a new one, remaining in an old one) may be an outcome of crisis. Where religion is newly embraced, or renewed, in time of crisis its potentially positive outcomes are predictable: it may provide transcendent reasons for the "unexplainable," such as the death of a loved one. Germ theories of disease can offer only knowledge; comfort derives from another realm. Religion thus becomes a point of security, serenity, and confidence, helping to make sense out of pain (theodicy).

When crisis strikes, the anger and sense of feeling cheated, or uncontrollably resentful, may be controlled by religious explanations. Those explanations can, however, take on negative aspects when they also become weapons with which to act out personal pain. Recriminations against those who refuse to share the religious "answer" to crisis, and the consequent ignoring of needs of others for alternative kinds of support and love, become a way of punishing self and others who live on.

The religious factor in dealing with a father's and family's crisis is thus one that should receive special attention in a presenting situation. Religion may "justify" a refusal by a father (or other family member) to join a family therapy, on the grounds that religion has provided the "answer," and none other is needed. No religion, however, is tolerant of uncharity toward strangers, let alone loved ones, and a therapeutic reply to religious resistance could use religious beliefs themselves as a starting point for counterbalancing religion-based resistance to help. It would be an error to assume that patients' religious practices, even where intense and orthodox before a crisis, remain internally qualitatively the same during and after a crisis. It is also necessary to look at the rejection of religion by a previously religious person, when crisis and pain have been extreme. That is sometimes a form of self-punishment, a refusal to take comfort from what formerly did comfort the individual.

Parent Roles as Religious Roles, Hierarchy, and Family Power

The father role is one that is highly regarded and rewarded in the religious orthodoxies, such as Judaism, Mormonism, Roman Catholicism, Islam. In all cases the male role is the orthodox basis for all sacramental functions; priestly/rabbinical/ministerial status, though they now encompass women in many denominations of Protestantism, and in Conservative, Reform, and Reconstructionist Judaism are male-only in the strictly observant faith communities. Male "headship" of the family, the obligations of men in the Covenant, male ordination and sacramental exclusiveness (Eucharist, Reconciliation, Orders, in the Catholic case, "smicha"—rabbinical ordination—in orthodox Judaism, and ministry/clerical status in fundamentalist Protestant, and Moslem, faith communities) impose duties on men, but also accord them power for fulfilling those duties. The power is both familial and communal. In the Mormon case, for example, all men are expected to be part of the priesthood, and this provides a religiously special status both in family and in larger church. Common folklore supports the notion that men raised in traditional Catholic, Jewish, Mormon, fundamentalist, or communal (Amish, Hutterite) settings would be "traditional patriarchs." There is no evidence that socialization alone would guarantee this. Hasidic Judaism (a branch of Jewish Orthodoxy marked by specific clothing, clustered neighborhoods, and whole-life-encompassing daily practices centered in the Hasidic community), the Amish, the Mormons, all groups, however "orthodox," do not experience total continued adherence by their young. Why does a man choose to stay in or to exit a traditionalist community that seems to support his maleness and father roles so powerfully? And why would an adult man enter such a community, as many do, according to evidence from Hasidic, Mormon, and Catholic sources?

One answer may lie in the degree to which entering or exiting a faith group affects family subsystems and family power. The benefits of well-defined subsystems and boundaries in families are well known to family therapists; confusion of parental and child roles and expectations is often dysfunctional where families do not maintain parent and child subsystem boundedness. A family hierarchy means that the lines of power are known, that expectations are known, that outcomes tend to be predictable. If religion in any way, and the religious orthodoxies particularly, enhance a sense of "safety" in clear lines of authority, then a religious outcome for family stability may be an asset for all family members.

There are correlative disadvantages, however, and these include a sense of "no limits but God" for those who are at the top of the hierarchy, that is, the fathers. Just as family myths may be the invisible glue that holds a family in a given pattern, and which persist because they are not openly discussed or questioned, so the top of a hierarchy tends to be less questioned. Authority may be a family glue, but it can also have abrasive qualities which undermine any coherence it could give. Where a religiously defined role is constantly challenged, such as father authority or "headship," and where there is much anger and contention, the question becomes why a given role is more important than love and resolution. The fears, uncertainties, and control that lie within a special religious role therefore become the issue that requires uncovering and accommodation.

The assertion of strong hierarchical power by a father may be compensatory for any number of other, sensed, inadequacies. Low levels of economic success, low esteem from others, strong-willed wives or children, educational or skill levels below those of community peers, have their compensation in "religious" power.

In all of these cases, the question must be not only what the religious factor does in a father's relationships, but whence it came in the first place. By uncovering the processes of which religion is an outcome, its potential dysfunctional power for self and family may be reduced or eliminated. Evidence that gender traditionalism is far more strongly related to adult affiliation than to childhood religion (Brinkerhoff & MacKie, 1988) highlights the need to examine religious choice as a support of parental and gender role decisions already made.

Examining the reactive/dependent variable nature of religious beliefs, values, and actions, may therefore be a major line of exploration for clinicians dealing with problems encountered by fathers and by their families.

Conclusion

The secular society is so called because of the many this-worldly values that compete with religious, other-worldly values in orienting beliefs and behaviors. Role definitions and actions for fathers, to the extent that they are or are not influenced by specific religious orientations, have effects on value transmissions to children, though these seem to be coexistent with gender expectations of children. No religious belief is compulsory; the most stringent orthodoxies lose children to less stringent lifestyles. Amish communities, Hasidic communities, orthodox communities of all types, compete with non-orthodox influences to retain children's loyalty and membership. Given this ultimately voluntaristic nature of religious membership, the choices made must be viewed as outcomes, perhaps more than as causes, of successive experiences and roles in the man's life course. The impact of religion on fatherhood is one that needs closely detailed, including qualitative, study, to determine whether and how religion can enhance that role for the father, and for his children.

References

Acock, A., & Bengston, V. (1978). On the relative influence of mothers and fathers: A covariance analysis of political and religious socialization. *Journal of Marriage and the Family*, 40(3), 509-520.

Brinkerhoff, M. B., & MacKie, M. (1988). Religious sources of gender traditionalism. In D. L Thomas (Ed.), *The religion and family connection: Social science perspectives* (pp. 232-257). Provo, Utah: Religious Studies Center, Brigham Young University.

Brutz, J. L., & Ingoldsby, B. B. (1984). Conflict resolution in Quaker families. *Journal of Marriage and the Family*, 46(1), 21-16.

Clark, C., Worthington, E. L. Jr., & Danser, D. (1988). The transmission of religious beliefs and practices from parents to firstborn early adolescent sons. *Journal of Marriage and the Family*, 50(2), 463-472.

De Vaus, D., & McAllister, I. (1987). Gender differences in religion: A test of the structural location theory. *American Sociological Review, 52*(4), 472–481.

Dudley, R., & Dudley, M. G. (1986). Transmission of religious value from parents to adolescents. *Review of Religious Research, 28*(1), 3–15.

Fichter, J. (1961). *Religion as an Occupation.* Notre Dame, IN: University of Notre Dame Press.

Franklin, C. W. (1984). *The changing definition of masculinity.* New York: Plenum.

Friedan, B. (1963). *The feminine mystique.* New York: Norton.

Gilligan, C. (1982). *In a different voice.* Cambridge, MA: Harvard University Press.

Hanson, S., & Bozett, F. W. (1986). Fatherhood: A library. In R. A. Lewis & M. B. Sussman (Eds.), *Men's changing roles in the family* (pp. 229–253). New York: Haworth.

Hendricks, L. E., Robinson-Brown, D., & Gary-Lawrence, E. (1984). Religiosity and unmarried black adolescent fatherhood. *Adolescence, 19,* 417–424.

Hoge, D. R., Petrillo, G., & Smith, E. I. (1982). Transmission of religious and social values from parents to teenage children. *Journal of Marriage and the Family, 44*(3), 569–580.

Johnstone, R. L. (1988). *Religion in society: A sociology of religion* (3rd ed.). Englewood Cliffs, NJ: Prentice-Hall.

Lenski, G. (1983). *The religious factor* (rev. ed.). Garden City, NY: Doubleday.

Marciano, T. D. (1978). Male pressure in the decision to remain childfree. *Alternative Lifestyles, 1*(1), 95–112.

Marciano, T. D. (1979). Male influences on fertility: Needs for research. *The Family Coordinator, 28*(4), 561–568.

Marciano, T. D. (1987). Families and religions. In M. B. Sussman & S. Steinmetz (Eds.), *Handbook of marriage and the family* (pp. 285–316). New York: Plenum.

Marciano, T. D. (in press). Corporate church, ministry, and ministerial family. *Marriage and Family Review, 15.*

Marzorati, G. (1989, January 29). Salman Rushdie: Fiction's embattled infidel. *The New York Times Magazine,* 24–27, 44, 47–49, 100.

Morgan, M. (1987). The impact of religion on gender-role attitudes. *Psychology of Women Quarterly, 11,* 301–310.

Sagi, A., Koren, N., & Weinberg, M. (1987). Fathers in Israel. In M. E. Lamb (Ed.), *The father's role* (pp. 197–222). Hillsdale, NJ: Lawrence Erlbaum Associates.

Sklare, M. (1971). *America's Jews.* New York: Random House.

Thomas, D. L. (1983). Family in the Mormon experience. In W. V. D'Antonio & J. Aldous (Eds.). *Family and religion: Conflict and change in modern society* (pp. 267–288). Beverly Hills, CA: Sage.

Thornton, A. (1988). Reciprocal influences of family and religion in a changing world. In D. L. Thomas (Ed.), *The religion and family connection: Social science perspectives* (pp. 27–50). Provo, UT: Religious Studies Center, Brigham Young University.

Weitzman, L. J. (1979). *Sex role socialization.* Palo Alto, CA: Mayfield Publishing.

Whitbeck, L. B., and Gecas, V. (1988). Value attributions and value transmission between parents and children. *Journal of Marriage and the Family, 50,* 829–840.

Wilson, B. (1982). *Religion in sociological perspective.* New York: Oxford University Press.

7

Environment and Fatherhood: Rural and Urban Influences

John DeFrain
E. E. LeMasters
Jan A. Schroff

A common thread in the fabric of folk wisdom in the United States down through the years has been that the city is the den of iniquity and the rural area is a haven of peace and tranquility. Urban life, however, has been scrutinized by innumerable observers far more carefully than rural life, and recent disasters in the agricultural economy bear fresh witness to the more accurate proposition that both city life and country life can be enormously challenging.

In this chapter, we will examine how these two different environments influence parents in their efforts to rear children as well as endeavor to paint a more realistic picture of rural life. The chapter begins with a section on the impact of urbanization on fathers and mothers in the United States. In this section, we will discuss the pluralistic nature of the city, the increased leisure of urban youth as compared to rural youth, the power of the youth peer group in urban areas, the impersonality and anonymity of the city, the pervasive nature of the urban mass media, and the urban ghetto. A second section of the chapter will focus on the positive aspects of urbanization: the advantages urban organization offers families and the relative affluence of the city compared to the country. The third section of the chapter will discuss special problems of rural fathers and mothers in the United States, including the dramatic decline in the farm population, the most recent wave of the continuing farm crisis, agricultural fundamentalism, resettlement, the impact of urbanization on farm parents and their children, the fact that farm parents often find themselves preparing their children for an urban-industrial world they themselves do not fully understand, the difficult realities of the rural economy today, and rural social class barriers farm families face. A final section of the article will comment on the need for future research in the area of rural fatherhood.

Writing the section on rural fatherhood was a rather difficult challenge, because much has been written about rural life in general, but little systematic research has been done on rural fathers in particular. We pored through the *Inventory of Marriage and Family Literature*, now published by the National Council on Family Relations, going back to the early 1960s. Fatherhood in general was seriously neglected by family researchers until there was a burst of enthusiasm for the topic during the mid- and late-1970s. Today, it is becoming increasingly difficult to publish a serious research article in the area of marriage and family relations without having included fathers in the study. This is a welcome development.

In the specific area of rural fatherhood, we were not successful in finding comprehensive studies focusing on fathers. There are, however, a few noteworthy studies that are helpful: Coleman, Ganong, Clark, and Madsen (1989), who found that rural parents emphasize intellectual and emotional development significantly more than urban parents, and emphasize social development significantly less than urban parents; Schumm and Bollman (1981), who concluded that rural and urban family relations do not differ substantially; Scanzoni and Arnett (1987) who found rural family members to be significantly more traditional than urban family members, especially in gender role prerence; and Kivett (1988), who found that rural adult sons play a relatively minor role in the support network of older rural fathers. Perhaps the greatest disappointment in our reading of the research literature was the apparent fact that no investigators have completed the rather obvious task of interviewing rural fathers themselves, and discussing in depth their specific beliefs and challenges in the context of the rural environment in which they live. Much has been written about rural life in general, but more direct study of rural parents, both fathers and mothers, is essential.

Defining Terms

At this point, it would be useful to say a few words about definitions. The terms "rural," "urban," and "suburban" are relatively simple to define from a layperson's standpoint, but they cause researchers some concern, for the terms can be thought of in a philosophical sense, a statistical sense, and a psychological sense.

"Rural," according to a standard dictionary, refers to the country, and "urban" refers to the city. These are distinct categories, in one sense, but in another sense they are simply points on a continuum, like black, gray, and white are points on a continuum. Thus, in most research projects, the investigators will define rural populations in some numerical fashion, e.g., those people living on a farm or ranch or town with populations of 2,500 or 5,000 or less. Similarly, cities can be put on a numerical continuum from small to large, and each of the gradations made is usually quite arbitrary, based on the needs and constraints of a particular research project.

The suburb, a point in between the city and the country, is also a bit murky to define; suburban people, in one sense, are often those who make their living in the city or have relatively close ties to the city, but do not live in the downtown.

To complicate matters, rural, urban, and suburban are also psychological, subjective states, i.e., "One can take the boy out of the country, but one cannot take the country out of the boy." There is a rural culture, just as there is an urban culture and a suburban culture. Though they are difficult to define precisely, they do influence people's thinking and behavior.

Perhaps any discussion of rural, urban, and suburban is doomed to break down in subjectivity. In short, even though we all may know what the terms mean, we're simply not too sure about how to define them.

Impact of Urbanization on Fathers
and Mothers in the United States

One major trend in history in the United States has been the steady urbanization of society over the years, the expansion of the urban population, and the decline of the rural population. In the second section of this article, we will outline some of the positive aspects of city life as it affects fathers and mothers, but in this section we discuss some of the major problems parents found themselves facing once they had left the farm and settled in the city.

Pluralistic Nature of the City

The city, in many ways, has functioned as the great melting pot of society in the United States. Urban fathers and mothers have been forced to function in relatively close proximity with families of extremely diverse racial, social, ethnic, and religious backgrounds. In rural areas, it proved somewhat easier to set up more isolated racial, social, ethnic, or religious enclaves. In urban areas, thus, it is often easier to find a wonderful richness and variety of people; this rainbow of families and lifestyles, however, often becomes a source of conflict. Sons and daughters in urban areas can more readily form friendships and bonds of love that ignore racial, ethnic, and religious lines, and parents often react with confusion and anger (Cornell, 1976; Handlin, 1952; Rogler & Cooney, 1984; Schwartz, Raine, & Robins, 1987).

Many observers have noted that cities tend not to be genuine melting pots, in which the elements meld together in racial, social class, ethnic, and religious harmony. Rather, cities tend to be segregated along racial, social class, ethnic, or religious lines, and the result tends to be more of a vegetable stew in which the various elements retain a good deal of their individually distinct characteristics.

In the more pluralistic city, children are exposed to an infinite number of "competing models"—Catholics, Protestants, Jews; lower-, middle-, and upper-classes; Blacks, Whites, Hispanics, Native Americans, Asians, Poles, Slavs, Germans; and so forth, *ad infinitum*. Children exposed to a wide variety of people may end up seriously questioning why their parents believe and behave in the ways they do, and many parents find this threatening (Cornell, 1976; Handlin, 1952; Rogler & Cooney, 1984; Schwartz, Raine, & Robins, 1987).

Farm families, on the other hand, can maintain their distinct values by maintaining distance from other families. And many rural areas today are segregated on racial, ethnic, social class, or religious lines. It is not difficult to find a small town or rural area in which almost everyone is White or Protestant or of Norwegian descent. The nearest individual from a "competing model" of life may be miles and miles away. In the city, however, the various cultural groups have more opportunity to interact; the possibility of conflict is also greater.

Increased Leisure of Urban Youth as Compared to Rural Youth

One major advantage farm fathers and mothers have over city parents is that it is relatively easier to keep farm children busy. On the farm, there are always chores to be done. The child has genuine status in the family, for important work must be done: feeding the animals, running the machinery, helping out around the house, and so forth. In the city, after the lawn is mowed and the table is set, parents are often hard-pressed to come up with responsibilities for their children that do not seem to be much more than carefully contrived busywork. Also, in the city, school is over at 3:30 p.m., and fathers and mothers are often still at work. So-called latchkey children roam the streets, where it is easy to get into trouble. The problems are compounded during the long summer breaks from school. Parents in affluent city neighborhoods can afford summer camp and other organized programs for their children, but in low-income areas, especially, kids with too much time on their hands can become a major problem (Schrag, 1967).

The present school year was not designed for urban parents and is an artifact of an earlier, more rural America. It conflicts with the urban work schedules of both fathers and mothers. Many larger school districts around the country are moving in the direction of year-round school programs, but solutions are not found without a great deal of public discussion because family needs are so diverse. Many two-job families would approve of year-round school programs for their children, which would eliminate childcare needs during the summer. But one-job families would not benefit from such options and would readily protest such programs for raising their taxes and threatening the sanctity of the family's summer leisure time together.

Rural parents have their own version of this type of dilemma. Many farm fathers and mothers work off the farm to supplement farm income. Community-sponsored childcare is even more difficult to organize and support financially in rural areas, and without adequate childcare options farm families are in a bind similar to what city families are in: children alone with too much time on their hands. The chores at home can still be done by the children after school, but farm work is one of the more dangerous occupations because of the equipment, animals, and isolation, and the threat of injury to lone youngsters is always present.

Public debate on these issues is likely to continue for many years before the wide variety of necessary options is fully instituted.

Power of the Youth Peer Group in Urban Areas

One result of increased leisure time for urban youths and close physical proximity with their friends is the rising power of the youth peer group. While rural young people may be saddled with chores and live, 5, 10, or 20 miles from their friends, urban youth may spend 30–50 hours a week with their peers. A powerful set of youth society norms of behavior and loyalties can readily emerge in such an environment, and the peer group can easily mount a challenge to the power and influence of their parents.

For example, there are an estimated 70,000 youth gang members in the Los Angeles area, and gang violence intertwined with a drug culture have created a problem that some observers believe is now nearly out of control. Rowdiness in rural areas, of course, is not unheard of. But the scale and intensity of the violence has escalated tremendously; thousands of heavily-armed teenagers now roam big-city streets (Burt, 1989).

Impersonality and Anonymity of the City

Urban parents often-times know little about the young people their children associate with, nor do they know much about the parents of their children's friends. In many cases, urban parents only know what their children choose to tell them about their friends. This makes it very difficult for parents to decide how to respond to the peer group. Is the peer group a threat to the parents' values? Or an ally? Urban parents often have little to go on, and young people can thus rather easily conceal deviant behavior from their elders. Parents end up taking a risk in most of the decisions they make. They rarely have complete knowledge or understanding of a particular friend of their child or knowledge of her or his peer group.

Family therapists, alcohol/drug counselors, and police officers hear story after story of parents who had no idea their children were into a wide variety of high-risk behaviors. This should not be particularly surprising, given the impersonality and anonymity the city fosters.

In rural areas, on the other hand, deviant behavior occurs, but on a less dramatic scale. Everyone knows everyone else. And as many smalltown critics note, everyone makes it a business of knowing everyone else's business. With so many eyes glued on young people, control over their behavior becomes somewhat more feasible.

Pervasive Nature of the Urban Mass Media

Urban fathers and mothers operate in an atmosphere that is in some respects like a circus or carnival or an enticing buffet of deviant behaviors. Hundreds of pitchmen surround the family, selling products and ideas and approaches to life often in direct conflict with the parents' values. Radio, television, newspapers, magazines, billboards, telephone hucksters all push their wares and values on the family, and parents often feel embattled. Rural parents, of course, can feel pressured by the media, but the intensity of this influence seems heightened in the crowded, highly-charged urban area because many forms of media are much more readily accessible in the city.

Urban Ghetto

As more affluent families migrated to the suburbs, much of the central area of cities in the United States has been left to low-income Whites, Blacks, Asians, Hispanics, and Native Americans. Public services in the central city are often lacking, because well-to-do taxpayers have fled to better surroundings. Schools are often in decay, and housing is often substandard. Homelessness has become a major problem for many urban families. Many rural parents face conditions of severe poverty, also, and many have fled the country to search for a better life in the city. Often-times opportunity has not materialized, however, for the urban ghetto in many areas has become synonymous with squalor, crowding, violence, alcohol and other drugs (Glazer & Moynihan, 1963; Hutchison, Searight, & Stretch, 1986; Landers, 1987; U.S. Riot Commission Report, 1968).

Positive Aspects of Urbanization

Societal attitudes toward the city have been ambivalent throughout history in the United States. On the one hand it has been portrayed as a depraved center of evil. On the other hand, it became a center of hope for millions of European immigrants in the late-nineteenth and early-twentieth century who arrived in this country too late to find free land and bent on making their fortune in a relatively wealthy society. And, more recently for poor rural black families during the Great Depression and World War II, the city held out the hope of a better life though this hope often was not realized.

Advantages Urban Organization Offers Families

There is no question that urban life causes many problems for parents, but there are a number of inherent advantages, also. These include: highly-organized school systems with many advantages for children that do not exist in rural areas, including a broader range of services for disabled and disadvantaged children; a full range of social services in both the private sector and the public sector; better medical and public health facilities; a relatively more tolerant atmosphere for racial and religious minorities; and greater opportunity for vertical social mobility (Gans, 1962).

Relative Affluence of the City Compared to the Country

Though poverty in the city is an enormous problem and has been in the news recently with the plight of the homeless before our eyes in the media, it can be argued with some merit that rural poverty may be even more insidious. The rural poor are somewhat outside the net of the nation's media, and seem to make headlines with less frequency than the urban poor. In the 1960s the media widely publicized the terrible poverty of the rural poor in Applachia, but major coverage of particular aspects of rural poverty was not forthcoming again until the mid-1980s when the farm crisis in the Midwest drew considerable attention. The mass media, based in urban areas, seems to be more cognizant of urban problems.

In the rural agricultural economy, there is no place for most low-income farm children. Their parents lack the knowledge, experience, and contacts to make a successful move to an urban area; and health, educational, and social services in rural areas are seemingly more difficult to obtain. This, of course, is not to make the bold claim that health, educational, and social services for low-income families in urban areas are adequate. The mind-set in the United States seems, in many respects, to want to focus on winners—the successful, rich, glitzy, and bold types who win the race—and ignore all others.

One minority group that has achieved a relatively high socioeconomic position in society in the United States, the Jews, is largely metropolitan in character. Jewish families, contrary to popular opinion, have tended to enter the socioeconomic system at the bottom rung. By skillful use of urban services, especially the school system and universities, a relatively high proportion of Jewish families have achieved a comfortable economic position in our society, though intolerance and bigotry against them still causes Jews a great deal of pain (Cherlin & Celebuski, 1983; Cohen, 1981; *Newsweek*, 1978; Selzer, 1972).

Special Problems of Rural Fathers and Mothers in the United States

Historically, the farm family in the United States has been stereotyped or romanticized almost beyond recognition. If we are not hearing a joke about some hopelessly ignorant hayseed, we are looking at a Thanksgiving magazine cover for a national magazine showing a prosperous middle-class farm family sitting down comfortably to a feast. Lower-class farm families rarely intrude into American thinking. But farm tenants, sharecroppers, farm laborers, and migrant farm workers travelling from one harvest to another are also part of the enormously diverse rural mosaic. Lower-class farm families are in many ways worse off than low-income urban families. The focus in this section will be on some of the special problems farm families face.

Dramatic Decline in the Farm Population

Up to this point our analysis has focused on urban fathers and mothers. The history of the United States has recorded a steady growth in urban population over the years, and because of a massive move to the city since World War I, farm parents now constitute a very small percentage of all parents in this country. Rural parents, in essence, have become a minority group, in not only a statistical but a sociological and psychological sense.

It is usually foolish to get into an argument over whose cross is the heaviest in life, but one would make the case that rural fathers and mothers in the United States are in a more difficult position than urban parents. Future shock has hit the Heartland in some ways harder than the city; the rural revolution in recent decades has been deep and widespread, and many farm families and communities have been left reeling (Burchinal, 1964; Farmer, 1986; Fremon & Wilson, 1976; Rowe & Lingren, 1986; Soth, 1965).

Mechanization of the farm has greatly reduced the demand for farm labor, and increased productivity has brought about a steady decline in the percentage of the United States population engaged in agriculture. In 1930 at the beginning of the Great Depression, 25% of the total population lived on the farm. By 1940, just before America's entry into World War II, 23% lived on the farm. In 1950, after the war's massive industrial build-up had in many ways revolutionized society, 15% of the population lived on farms. By 1960, the figure had dropped further to 9%; by 1970, 5%; and by 1979, it was only 2.8% (U.S. Department of Commerce, 1980). During the 1980s, the most recent wave of the farm crisis forced more families off the land, and the percentage continued to drop. One man who left the farm he grew up on in the Midwest during the Great Depression described the situation to us in very human terms: "When I left to go to the university in 1936, there were 17 family farms in my neighborhood. Today, 50 years later, there are only six. Can you imagine what that does to the businesses, to the school, to the churches, to the sense of community people have?"

Most Recent Wave of the Continuing Farm Crisis

Though there is evidence today that farm income has once again stabilized, it is clear that the 1980s were not a good time in general for agriculture in the United States, and difficult economic times exacerbated the many challenges that rural parents normally face. During the worst of the current rural economic crisis, the U.S. Department of Agriculture reported that almost a third of the full-time farm families in America were in "serious financial difficulty" (Rowe & Lingren, 1986).

It would be useful at this point to give a brief, simple explanation to a chronic, bitterly difficult problem. The roots of the farm crisis of the 1980s were set down in the inflationary spiral of the 1970s. Though farmers tend as a group to be financially cautious and conservative and averse to taking on major debts, several factors contributed to a debtor crisis: agricultural exports increased dramatically in the 1970s, causing a wave of money to rush into the farm economy and a wave of enthusiasm; interest rates were relatively low, making heavy borrowing more palatable to farmers; the value of land was rising rapidly; the United States government and lenders became caught up in the euphoria of good times. Many farmers, businessmen, politicians, and lenders became carried away by the spirit of the times. Many people bought land and expensive equipment in order to expand their operations. Good times, it seemed, would last a long time. It seemed foolish not to borrow and expand for the risk seemed minimal.

The most recent analogy to this situation is the euphoric spirit which permeated financial circles in the years before the stock market plunged dramatically in late 1987. For a time it seemed to many people as if the stock market would climb forever and everyone would grow rich. Simply pour your precious savings into the market. Bubbles, however, tend to burst.

The agricultural bubble burst in the early 1980s. International agricultural exports dropped dramatically as the value of the United States dollar rose, making products from the United States more expensive to purchase overseas. A worldwide recession and hard times slowed agricultural sales. Land values plunged, but interest rates skyrocketed leaving farmers in a desperate bind. They owed their creditors vast amounts of money, but since their land had declined dramatically in value, farmers could not borrow enough on the collateral to service their debts.

Farmers could not pay their bills, and the wolves were soon at the door. Desperate turmoil and pain were widespread in the rural United States during the 1980s. Economic indicators today may tell us that the worst is perhaps over, at least for now, but bitter memories and classic intra- and interfamily struggles over who was to blame and what to do next continue to cloud the air.

Rowe and Lingren (1986; Row, Williams, Lee, & Johnson, 1985) surveyed a random sample of farm and ranch families in one hard-hit state, Nebraska, in 1985 during the depths of the agricultural crisis. Six hundred and fifty families participated in their survey. Rowe and Lingren reported that fully 58% of the families said they were in an economic "holding action, barely able to survive." Imagine trying to be a good father or mother, focusing on the growth and development of your children, and yet being financially "barely able to survive." Rowe and Lingren found in their survey that, as one would expect, marriage relationships and parent–child relationships suffer during times of economic turmoil.

Family members, especially the father in those families where he has been assigned the "traditional" father's role, tend to focus on money problems; love and concern and affection for each other tends to be put on a back burner during these times. Primary survival needs take precedence. Disputes over who is to blame for the disaster heat up; family members argue more over how dwindling money supplies are spent; the older generation blames the younger generation if the land is lost in foreclosure to the creditor, and so forth.

Rural people are especially prideful of their self-sufficiency. Being one's own boss is an important plus when farmers outline the pros of their profession. Also, a distinct strain of the "Root hog or die!" mentality tends to pervade the Heartland. In short, if you can't make it on your own, tough luck.

But community mental-health centers in rural areas reported a dramatic increase in the number of farm families coming in for counseling during the crisis. This was surprising, for farmers traditionally tend to avoid counselors. "They take special pride in their self-sufficiency and independency, so that their willingness to turn outside for help is indicative of their desperation," South Dakota psychologist Farmer wrote (1986).

Churches played an important role in trying to solve critical problems of debt, frustration, violence, an increase in suicides, and genuine hunger during the crisis, as did the Cooperative Extension Service. Extension has served rural America for many, many years, and counseling, education, mediation, and farm crisis workshops were valuable services provided for many farm families. One Extension family life specialist we know well was near collapse after conducting 28 farm crisis workshops all across the state in a short span of time. The magnitude of the problems and the pain families brought to the workshops was almost staggering to the professional.

Agricultural Fundamentalism

Rural people have an almost religious attachment to the land, an intense bond of love for the earth and its plants and animals. The farm or ranch is a collective effort of living family members in unity with early generations of family members who pioneered in their efforts to make the land fruitful. "You can't place a dollar amount on the independence we have," one farm wife told Farmer (1986). The freedom of being your own boss, even though the work can be terribly difficult, is very important to rural people. Other benefits: living close to nature; privacy and quiet; the opportunity for husbands and wives to share a career; the chance to pass on the fruits of your life and your land to your children; a tightly-knit family life; close ties with neighbors. All these values become the ideology of the Heartland, heavily laden with religious overtones.

Some observers argue that many rural people are overzealous in their defense of the rural life. These observers argue that many farmers are guilty of "agricultural fundamentalism," which could be defined as extreme praise for rural life and high and irrational criticism of city life. To the "ag fundamentalist," rural is good, urban is bad; rural is free, urban is slavery, and so forth.

Critics of ag fundamentalism counter that rural areas are full of problems, and not all these problems can be blamed on greedy city people. It has been said that child abuse thrives in the shadows. Social workers, counselors, and public health nurses, for example, are well aware that isolated farms or ranches can be fertile seedbeds for the physical, emotional, and sexual abuse of children. If parents do not have other adults around to support them and model positive behavior, it is not difficult to predict that some parents will exhibit deviant behaviors. Similarly, the extreme isolation in many rural areas can readily contribute to alcohol and other drug abuse, to spouse abuse, and to suicide.

Divorce rates in rural areas tend to be lower than in urban areas. An ag fundamentalist explanation of this might be, simply put, that rural families are happier than urban families. A more likely explanation, however, is that rural women do not have as many options off the farm as urban women have outside the home. Rural women, it can be argued, find it more difficult to support themselves economically if they leave their husbands. They feel more trapped and stay in poor marriages much longer than they should and longer than do urban women. Some observers believe that rual areas tend to be more conservative than urban areas, and that male dominance is more pronounced. The city, bombarded continuously by new ideas and new people, does not seem to hold to tradition as doggedly as rural areas.

Gang violence is in the news today as urban areas are awash in alcohol and illegal drugs and besieged by heavily armed youth. Rural areas are not overrun by gangs, but one cannot forget the Posse Comitatus and other white supremacist groups based in rural areas who have armed themselves against the devils they have created to inhabit their worst nightmares: Russian, Jews, Blacks, and others who these benighted rural people feel are out to destroy "God's Country."

One white supremacist father we interviewed recently, for example, had joined a rural defense group armed with automatic weapons, 180,000 rounds of ammunition, and bull whips. The commandos and their families had built their fortress on high ground near the Missouri River. They dug earthworks, trained energetically for attack from enemy forces, and watch *Rambo*, *Red Dawn*, and other simple-minded movies on their VCR to supposedly "educate" themselves about the threat from outside. Who, we asked, would want to invade a hog farm overlooking a town of 230 on the Missouri River in Nebraska? Russians, perhaps, the father replied. Or Blacks from Omaha led by Jewish bankers.

Although prejudice can more readily be found in urban areas today, it is not uncommon in the rural United States.

There is no question that agricultural fundamentalism and other strains of hard-headed ignorance can be a problem in rural areas today. The farm crisis of the 1980s added greatly to the difficulties farmers face even in times of relative plenty, and frustration kindled the drive to find scapegoats for rural misery.

Difficult Realities of the Rural Economy Today

Though it is hard to imagine that the farm and ranch population could fall much more than it already has, there still may be no place for many farm children in the farm economy of tomorrow. To try to stay in farming remains a calculated risk. Only well-educated, well-financed farm youths can hope to survive in the agricultural world of the future. Today's farms are larger, more expensive, more mechanized, more scientifically managed, and managed in a more complex corporate mold than ever before. Poor farmers and small farmers have little space to maneuver in such a world of imposing "agribusiness," and end up working in marginal agricultural nooks and crannies which often provide little shelter from great national and international trends that buffet even the biggest businesses. Many farmers—both fathers and mothers—work full- or part-time in town to keep the farming operation afloat. The farm can easily become a financially and emotionally draining hobby or moonlighting operation that never bears much economic fruit.

Resettlement

The majority of farm youth today will probably end up resettling in a more urbanized area. They will leave the farm, as youth have for decades, for a number of reasons. Many will leave because they want to , for long hours and hard physical labor offer little appeal to many. And many others will leave in spite of the fact that they love the rural life and wish to stay. These young people leave the farm and rural areas because they are forced out by hard times.

Because of the farm revolution, farm youth from low-income families have little chance for vertical social mobility. Migration to the town or city has offered the best hope for these young people, and better-informed farm parents have known this. The children of other parents have tended to find out the hard way. As one farm father told us, "I have operated this dairy farm for over 30 years with only 2 weeks' vacation in all that time. I have made a good living and want to turn the farm over to my son. He says he wants no part of it—too much work. I can't understand what's happening to kids today." The farmer finally sold his farm and retired.

Economists call the mass migration from rural areas to urban areas "agricultural readjustment." This term probably works well when one is looking at a computer print-out covered with minute numbers and trend lines. But "agricultural readjustment" becomes a bloodless piece of academic jargon to those who work in the trenches with distressed rural families. "Agricultural readjustment" simply does not convey the emotion, the sheer grit and pain that scrapes one's soul when listening to a farm father or mother go into a spiritual free-fall. The term "rural refugees" is much more precise, we believe, in describing how many individuals and families make their way from the farm to the city. Any time of momentous and difficult transition in a group of people's lives fraught with anger, violence, suicide, depression, and despair deserves better words to describe it than the emotionless "rural readjustment."

Impact of Urbanization on Farm Parents and Their Children

Rural fathers and mothers struggle to internalize their rural values and way of life in their children, but in many ways they are swimming upstream for American society has clearly gone in the urban direction. The mass media, the automobile, the consolidated school, and the general mobility of the American population all increasingly subject farm children to urban values and the urban way of life.

Farm Parents Often Find Themselves Preparing Their Children for an Urban-Industrial World They Themselves Do Not Fully Understand

In many ways, farm parents today have problems similar to those that immigrant parents have faced. Farm parents often find themselves struggling to prepare their children for life in an urban world they do not clearly understand. Historically, education has not been important on the farm. People willing to do hard physical labor could get by. Skill at handling animals was more crucial than skill at handling people. Today, however, urban pundits caution us not to "work harder," but to "work smarter."

Furthermore, trade unions, sex equality, racial integration, the Gay and Lesbian rights movement, cohabitation, and other more liberal approaches to social, religious, and moral issues that have never been particularly popular or understood in rural areas are powerful influences in urban areas today. Rural children making the transition to the city are forced to learn more about these systems of belief, and rural fathers and mothers may not be much help to their children in the process. Rural parents may, in fact, be greatly disturbed on hearing about the kind of world their offspring are struggling to survive in.

Implications

There are a number of implications which may be drawn from this discussion of rural and urban influences on parenthood specifically, and fatherhood in particular. These implications may prove useful for those professionals who work closely with rural families.

1. Professionals working with rural families need to develop a balanced view of rural living in general and rural fatherhood specifically. The Agrarian Myth has elements which ring true, for the beauty, solitude, and independent style of life in rural America are attractive to many people. But professionals cannot afford to be lulled into thinking all is well. The dark dynamic of enmeshment in rural families can grow in the open spaces and isolation. There is little evidence to lead one to conclude that dysfunctional communication patterns, family violence, alcohol and other drug abuse, sexual abuse, and suicide are any less likely to occur simply because one lives on a farm rather than in the suburbs or inner city. Family problems can thrive in the shadows.

2. Rural fathers, indeed, may have more influence on their wives and children because there are fewer "competing models" in rural areas. This influence on the family can be, of course, both positive and negative. In our society we tend to assume mostly positive things about family interaction in rural families, because much of what we feel and believe about rural life comes from photographs on the covers of glossy national magazines of middle-class farm families sitting down to Thanksgiving dinner. Other more negative images do not generally get as enthusiastic a treatment

from the national media, though the recent coverage of the latest farm crisis was a breath of fresh air in this regard.

3.   The farm crisis, which perhaps is best defined as a chronic problem rather than acute and short-lived circumstance, continues today whether the media and the politicians agree or not. American society is faced with a long-term decline in rural population and the problems attendant with the decay of a population base: the loss of schools, churches, businesses, jobs, and other social supports which make rural living attractive. Whole communities have been shattered by the farm crisis; morale disappears and blows across small towns and fields like a dry wind.

4.   For rural fathers of a traditional orientation, still psychologically saddled with the responsibility of providing for the financial needs of their families, the farm crisis is a chronic problem. When a man is forced to spend many of his waking hours worrying about money, this can have serious effects on his relationships with his wife and children. Rural fathers, trained from birth to be independent and strong, often find it difficult to communicate their pain and feelings of isolation. The strength these men need to meet the challenge of the elements and the global economy can become a double-edged sword: they sometimes are strong enough to be silent about their pain, but not strong enough to talk about it. This can lead to a silent rage which fouls the air in a family, or genuinely dangerous violent outbursts. One family therapist once complained about working long hours with verbal, white-collar, middle-class, well-mannered husbands and wives who discussed their differences in an anti-septic, intellectual, almost genteel manner. She stopped complaining when a farm father explained how he disciplined his wife with a tractor chain. Such behavior is certainly not representative of rural fathers in general, but professionals working with rural people know that in some families an undercurrent of mayhem lurks.

5.   The farm crisis adds fuel to an already naturally conservative rural environment, and long-held prejudices about minorities, politicians and businessmen can become intensified. Programs which increase multicultural understanding will serve rural families well, for these families have to learn to deal successfully with a wide variety of individuals and groups in our increasingly complex world.

6.   Though the divorce rate in rural areas is consistently lower than in urban areas, this is no reason for concluding that rural marriage is in general any stronger than urban marriage. Rural

women often have few opportunities for work off the farm or out of the small town if the marriage is not going well. It is not unreasonable to hypothesize that the percentage of "holy deadlocked" marriages may actually be higher in rural than urban areas. For this reason, efforts to develop marriage and family enrichment programs in rural areas are to be applauded. Marriages, especially, can be the greatest source of strength for spouses enduring critical times, and yet marital communication often diminishes during these periods of crisis.

7.   In many rural areas there is a dearth of positive activities for adolescents and young adults. Young people often describe cruising main street, drinking, and sex as the major sources of recreation in their home towns. Recreational activities for young people, and for whole families could help improve the morale of rural areas. Many rural fathers appear lost in the work ethic, not knowing how to slow down and relax. Professionals working with communities could design programs which enhance rural fathers' relationships with their families for the benefit of all.

8.   Finally, much of the discussion in this chapter has focused on the economic challenges rural families face because of the chronic, long-term decline of the rural population, and the problems posed by an increasingly complex global marketplace. The authors have chosen to do so because rural fathers and mothers do not operate in a vacuum anymore than do urban fathers and mothers. A black father trying to raise his children in the South Bronx, a desperately poor area of New York City, is caught up in an environment beyond his control. Similarly, a rural father only has so much power to positively influence the lives of his children. Today, there is an almost palpable fear in many rural areas, and families living in these difficult environments are seriously effected. Professionals seeking to be of service to rural families need to be acutely aware of the challenges the rural environment poses for parents. Solutions to the intra-family problems which come to professionals' attention each day will be found working on a number of fronts. Family therapists, social workers, teachers, ministers, doctors, nurses, and health care professionals, lawyers, and others who work with families on an individual basis will continue to provide direct, essential aid for specific problems. Politicians, economists, business people, social policy makers, and others concerned with the bigger picture need to work hand-in-hand with those direct service providers so that the greater society

can move in a positive direction. We cannot afford to simply work with individual families and ignore structural problems pervading rural society as a whole. The strength of the rural economy effects rural families. The strength of rural schools, churches, businesses, so on and so forth. All these institutions influence, both positively and negatively, the health of rural families. Those who work directly with rural fathers and mothers are in a unique position: their observations and recommendations in the political arena can have a great and positive influence on the development of social policies desperately needed to support rural parents.

Research Needs In The Area Of Rural Fatherhood

Rural fatherhood is sufficiently important to merit closer examination. Although we could find bits and pieces of research on rural fathers scattered here and there, we were not able to find any comprehensive studies which focused specifically on them.

Good sources of support and advice for researchers interested in studies focusing on rural living would be the Farm Families Focus Group of the National Council on Family Relations, and members of various on-going regional research projects in land-grant school institutes of agriculture and home economics funded by the USDA.

Perhaps the most disappointing gap in the research literature on rural fatherhood is that no one seems to have done the rather obvious task of interviewing rural fathers themselves. Many words have been written about rural life, and as reviewers we felt relatively comfortable extrapolating from this literature to the effects of a rural environment on rural parents. But, the most sound approach would obviously be to ask the rural parents themselves. We would propose, then, a major exploratory study of rural fathers and mothers, comparing them to a sample of urban fathers and mothers. The study could be conducted by mailed survey, reaching a large number of fathers in a large geographical area. But we believe it would be quite useful to develop the questionnaire after conducting 50 to 100 in-depth sets of family interviews. In these interviews, researchers would individually talk with fathers, mothers, and children. Issues of particular interest would include:

1. the strengths and stresses of rural and urban families (for example, are rural families stronger than urban families because they live in close proximity and share common goals and tasks?)

2. parenting attitudes and behaviors of rural parents as compared to urban parents

3. family cohesiveness among rural families compared to urban families (for example, are rural fathers closer to their children because they work closer to them?)

4. how rural as compared to urban parents deal with "competing models" (for example, do rural fathers exert more influence on the formation of their children's values than urban fathers?)

5. how rural as compared to urban parents maintain influence on their children during leisure hours

6. the power of the youth peer group in rural and urban areas

7. the extent to which rural and urban parents know their children's friends and families; and how well rural and urban parents think they know what their children are doing when with the peer group

8. the effects of the mass media on rural and urban parents and children

9. the effects of separation, divorce, and remarriage on rural families as compared to urban families

10. how economic problems influence parenting behaviors in rural families

11. much farm income today comes from government price supports, which many people see almost as a type of welfare system for farm families; there needs to be an assessment of the extent to which long-term dependence on government financial support effects the morale, selfesteem, and individual integrity of rural fathers and mothers

12. how the declining rural population affects rural families

13. the extent of "agricultural fundamentalism" among rural families, and how this affects family relationships and decision-making

14. the extent of the "rural refugee" problem and how farm families make the transition to the small town or city

15. the extent of farm parents' difficulties in preparing their children to live in an increasingly urbanized America

16. the difficulties farm parents face in preparing their children to face a world in which agriculture is becoming increasingly more expensive, more mechanized, and more scientifically managed than ever before
17. how farm parents help their children make the transition to city life when there is no place for the farm children in the rural economy?

We do not expect one study to be able to adequately answer all of these questions. What these questions do suggest, however, is that there is a great deal of very useful research that could be done to better understand the strengths of rural parents and the stressors they face.

Conclusion

The most recent wave of the farm crisis reminds us once again that rural life, as life anywhere else, is a bittersweet experience. Farm population continued to decline in the 1980s. Perhaps it will stabilize now, at least for awhile. If that occurs, the rural way of life will continue to bring its unique satisfactions to a small but distinctly important minority of families in America. If a new series of problems disrupts the delicate balance of our global agricultural economy, however, rural fathers and mothers will once again be forced to endure a wrenching, perhaps brutal period of transition.

There is a need for researchers and clinicians sensitive to the needs of rural fathers and mothers today. In the event of another downturn in the farm economy, there will be even more need for those skilled in helping families move from one way of life to another.

Rural life and urban life are clearly different, and these inherent differences influence the ways in which parents rear their children. These differences also make the researcher's task more difficult, for generalizations about parenthood are more challenging to construct given the complexities of what becomes, in essence, cross-cultural research comparing rural and urban fathers and mothers. The complexities, however, add a richness to the tapestry of the institutions of fatherhood and motherhood, and insure the investigator that the research enterprise will be rich in its challenge and difficult enough to keep one's interest from dwindling for a long time.

Rural/urban differences also remind the family life educator and family therapist, once again, to never forget that each family is unique and must be understood from a fresh, open-minded perspective. Researchers and theoreticians in the emerging field of family science are energetically collecting data and constructing general theories to describe, explain, and predict various aspects of family behavior. This is, indeed, a worthy endeavor. The work done by clinicians complements and enhances the work of the researchers and theoreticians. Many clinicians often see each family as being uniquely individual and difficult or impossible to fit into a mold or theoretical box. The clinician's first instinct is often to see each family almost as if it were a marvelous, rare or newly discovered species on the face of the earth. This clinical mind-set is eminently useful and valid, for it helps the clinician retain interest in the challenge of family therapy; and, by holding on to a healthy skepticism when it comes to theories about families in general, the clinician remains open to nuance and creative approaches to therapy for particular families. Canned therapy is no better than TV dinners.

Families share many things in common, no doubt, but at the same time we do them a disservice by jumping in too quickly and buying into particular stereotypic models. All families simply are not the same. And all rural families are not the same, either. They share a richness and diversity that rivals the complexities of urban families. Dedicated family professionals endeavor to better understand the complexities inherent in families so that they may be of some service to these families. The process of gaining this understanding is a most difficult, baffling, and delightful challenge.

References

American heritage dictionary of the English language. (1979). Boston: Houghton Mifflin.

Burchinal, L. B. (1964). The rural family of the future. In J. H. Copp (Ed.), Our changing rural society (pp. 159–197).

Burt, K. (1989). The community's response to gang violence. An audiotaped interview with Burt, a San Diego prosecutor. Lincoln, NE: University of Nebraska, Department of Human Development and the Family (March).

Cherlin, A., & Celebuski, C. (1983). Are Jewish families different? Some evidence from the general social survey. *Journal of Marriage and the Family, 45*, 903–910.

Cohen, S. M. (1981). The American Jewish family today. In M. Himmelfarb & D. Singer (Eds.), *American Jewish year book* (pp. 136–154). Philadelphia: Jewish Publication Society.

Coleman, M., Ganong, L. H., Clark, J. M., & Madsen, R. (1989). Parenting perceptions in rural and urban families: Is there a difference? *Journal of Marriage and the Family, 51*, 329–335.

Cornell, G. (1976, May 28). Divorce among Jews called shocking trend. *Wisconsin State Journal*, section 5, p. 4.

Farmer, V. (1986). Broken heartland. *Psychology Today*, April, pp. 54–62.

Fremon, S., & Wilson, M. (Eds.) (1976). *Rural America*. New York: H. W. Wilson.

Gans, H. J. (1962). *The urban villagers*. New York: Free Press.

Glazer, N., & Moynihan, D. P. (1963). *Beyond the melting pot*. Cambridge, MA: Harvard University and M.I.T. Press.

Hutchison, W. J., Searight, P., & Stretch, J. J. (1986). Multidimensional networking: A response to the needs of homeless families. *Social Work, 31*, 427–430.

Kivett, V. R. (1988). Older rural fathers and sons: Patterns of association and helping. *Family Relations, 37*, 62–67.

Landers, S. (1987). Homeless families. *The American Psychological Association Monitor, 18*, 1, 4.

Newsweek (1978). Civil liberties: Skokie and the Nazis. July, p. 31.

Rogler, L. H., & Cooney, R. S. (1984). *Puerto Rican families in New York City: Intergenerational processes*. Maplewood, NJ: Waterfront Press.

Rowe, G., & Lingren, H. (1986). How farm/ranch families cope with economic distress. *Fact sheet*. Lincoln: University of Nebraska, Institute of Agriculture and Natural Resources, Cooperative Extension Service, Department of Human Development and the Family.

Rowe, G., Williams, R., Lee, P., & Johnson, S. (1985). The impact of economic stressors on rural and urban family relationships. In R. Williams, H. Lingren, G. Rowe, S. Van Zandt, P. Lee, & N. Stinnett (Eds.). *Family strengths 6: Enhancement of interaction* (pp. 341–354). Lincoln: University of Nebraska, Department of Human Development and the Family, Center for Family Strengths.

Scanzoni, J., & Arnett, C. (1987). Policy implications derived from a study of rural and urban marriages. *Family Relations 36*, 430–436.

Schrag, P. (1967). *Village school downtown*. Boston: Beacon Press.

Schumm, W. R., & Bollman, S. R. (1981). Interpersonal processes in rural families. In R. T. Coward & W. M. Smith, Jr. (Eds.), *The family in rural society*. Boulder, CO: Westview Press.

Schwartz, J., Raine, G., & Robins, K. (1987, May 11). A 'superminority' tops out. *Newsweek*, pp. 48–49.

Soth, L. (1965). *An embarrassment of plenty.* New York: Thomas Y. Crowell.

U.S. Department of Commerce. (1980). *Statistical abstract of the United States* (101st Ed.). Washington, DC: U.S. Government Printing Office, 685.

U.S. Riot Commission Report. (1968). New York: Bantam.

Selzer, M. (Ed.) (1972). *Kike! Anti-semitism in America.* New York: World Publishing.

8
Effects of Organizational Culture on Fatherhood

Gary L. Bowen
Dennis K. Orthner

We are not hapless beings caught in the grip of forces we can do little about. Organization has been made by man; it can be changed by man. The fault is not in organization, in short; it is in our worship of it.

William H. Whyte, Jr.
The Organization Man, p. 13

Jim is employed as a senior accountant by a large multinational accounting firm with over 450 employees. Last January marked his 10th anniversary with the firm. He has been married for 8 years and is a father of two boys, ages 5 and 2. His wife, Paula, is employed as a real estate salesperson. Jim considers his family his most important priority, and describes himself as an active and involved parent. However, his job often involves frequent travel that requires him to be separated from his family for more than 100 days per year. As a consequence, his wife, Paula, assumes a disproportionate level of responsibility for the day-to-day care and rearing of the boys. When asked to describe his employer's sensitivity to the increased interest of fathers like himself in being active and involved co-parents, Jim frowns. Although he mentions that the firm has recently implemented flexitime and part-time employment with benefits as a result of initiative from female support staff with family responsibilities, he considers his employing firm to still be working from the old assumptions of male bread-winners and female homemakers. Jim expresses reluctance to challenge these assumptions. Although he does not consider himself a "hapless being" as described by William Whyte above, he does feel trapped in processes that he considers much larger than himself: the organizational culture of the firm in respect to the priority of work and family roles for men and women in society. However, he is optimistic that men will have greater work and family role flexibility in the future.

Recent studies have suggested that men, like Jim, are becoming less traditional in gender-role orientation and are assigning greater importance to socioemotional role performance in the family. Many men are no longer content with being defined just in terms of breadwinning, their traditional role in the family; they also want to be husbands and fathers of presence, both physically and psychologically. This is particularly true of the fathering role. The new breed father is on the rise: men who wish to be full participants in the care and rearing of their children (Lamb, 1987; LaRossa, 1988).

Despite these value shifts among men toward an expanded definition of fathering, the actual performance of caretaker and nurturing roles by fathers in intact families, like Jim, still lags significantly behind the time and energy that mothers give to these roles (Atkinson, 1987; Coverman & Sheley, 1986; Lamb, 1987; Levant, Slattery, & Loiselle, 1987; Pleck, 1985; Repetti, 1987). Even in dual-earner and dual-career households, the care and rearing of the children fall largely to the wife/mother (Hertz, 1986). Hertz (1986) recently concluded that "men have yet to significantly expand their static provider role of father into a fully active role of fathering" (p. 132). There is a clear gap for a growing number of men between their expanding role orientations as fathers and their actual role performance in the family.

To explain the discrepancy between individual orientations toward roles in the family and actual role behavior, investigators have sought to identify variables that may mediate this relationship (Bowen, 1988a; Pleck, 1985). For example, Bowen (1988a) recently identified three categories of such variables: (1) the contrasting role orientations and perspectives among family members, (2) the relative presence or absence of personal resources and relational skills that are necessary for role performance, and (3) the nature and magnitude of intrafamilial- and extrafamilial-level constraints that may serve as obstacles to actualizing individual orientations in behavior.

This chapter focuses on the potential impact of organizational culture on the role performance of employed fathers in intact families: a potential structural constraint to expanded role performance by fathers. The question to be addressed is: To what extent do the set of assumptions, expectations, and norms in the workplace toward the work and family demands and responsibilities of employees impact upon the role behavior of fathers? Despite the considerable discussion in recent years of the concept of organizational culture, the increased attention to the influence of organizational culture on the attitudes and role performance of employees, the expanding interest in the reciprocal interface between work and family, and the burgeoning attention on fathering over the last decade, the impact of organizational culture on the role performance of fathers has been virtually ignored. Relatively more attention has been given to the impact of specific work demands (e.g., the timing and scheduling of work, relocation, and family separation) and employer-related benefits and policies (e.g., flexitime, provision of child care) on the nature of work and family linkages among men with family responsibilities. (e.g., Kamerman & Kahn, 1987; Piotrkowski, Rapoport, & Rapoport, 1987; Pleck, 1985; Voydanoff, 1987).

This chapter is divided into three main sections. In the first section, the concept of organizational culture is discussed, and a working definition is provided, including the parameters of the concept for purposes of the present review. In the second section, the review examines the link between organizational culture, work behavior, and fathering. The changing assumptions and responses of Corporate America to the family-related demands and responsibilities of employees are reviewed within a historical perspective. Selected factors are identified which are resulting in a shifting organizational framework toward greater sensitivity and responsiveness to the family situations and responsibilities of employees, and an important distinction is drawn between organizational behavior and organizational culture. A conceptual model is proposed for examining the relationship between organizational culture and fathering. This model considers the relative salience of work and fathering roles for men in the context of traditional and symmetrical organizational cultures. Hypotheses are developed for guiding future research into this area of inquiry. In the third section, pressures for and implications of expanding organizational sensitivity and responsiveness to the family situations and needs of employees are discussed in the context of future implications for fathering. The chapter concludes with a summary and a call for future research.

Concept of Organizational Culture

> Organization of itself has no dynamic. The dynamic is in the individual and thus he must not only question how the Organization interprets his interests, he must question how it interprets its own.
>
> William H. Whyte, Jr.
> *The Organization Man*, p. 397

In recent years, the concept of "organizational culture" has become a key notion to understanding organizational dynamics and excellence in American businesses (Deal & Kennedy, 1982; O'Toole, 1979; Peters & Waterman, 1982; Schein, 1984; 1985). Like other societal institutions and organizations, work organizations have cultures— rules and expectations for behavior within the work group that arise through both the deliberate actions of leadership and the on-going interaction of group members (Schein, 1984, 1985; Silverzweig & Allen, 1976). Typically unwritten and often unspoken, this culture gives the organization a certain style and character and may have considerable impact upon the values, attitudes and actions of employees in both work and nonwork domains.

Formal definitions of organizational culture in the literature vary greatly, and ambiguity exists in separating the definitional boundaries of the concept from the functions it serves for the organization (Schein, 1985). Deal and Kennedy (1982) define organizational culture as "a system of informal rules that spells out how people are to behave most of the time" (p. 15). Preferring the concept of "organizational ideologies" to "organizational culture," Harrison (1972) defined these ideologies as "systems of thought that are central determinants of the character of organizations" (p. 119). Harrison (1972) describes these ideologies as having an important influence on an organization's decision-making strategies, its use of human resources, and the nature of organizational-environmental relations. From Harrison's perspective, organizational ideologies do more than provide a set of "proscriptions" and "prohibitions," they establish a basis for the type of behavior that is preferred. According to Harrison (1972), a key function of these ideologies is to define the nature of the relationship between the employee and the organization, a "social contract" that underscores the responsibilities of the organization and the individual vis a vis one another.

Perhaps the most comprehensive definition of organizational culture is provided by Schein (1984):

> the pattern of basic assumptions that a given group has invented, discovered, or developed in learning to cope with its problems of external adaptation and internal integration and that have worked well enough to be considered valid, and, therefore, to be taught to new members as the correct way to perceive, think, and feel in relation to those problems. (p. 3)

Schein's definition of organizational culture is broader than the definitions offered by Deal and Kennedy (1982) and by Harrison (1972) above and focuses more its evolvement, its functions for the organization, and its source of change. Because of its comprehensiveness, Schein's definition of organizational culture will serve as the broad working definition of organizational culture in the present chapter.

Several caveats are important to note in the systematic study of organizational culture as both an independent and dependent variable in social research. First, within any one organization, multiple subcultures may exist, each with their own distinctive set of norms or preferred behaviors (Schein, 1984; Silverweig & Allen, 1976). These subcultures may be more or less compatible in their prescriptions and prohibitions for behavior. The presence of multiple subcultures is particularly likely in organizations that have strong structural dimensions and divisions (Schein, 1984).

Second, the influence of organizational culture on the behavior of the individual or small group may vary. Its influence may depend on such factors as the strength of organizational leadership, the need for and the attractiveness of rewards for conformity, the perceived costs for nonconformity, and the strength and compatibility of cultures from other institutions in which the individual may also be involved, such as the family (Harrison, 1972; Schein, 1984, 1985).

Third, the nature of organizational culture is dynamic and fluid, and, at best, represents a negotiated order among individuals and sub-units in the organization in an attempt to accomplish its mission and to function as a group (O'Toole, 1972; Schein, 1984). Working agreements in organizations are in a constant state of process, and are created, renegotiated, and consolidated through an on-going process of diplomacy, bargaining, and negotiation (Mangam, 1981). As recently concluded by Mangam (1981): "personal relationships acting in the social process create and uphold the rules, the rules do not create the process" (p. 200).

Fourth, although the nature of organizational culture may have a tremendous impact on how individuals in the organization think, act, and feel, they may not be totally conscious of the influence of this culture on their actions. According to Schein (1984, 1985), aspects of organizational culture that have worked well for its members may be taken for granted and dropped from consciousness (e.g., business should be profitable). These underlying organizational assumptions can only be uncovered through a kind of "focused inquiry," including observations of group process over time and in-depth interviews with organizational members (O'Toole, 1979; Schein, 1984).

Fifth, it is important to distinguish between more objective features of the organizational culture which are based on the beliefs among a group or groups of members in the organization, and the subjective perceptions of organizational culture for any one member of the organization. In the present analysis, we are interested in the latter perspective.

Lastly, the nature of the organizational culture may not be necessarily productive or healthy for the organization nor for the individuals that work within them (Schein, 1984). As described by Kilmann (1985), "cultural ruts" or "habitual ways" of thinking and acting can develop within organizations that both limit their ability to adapt to changing dynamics in the marketplace and to be responsive to emerging employee needs and concerns. However, behavior in organizations that has worked well in the past may persist although it is outdated and no longer functional for the organization or its employees. An excellent case in point was the tacit denial by the American Automotive Industry in the late 1960s and early 1970s of the potential attractiveness of Japanese imports to the American population. A more recent example has been the attempt by Corporate America to respond to the new demographics of the American workforce and the changing dynamic between work and family in American society with the personnel policies and practices of the 1950s (Blankenhorn, 1986).

This chapter is primarily concerned with only one aspect of organizational culture: the level of awareness, sensitivity and responsiveness of leadership in work organizations to the interdependency between the work and family demands and responsibilities of employees with dependent children, including how the changing role orientations of men and women in society are resulting in a broader definition of fatherhood for an increasing number of fathers. Of particular interest is the mediating role of organizational culture on the level of paternal involvement in child care and child rearing. It is assumed that organizational awareness and sensitivity to the family demands and responsibilities of its employees will influence the employer's receptivity to organizational policies and practices that enable employees to better integrate work and family demands and responsibilities. However, it is not assumed that organizational culture and organizational behavior are necessarily syntonic.

Organizational Culture, Work, and Fathering

> The young men have no cynicism about "the system" and very little skepticism—they don't see it as something to be bucked but as something to be cooperated with.
>
> William H. Whyte, Jr.
> *The Organization Man*, p. 129

The organizational and work context of fathering has not traditionally attracted a great deal of attention from social and behavioral scientists. Much more research has been conducted on mothers because of the more profound changes that have occurred in the labor force participation rates of women. In contrast, the proportion of men who are employed has remained high and their work roles have generally accorded them more status, in society and the home, than their family roles.

This section first explores the work context of fathers and the potential influence of work involvements on fathering behaviors and family life. Next, the evolving nature of organizational culture is examined, especially in helping employees better balance work and family demands and responsibilities. It is argued that despite recent organizational initiatives on behalf of the family situations of employees by a small but growing number of employers, Corporate America remains quite traditional in its views toward the work and family roles of men. This section concludes by proposing a heuristic model for conceptualizing the link between the organizational culture of the work setting and the fathering behavior of its male employees which is intended to encourage research on this important relationship.

Work Context of Fathering

During the 1950s, the study of work and fathering was given a boost by several sociologists who suggested that the work context of the family influenced child rearing patterns and subsequent intergenerational mobility. Miller and Swanson (1958), for example, hypothesized that wives of men who worked in "bureaucratic" settings, in which there is an emphasis on security and accommodation, were more likely than the wives of men who worked in "entrepreneurial" setting, in which there is an emphasis on initiative and risk taking, to describe styles of childrearing that were more oriented toward the development of interpersonal skills and accommodative behavior in children. On the other hand, the childrearing patterns of the wives of men who worked in "entrepreneurial" settings were hypothesized to be more oriented than those of "bureaucratic" wives to the development of individual achievement, self control, and independent behavior in children.

While there is some intuitive appeal to the hypothesis that the father's work setting influences parental values and behavior, Miller and Swanson found only partial support for their hypotheses when tested on a sample of Detroit women. In addition, attempts to replicate their findings have been unsuccessful when examined for families in the United States (Caudill & Weinstein, 1969; Franklin & Scott, 1970). It has been suggested by Bronfenbrenner and Crouter (1987) that the lack of subsequent support for Miller and Swanson's hypotheses may result from the progressive shift of entrepreneurial settings in the United States toward greater bureaucratization.

Kohn (1963, 1969) extended Miller's and Swanson's analysis by proposing a link between the characteristics of the father's job and its effects on the characteristics of parenting behavior. This research demonstrated that fathers who worked in environments that provided considerable autonomy and control tended to produce children who were more independent and self-reliant. In contrast, when the father's job demanded more supervision and control by others, children were expected to be more compliant at home and at school. Subsequent studies have generally confirmed these relationships (see Gecas, 1979, for a review of this research).

The earlier research by Miller and Swanson (1958) and Kohn (1963, 1969) has been heuristic to continued research on the influences of occupational variables on family-oriented values and processes. For example, there is increasing evidence that the work involvement of fathers does influence their parental behavior and family outcomes. Studies of family time generally find that men who work longer hours have less time available for parental or shared marital activities (Berk & Berk, 1979; Juster & Stafford, 1985). These findings have generally been interpreted from a role scarcity perspective to reflect the fact that there are only so many hours in a day and that work hours take away from family time. However, Clark, Nye and Gecas (1978) found that this assumption may not always be accurate. In their study, they found that the length of the work week had little or no influence on the marital role involvements of husbands beyond the influence of control variables in their analysis. The authors suggested that the effects of the length of the husband's work week on their marital role performance may be contingent on the role priorities and expectations of the husbands and wives in marriage. Thus, it appears that family values and expectations may be an important intervening variables in the relationship between the job requirements of men and their level of involvement in the family.

Despite important qualifications in the literature on the nature of work and family linkages, in general, the available literature does suggest that the organizational context within which men are working can influence the set of values that pervade the family and set parameters around fathering expectations (Aldous, 1969; Bowen, 1988b; Bronfenbrenner & Crouter, 1982; Kanter, 1977b; LaRossa, 1988; Piotrkowski, Rapoport, & Rapoport, 1987; Pleck, 1985). This is especially true in what Bowen and Orthner (1989) refer to as "organizational families." In these families, the work and family environments are much more contiguous and the values of the organizational culture are more likely to transpose themselves on family roles. This is more common in some corporations, among the clergy, and in higher risk organizations such as the police and military services. For example, the clergyperson may live on the parish grounds and be subject to on-going demands of parishioners. Likewise, the military father often lives on the installation and the nature of the job requires that he be available for duty 24 hours a day.

Fathering within the context of an organization family places special demands on the family. Organization values are more visible and they can be more easily reflected in family rules and behavior (Segal, 1989). For example, in a large study of adolescent children growing up in military and nonmilitary families, it was found that relationships between boys and their fathers were especially strong among the military youth (Orthner, Giddings & Quinn, 1987). Furthermore, the researchers reported that the psychological profile of the male youth from military families was much more positive than the female youth. The females growing up in military families exhibited lower self-esteem, higher alienation, and more depression than their nonmilitary counterparts. The results were interpreted to suggest that the highly masculine organizational culture of the military resulted in higher than normal levels of attachment between boys and their fathers. At the same time, these organizational values caused conflict for female youth and weakened their attachments to their fathers, families, peers and themselves.

Research on the influence of the work context on fathering is still in its infancy but it is clear that the larger cultural context for fathering is changing rapidly today (Mancini & Orthner, 1988). As more women move into the workplace, there are accompanying increased expectations for more participation by fathers in childrearing and household tasks (LaRossa, 1988). This is leading to the current cultural clash between the traditional socialization of men to be breadwinner fathers, the emerging societal expectations for participatory fatherhood, and organizational cultures which promote the primacy of work for both men and women.

Pro-Family Workplace: Myth or Reality for Fathers

Historically, there has been little reason to study the relationship between organization culture and the role performance of fathers in intact families. Neither environment permitted significant variation. The culture in work organizations was based on a strong "masculine ethic" which denied potential conflict between the goals of the organization and those of the individual (Kanter, 1977a; Whyte, 1956). On the other hand, the success of fathers was evaluated primarily on one criterion: their ability to be good economic providers for their families—their only legitimate role in the family (Orthner, 1981). From this traditional perspective, the roles of men and women were clearly differentiated with men performing the economic role and women responsible for the home and care of the children.

Paralleling the womens' liberation movement, the improved opportunities for women in the paid labor force, and the transition toward less traditional gender-role orientations for men and women, there is emerging evidence in both the popular media and the scientific press that a growing number of work organizations are evolving to be more supportive of the family responsibilities of employees and that an increasing number of fathers are showing greater interest in expanding their role responsibilities. However, questions remain as to the extent and depth of these changes among men, and whether they may be more rhetoric than real.

During the nineteenth century, there was significant economic shift in America as men left the farms in great numbers to assume a role in industry. Families were transformed from units of production to units of consumption, and the roles of men and women became highly differentiated with men tied to workplace and women tied to home and family. Although largely restricted to the middle class, the traditional family with the husband as the provider and the wife as the expressive hub of the family became the ideal. During this era, fatherhood became synonymous with being a good provider (Lamb, 1987).

As the large corporation emerged as a dominant organizational form in the early twentieth century, it was imbued with a strong "masculine ethic" that helped to legitimate the authority of a burgeoning class of managers (Kanter, 1977a). This "masculine ethic" stressed the importance of rationale, unemotional decisionmaking which was based on logical and unemotional analysis. As a management principle, it was undergirded by the traditional division of labor among men and women in society at that time and reinforced by early management theories, such as Taylor's theory of "scientific management" (Taylor, 1947). These theories rejected "intuition" as a decisionmaking strategy and stressed "rationality" as the ideal

(Kanter, 1977a). Since "rationality" was considered a male virtue, this "masculine ethic" became the basis for excluding women from jobs as managers, limiting their work roles primarily to clerical and support functions. Unfortunately, it also became a basis for excluding men from active participation in their families, a barrier for men becoming active and involved participants in child care and child rearing. Kanter (1977b) has referred to this segmented view of work and family responsibilities which is differentiated along lines of gender as "the myth of separate worlds" (p. 8).

Given this traditional perspective, there was little reason for work organizations to give recognition to the family interests and responsibilities of their employees. Although "company welfarism" peaked during the 1920s—a decade of company towns, company houses, and company stores—these services represented the height of corporate paternalism (Kamerman & Kingston, 1982). Rather than being supportive to the family responsibilities of employees, they gave the organization an encompassing power over employees and were intended, in part, to discourage the organization of trade and labor unions (Kamerman & Kingston, 1982). From this traditional model of organizational culture, as long as men were being compensated adequately for their services, they were fulfilling their roles in the family. Of course, this operating principle was based on the assumption that work was the primary life pursuit of men; further, it assumed that women were attending to home and family responsibilities so that men could devote their time, energy, and loyalty to the organization without family reprecussions. Work organizations were greedy for the time and energy of men, and, as William Whyte concluded in his 1956 volume, denied potential conflict between the goals of the organization and those of the individual. As early as 1956, Whyte described this "social ethic" that reified the organization as "static," "delusory," and "ill-suited to the needs of 'modern man'" (pp. 396–397). He asserted that the emphasis on group at the expense of the individual was detrimental not only for the individual, but also for the organization. Whyte saw conflict between the organization and the individual as inevitable and normal, requiring continuous realignment on the part of both the organization and the individual, not just the individual alone.

Organizations today continue to remain "greedy" for the time, energy, and commitment of their employees (Segal, 1989). However, dramatic changes have occurred in American society since the mid-

1950s that have prompted an increasing number of organizations to critically reexamine their traditional assumptions toward both the roles of men and women in society and the relationship between the work and family demands and responsibilities of employees. Some of these changes include a substantial growth in the labor force partici- pation of married women, including those with young children in the household (Hayghe, 1986; Teachman, Polonko, & Scanzoni, 1987); a significant increase in the number of employed women in more prestigious, higher paying occupations (Reubens & Reubens, 1979); the emergence of dual-career couples, couples for whom the career of both the husband and wife is important (Sekaran, 1986); a decline in the share of households headed by married couples and an increase in the number of families headed by single parent men and women (Glick, 1984; Teachman, Polonko, & Scanzoni, 1987); a convergence of new, more egalitarian gender-role preferences among men and women (Bowen, 1987; Bowen & Neenan, 1988; McBroom, 1984); the emergence of the "new-breed" worker, workers who are particu- larly likely to question the cost of success in the work place, especially when this success compromises opportunities for a quality family life (Nieva, 1985; Yankelovich, 1979); rising demands by working par- ents for their employers to develop workplace policies that are more supportive of their family responsibilities (Blankenhorn, 1986); and a move toward more democratic and participatory styles of manage- ment and decision-making in work organizations that follow more of human relations models of management (Crouter, 1984; McGregor 1960; Ouchi, 1981).

These demographic, value, and social changes were preceded by critical events during the 1930s and 1940s, including the Great Depression and World War II, that challenged the narrow role assumptions for fathers and demonstrated the ability of large numbers of women to contribute meaningfully in the labor force and as sole providers for their families. Combined, they have resulted in a growing awareness among employers of the potential conflict be- tween the values and interests of employees and those of the organi- zation, more specifically, the interdependence between the work and family demands and responsibilities of employees (Bowen, 1988b; Kagan, 1983; Kamerman & Kingston, 1982; Louis Harris and Asso- ciates, Inc., 1981).

Although estimates vary on the scope of development and the level of expenditure, there are indications that this growing awareness among employers of work and family linkages has resulted in an expansion of family-oriented policies and services over the last decade (e.g., Bureau of National Affairs, Inc., 1986; Kamerman & Kahn, 1987; Kamerman & Kingston, 1982; Ozawa, 1980). The implementation of these family-oriented policies and services for employees now includes flexible alternatives in the scheduling and hours of work, extended maternity leave provisions and benefits, paid personal days for child and family responsibilities, information and referral services, expanded relocation assistance, and even corporate childcare services.

Despite these trends which on the surface should have positive implications for fathers who wish to become more active in their paternal response, there are indications that the response of Corporate America has lagged behind changing trends and dynamics in work and family (Blankenhorn, 1986; BNA, 1986; Bowen, 1988b; Friedman, 1987; Kamerman & Kahn, 1987; McNeely & Fogarty, 1988; Raabe & Gessner, 1988; Stillman & Bowen, 1985). Many senior managers remain skeptical about the benefit/cost ratio of expanding family-related supports to employees and their families (BNA, 1986; Bohen, 1984). In addition, in some ways, the move by employers to develop a more pro-family workplace reflects the same paternalistic attitude of the past, not necessarily a move toward a more androgynous workplace.

A key question concerns whether these behavior changes in organizations also represent a change in the underlying organizational ideology on an interpersonal level in work organizations toward greater awareness and sensitivity to the work and family dilemma for employees. In other words, do these actions represent a genuine concern for the well-being of employees that are reflected on a day-by-day basis throughout the organizational hierarchy in work organizations, or do they arise without an underlying commitment to the values that the changes supposedly represent: from a simple profit motive, a paternalistic attitude, or a desire to gain firm control over employees? Unlike the situation for fathers today where the values for more involved parenting seem to have changed more quickly than their actual role performance in the family, the converse seem true of family-support initiatives in work organizations today: organizational behavior in support of the family lives of employees is hypothesized to be changing faster than the underlying organizational ideology (Raabe & Gessner, 1988; Stillman & Bowen, 1985).[1]

In many ways, this culture remains very traditional, especially for men (Raabe & Gessner, 1988). The permeability of work and family role boundaries for men remain unidirectional where work demands are allowed to intrude upon family role performance, but not vice versa (Pleck, 1977). For instance, Raabe and Gessner (1986) found "organizational resistance" to discussions of paid paternity leave in their study of family-supportive policies in 30 firms in New Orleans. From their interviews with the personnel managers of the firms that they studied, Raabe and Gessner concluded that traditional assumptions of parenting responsibilities continue to dominate. In addition, it is interesting that no one has yet to suggest a "daddy-track" for men who wish to pursue both a career and fatherhood that would parallel the "mommy-track" that was recently introduced by Felice Schwartz (1989), the head of Catalyst, a nonprofit organization that advocates for the career advancement of women. To the extent that work is important for men, such a gender-role traditional organizational culture is hypothesized to serve as a considerable obstacle to men who wish to be more active and involved fathers.

Conceptual Model

To date, the study of the effect of the father's occupation on family life has followed four main tracks: (1) the effect of father's job loss on both the status of the father in the family and family relationships; (2) the effect of the father's occupational position on his child rearing orientations and behaviors; (3) the long-range effects of father's employment and socioeconomic status on child development; and (4) the conflict between the father's work demands and responsibilities and his level of family participation and performance of family roles (e.g., Aldous, 1969; Aldous, Osmond, & Hicks, 1979; Bronfenbrenner & Crouter, 1982; Hoffman, 1986). Despite the considerable attention that has been given to the effect of organizational culture on the work attitudes and performance of men in the organizational literature (e.g., Silverzweig & Allen, 1976; Schein, 1985), there has been a lack of systematic attention to the effect of organizational culture per se on the role performance of fathers in their families. However, in a recent article on corporate supports for the family lives of employees, Bowen (1988b) advanced a conceptual model that depicted organizational culture and philosophy as indirectly effecting role performance in the family via its influence on both structural and dynamic features of the work environment. In addition, the model as developed by Bowen underscored the reciprocal interplay between organizational culture, the employee's perceptions and circumstances, and both work and family role performance.

Given the lack of empirical data on the relationship between organizational culture and fathering, a structural effects model is advanced that builds on the recent modeling effort by Bowen (1988b) and the classic research which was conducted by Blau (1960) nearly three decades ago that attempted to isolate the effects of group values from individual values on behavior. Based largely on role theory (Biddle, 1986; McCall & Simmons, 1978) and a person–environment fit perspective (Moos, 1986; French, Caplan, & Harrison, 1982), the proposed model focuses on how organizational culture may mediate the relationship between the relative salience of work and fathering orientations among men and their actual role performance as fathers in the family. Although the effect of organizational culture on fathering behavior may be direct and independent of the father's individual orientations (cf., Blau, 1960), for purposes of the present analysis, the relationship between the individual orientations of fathers and their actual role performance as fathers is conceptualized as contingent on the nature of the organizational culture. The most extreme example of such a contingency effect is where the relationship between the individual orientations of the fathers and actual fathering behavior are inverse, contingent on the nature of the culture of the organization concerning the rights and responsibilities of fathers. As a beginning framework, it is hoped that the model will be heuristic to future modeling and research efforts which attempt to depict and understand the relationship between organizational culture and fathering.

Figure 8.1 depicts the conceptual model. For reasons of simplicity, its two continua have been reduced to simple dichotomies to form a two by two typology. On the horizontal dimension, two types of organizational cultures are identified: traditional and symmetrical. Traditional organizations are defined as those organizations that lack awareness of as well as genuine concern and sensitivity to the potential interest of men to play active and involved roles as fathers in the family. These organizations tend to have very stereotypical views about the roles and responsibilities of men and women in the care and rearing of children. Even when organizational supports are present for helping employees better meet their family demands and

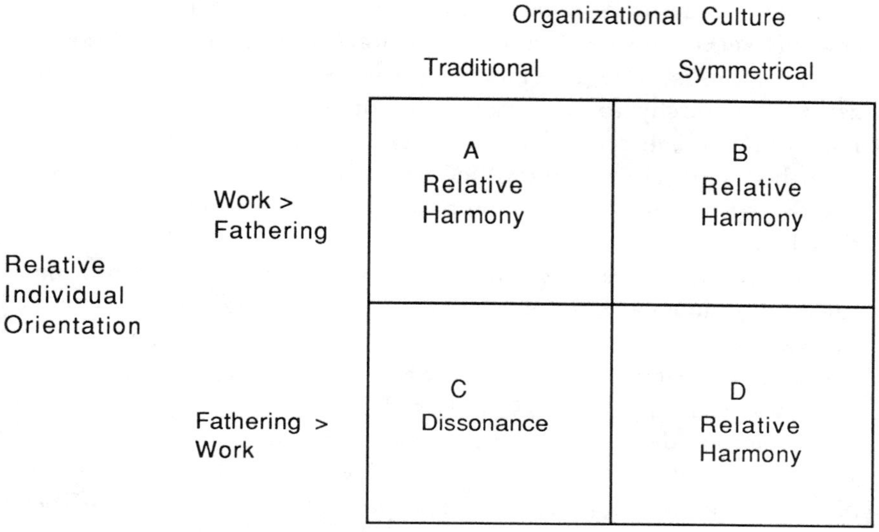

Organizational Culture

	Traditional	Symmetrical
Work > Fathering	A Relative Harmony	B Relative Harmony
Fathering > Work	C Dissonance	D Relative Harmony

Relative
Individual
Orientation

Figure 8.1   A structural effects model.

responsibilities, these supports are often founded on paternalistic principles, profit motives, and are geared for the most part to female employees. The vast majority of employers in the United States would be hypothesized to fit this traditional description of organizational culture.

On the other hand, symmetrical organizations represent a small but growing number of employers in the United States (Blankenhorn, 1986). While the "bottom line" may also be an important consideration for these employers, they have a keen awareness of work and family dynamics and have a genuine interest in assisting their employees in achieving their aims and goals in both work as well as in nonwork domains. In these firms, family concerns are more than just a female issue: they are equally important for men. The modus operandi is "partnership" and "cooperation" between the work organization and its employees: a win-win situation for both the organization and its employees in accomplishing their respective missions. Interestingly, these organizations may actually have fewer formal supports and workplace initiatives to help employees balance work and family demands than traditional organizations. However, among employees, there is little or no hesitation to make special requests in order to respond to family needs and considerations. The key difference between symmetrical organizations and traditional organizations is the depth of awareness within and across the organizational hierarchy to the importance of being responsive to the family-related concerns of both men and women. From coworker to front-line supervisor to the Chief Executive Officer, the family demands and responsibilities of employees are built into the organizational equation.

On the vertical axis, the relative salience of work and parenting roles for individual fathers are depicted. These individual orientations are conceptualized as cognitive, serving as a basis for choice and as a guide for action. Although the orientations of men toward their work and fathering roles as well as the interrelationship between these roles are defined as variables that may change in response to a variety of familial and extra-familial influences, the relative salience of these two roles for men are conceptualized for purposes of the model into a simple dichotomy: (1) work roles are more salient for the individual than fathering roles, and (2) fathering roles are more salient for the individual than work roles. All else being equal, the stronger the salience of a given role, the higher the probability of behavior being invoked across situations that is consistent with that role (Stryker, 1968). In the present case, we make one exception to all else being equal: the nature of the culture in the organization concerning fathering behavior.

As Figure 8.1 hypothesizes, there would be relative harmony for fathers in cells A, B, and D. In both A and D, the relative salience that fathers give to their work and fathering roles is syntonic to the culture of their work organization. In these situations, we would hypothesize that the fathering behavior of these men would be consistent with the relative salience of their work and fathering roles. Although the role orientations of fathers in cell B are not in sync with the nature of the culture of their employing organization, these situations are still hypothesized as being relatively harmonious. Specifically, even though these fathers give greater priority to their work roles than to their roles as fathers, and, all else being equal, would be hypothesized to be more likely to perform work roles at the expense of fathering roles, these fathers may find it satisfying to know that their employing organizations are supportive of more expanded definitions of fathering behavior. Such a situation provides them with greater role latitude and may actually influence their individual orientations to work and family roles over time—a situation that Levinger (1986) refers to as dispositional transformation.

Cell C combines fathers where the relative salience of work and fathering role favors fathering with their employment in a traditional organizational culture. Given the respective literature on the increased salience of fathering roles for men and the lag in significant shifts in the nature of organizational culture for men, it is hypothesized that an increasing number of men are finding themselves in this situation. A situation of dissonance, it is further hypothesized that this situation helps to explain the discrepancy in the literature between the changing orientations of fathers toward being more active and involved parents and their actual behaviors as fathers. In these situations, the nature of the organizational culture is hypothesized to serve as a structural constraint to men in becoming involved in all aspects of child care and child rearing.

Despite its simplicity, the model provides a rich source of hypotheses for guiding empirical research into the nature of the relationship between organizational culture and fathering. In addition, the model could easily be made more sophisticated by adding more refined categories to its horizontal and/or vertical axes. For example, a third organizational type could be added on the horizontal dimension between the traditional and symmetrical organization: the transitional organizational culture. Other contingency effects could also be added to the model. For instance, the expectations of the wife for the father's work and fathering behavior could be added to the model, a variable that Bronfenbrenner and Crouter (1982) consider as necessary to fully determine the mutual influence of work and family roles for men. This could be simply done by conceptualizing the level of agreement between the husband and wife on the vertical axis concerning the relative salience that the father gives to his work and fathering roles.[2] From this perspective, situations of maximum harmony for fathers would involve consensus with their wives about the level of relative salience that they give to their work and fathering roles as well as their location in an organizational culture that supports their role orientation toward work and fathering roles. On the other hand, situations of maximum dissonance for fathers would involve a lack of husband and wife consensus about the relative salience that they assign to their work and fathering roles as well as location in an organizational culture that is also at dissonance with their respective role priorities as workers and as fathers.

Organizations and Fathering:
Future Prospects

> He must fight The Organization. Not stupidly, or selfishly, for the defects of
> individual self-regard are no more to be venerated than the defects of co-
> operation. But fight he must, for the demands for his surrender are constant
> and powerful, and the more he has come to like the life of the organization
> the more difficult does he find it to resist these demands, or even to recognize
> them.
>
> William H. Whyte, Jr.
> *The Organization Man*, p. 404

Organizational cultures, like most cultures, change ever so slowly.
Corporations and other large-scale organizations typically have
vested interests in maintaining their own styles or modes of operation, whether those models are related to production or to personnel
practices. Through personnel selection, training and socialization,
organizations and their supportive cultures develop their own inertia
that discourages change, even when new norms and values would
seem to benefit both the organization and its people. Kilmann
(1985) refers to these as "cultural gaps," disconnects between what
an organization's behavior should be and what the norms and values
of the organization will permit. Cultural gaps occur when either the
norms of the larger society or the expectations of organization
members have changed to a larger degree than the organization's
own policies or values.

Organizational support for the roles and responsibilities of
fathers is increasingly reflected in this cultural gap. Societal and
family pressures for fathers to participate more fully in household
responsibilities are increasingly clashing against the unchanging demands placed on men by work organizations. Even though there is
an acknowledged crisis in parent-child relationships today (Levine,
1976), organizations have not typically changed their work expectations or reward systems to permit men more opportunities for
participatory parenthood. Instead, work weeks today remain just as
long as a few decades ago; company required relocations continue
almost unabated; paternity leaves are lobbied against; and men who
take too much time off for their families (even evening and vacation
time) are penalized in the promotion and merit process.

There are a number of pressures, however, for organizations to reduce the size of the cultural gap between what a small but growing number of fathers want and what organizational policies will permit. These pressures are coming from several sources, including organizational competition, government mandates, women's groups, and fathers themselves. Of these, the most widely observed is the growing influence of women on organization policies and practices. Women's groups have been vocal proponents for more flexible leave policies, flexitime, company sponsored child care and new personnel management initiatives (Fernandez, 1986). These pressures have been initiated primarily out of the self-interests of the women involved but they have had much more far-reaching consequences. As the discussions and debates over the need to reduce work and father conflicts have increased, men too have benefited and often joined with women in encouraging organizational changes. Still, it is clear that men tend to be more the benefactors than the initiators of these debates and all too often, family policies are still couched as a "women's issue" rather than as a parental issue (Voydanoff, 1985).

The role of government in encouraging changes in organizational policies and culture is still in its infancy, at least in the United States (Kamerman & Kingston, 1982). The old adage, "What is good for General Motors is good for the U.S.A.," still lives in the minds of many government policymakers. Thus, both federal and state legislation tends to respond to the interests of corporations and to be benign in directing companies to make pro-family changes. Instead, subtle encouragements are offered that have only minor influence over company practices. For example, the federal government in 1981 included in its tax reform act the ability of employers to set up a child care plan and deduct expenses from employees. However, there were no requirements to set up the plan and there was no promotion of the tax benefits either to the company or its employees. Few fathers or mothers, therefore, saw any positive consequences from this act, even though it was designed to help them. In contrast to most Western countries, the U.S. has no nation-wide policies on parental leave, part-time employment, vacations, medical care coverages, or other family-related work practices. Thus, fathers do not benefit from governmental pressures to change organizational practices which might allow them more opportunities for parenting.

While government encouragement for organizations to support parenting is lacking, some industries are beginning to force changes on themselves. Relatively low unemployment and a healthy economy have increased the competition for young, especially well-educated, workers. This competition for skilled workers is beginning to encourage companies to expand their benefits and introduce new policies in order to attract and keep good employees (Orthner & Pittman, 1986). Fathers are benefiting from these changes as companies in highly competitive industries are offering more inducements to them that make it easier in balancing their work and family roles. Thus far, these changes have been most noticeable in higher technology firms that need to attract younger adults with the newer skills. But this pattern is likely to expand as the competition for labor grows and as international competition increases. More and more companies are competing internationally or becoming multinational and this puts increased pressure on work organizations and the government to develop policies that are more comparable to those in competing industries and countries.

Finally, pressures for change in organizational cultures are coming from fathers themselves. Some men are noticing the disconnect between what they say about the importance of being fathers and what they find themselves *not* doing in support of their words (Lamb, 1987). When parental roles are blocked by organizational demands or expectations, some men are leaving their employers in favor of other companies who do recognize their parental ambitions. Still others are embarking on new entrepreneurial opportunities that give them more freedom to participate in family activities. As an example, the marketing vice-president of a major food company resigned to become a university professor (at one-third the salary) when he learned that his children did not feel they even knew him. This father is still the exception rather than the rule, but it appears that there is a new generation of men who are willing to agitate for change in organizational norms and values or willing to leave those organizations that are unwilling to recognize their paternal interests.

What will the future bring for fathers and for the cultural gap around parental values and practices that still pervade many organizations? It appears that the general cultural drift is in the direction of organizational cultures permitting more flexibility for men who elect to participate in the rearing of their children. There does not appear to be a wholesale shift under way from what was earlier termed "traditional" to "symmetrical" oriented cultures, but the move is clearly in that direction. Executive workshops and conferences around the subject of work and family issues are becoming increasingly common and they are attracting growing numbers of participants from both labor and management (Conference Board, 1985). Often, these meetings are accompanied by a speech from a senior corporate leader (usually male) who expresses his concern about his own family frustrations, as well as those of the people with whom he works.

If the drift toward symmetrical organizational cultures is to continue or even accelerate, two conditions are probably necessary. First, the economy must continue to be healthy and unemployment rates must remain low. A major driver behind the softening of the performance-oriented belief systems of most organizations is the competition for high quality personnel. Many organizations today are introducing radically new family-oriented policies only because they believe that this is the best way they can attract and keep the best people. A case in point is the recent labor contract agreed to by American Telephone and Telegraph Company (AT&T), a company where the majority of employees are women. Under this agreement, AT&T breaks new ground in providing comprehensive support benefits and services for employees with child and elder care responsibilities (Perkins, 1989). Organizations are slowly learning that pay alone is not sufficient to induce employees, especially parents, to be loyal to employers.

A second condition that will promote organizational change is continued pressure from women, both at home and on the job. Most scholars agree that the changes men have made thus far in their parental and household roles have come about largely as a result of pressure from women, not necessarily from men themselves (Lamb, 1987; Orthner, 1981; LaRossa, 1988). Men appear to be somewhat ambivalent about shifting their primary source of personal gratification from work to the family, despite much of the rhetoric in that direction. Research has shown that men can successfully accommodate higher role performance and competence in both work and family spheres, but the catalyst for this accommodation comes from the support of their wives (Clark, Nye, & Gecas, 1978). When wives do not provide encouragement for father and husband involvement, men are much less likely to participate in family roles (Benokraitis, 1985).

On the job, men are likewise able to take advantage of the pressure from women to change organizational values toward balancing work and parenthood. This coat tail strategy has been less risky for men thus far but it has resulted in a narrowing of the benefits from organizational change primarily to women. As long as the pressure to change the organizational culture comes from women, the predominant "masculine ethic" of the organization (Kanter, 1977a) will not be changed but will only be modified to accommodate females as second-class employees. This is a major concern for those who have been observing this trend thus far (e.g., Voydanoff, 1985). If this continues to happen, the benefits for men as fathers will only be slightly improved. This has been already demonstrated in some European countries where men are permitted by law or policy considerable freedom to participate in parental roles but then they are discouraged by their organizational cultures from taking advantage of these benefits. The sooner family and dependent care issues are expanded to include both fathers and mothers, the better.

Summary and Conclusions

> But what is the "solution"? many ask. There is no solution. The conflict between individual and society has always involved dilemma; it always will, and it is intellectual arrogance to think a program will solve it. Certainly the current experience does suggest a few steps we can profitably take, and I would like to suggest several.
>
> William H. Whyte, Jr.
> *The Organization Man*, p. 397

At the present time, it does not appear that organizational cultures are antifatherhood. Instead, it might be said that they are ambivalent toward parenthood in an attempt to foster those practices that promote organizational performance and success. Echoing the concerns raised in this chapter, Gutek, Nakamura and Nieva (1981) observe:

> At the present time, most employers do not consider the welfare of their employees as family members to be an organizational concern. Company policies and practices, therefore, for the most part, are designed and enforced as though the employees either had no competing concerns or that responsibilities outside their jobs are naturally subordinate to their work demand. (p. 12)

If the organizational cultures at work are ambivalent about participatory fatherhood, the culture of the larger society provides little in the way of encouragement for organizations to change. While it is true that fathers are spending more time with their children than a decade ago (Juster & Stafford, 1985), it does not appear that they are taking significantly greater responsibility for their children. LaRossa (1988) summarizes current research to indicate that the dominant pattern today is a "technically present but functionally absent father" (p. 454). Although fathers are now more likely to spend time in one-on-one interaction with their children, mothers continue to carry a disproportionate level of responsibility for the day-to-day care of children. LaRossa goes on to indicate that the cultural belief that fathers should participate more in childrearing is increasingly reflected in the public media but that fathering behaviors are clearly lagging behind these expanding expectations.

Given this incongruency behind values and behavior in the larger society, most organizations are unwilling to undertake radical changes in their own values and expectations, at least with regard to fatherhood. Critical examinations of organizational cultures are becoming more common today but these reviews are typically targeted toward factors that inhibit communication and productivity, not employee satisfaction or work and family conflicts (Kilmann, 1985). Until organizations see short and long-term benefits in their "bottom-line" profits and performance from improved family well-being and participation, deliberate overhauls of organizational cultures are unlikely to be made.

What strategies can be used to encourage organizations to consider reviewing their official and unofficial policies and practices toward fatherhood? First, more research is needed into the contributions that family factors have for personnel recruitment, retention and performance. This research is currently lacking since most studies either examine work and family factors independently or they focus on the influences of work on family adjustments. Organizational change is usually easier when there is a body of research and theory that undergirds major transformations. Without this, significant changes are considered risky and managers are unlikely to threaten their jobs by proposing major changes.

Second, women need to include men more actively in their strategies for improving organizational benefits and policies for families. Some attempts at organizational change have been pushed and/or perceived as uniquely the concern of women when in fact the interests have included men as well. If men and women cooperated more closely in developing and implementing strategies for change, the organization may view the recommendations more broadly. Fathers would then become co-stakeholders in the change, not just beneficiaries by default.

Third, and lastly, government reviews of organizational policies regarding work and family roles of employees should be encouraged. Just as the federal government has had a vital role in stimulating health and education policies in the face of some strong cultural barriers, issues of equal employment opportunity, corporate productivity and family well-being must be examined despite barriers that may lie in organizational cultures. The ability of fathers to share in the rearing of their children is no longer just a nice gesture, it has become a national concern. Women have been bearing the stress of the expanding economy by increasing their employment obligations outside the home without significantly decreasing their family involvements and responsibilities. With most mothers and fathers now in the labor force, the family system today is under heavy demands but mothers are still primarily responsible for the care of children. A healthy two-parent system of childrearing is needed as the burden of childrearing has become increasingly unfair. Work organizations need to be encouraged to support participatory co-parenthood, not just because it is in the best interests of the company, but also because it is in the best interests of the society.

In conclusion, the evidence we have reviewed suggests that work organizations can and do play a major role in the behaviors and attitudes of fathers. The ability of men to fulfill their parental responsibilities is both conditioned by and inhibited by the work organizations of which they are a part. Organizational cultures serve in a quiet but strong way to reinforce traditional fatherhood roles and thereby limit the opportunity of men to take advantage of the new cultural prescriptions which are encouraging them to take greater responsibility for the rearing of their children. Unless these organizational pressures are mitigated, however, fathers will continue to be pulled away from their families and haunted by the messages in songs like "Cats in the Cradle," which they all too often hear going to and from their jobs, songs describing fathers who are never quite able to find the time to experience those special and often unanticipated moments of opportunity with their children.

Notes

1. It is not unusual for behavioral changes to precede large-scale value shifts in society. A good example is the civil rights movement that began in the early 1960s where changes in social values lagged behind behavioral changes in society. However, unless values begin to shift to become supportive of behavior changes, the behavioral changes can be underminded.

2. See Christensen (1964) who presents a paradigm of harmony and dissonance which is based on the interaction of husband and wife values within the context of their external system.

References

Aldous, J. (1969). Occupational characteristics and males' role performance in the family. *Journal of Marriage and the Family, 31*, 707–712.

Aldous, J., Osmond, M. W., & Hicks, M. W. (1979). Men's work and men's families. In W. R. Burr, R. Hill, F. I. Nye, & I. L. Reiss (Eds.), *Contemporary theories about the family*, Vol. 1 (pp. 227–256). New York: Free Press.

Atkinson, A. M. (1987). Father's participation and evaluation of family day care. *Family Relations, 36*, 146–151.

Benokraitis, N. (1985). Fathers in the dual-earner family. In S. M. H. Hanson & F. W. Bozett (Eds.), *Dimensions of fathering* (pp. 243–268). Beverly Hills: Sage.

Berk, R., & Berk, S. F. (1979). *Labor and leisure at home.* Beverly Hills, CA: Sage.

Biddle, B. J. (1986). Recent developments in role theory. *Annual Review of Sociology, 12*, 67–92.

Blankenhorn, D. (1986). A pro-family workplace. *Youth Policy, 10*, 20–21.

Blau, P. M. (1960). Structural effects. *American Sociological Review, 25*, 178–193.

Bohen, H. H. (1984). Gender equality in work and family: An elusive goal. *Journal of Family Issues, 5*, 254–272.

Bowen, G. L. (1987). Changing gender-role preferences and marital adjustment: Implications for clinical practice. *Family Therapy, 14*, 17–33.

Bowen, G. L. (1988a). Family life satisfaction: A value-based approach. *Family Relations, 37*, 458–462.

Bowen, G. L. (1988b). Corporate supports for the family lives of employees: A conceptual model for program planning and evaluation. *Family Relations, 37*, 183–188.

Bowen, G. L., & Neenan, P. A. (1988). Sex-role orientations among married men in the military: The generational factor. *Psychological Reports*, 62, 523-526.

Bowen, G. L., & Orthner (1989). (Eds.). *The organization family: Work and family linkages in the U.S. military*. New York: Praeger.

Bronfenbrenner, U., & Crouter, A. C. (1982). Work and family through time and space. In S. B. Kamerman & C. D. Hayes (Eds.), *Families that work: Children in a changing world* (pp. 39-83). Washington, DC: National Academy Press.

Bureau of National Affairs, Inc. (BNA). (1986). *Work and family: A changing dynamic*. Washington, DC: The Bureau of National Affairs, Inc.

Caudill, W., & Weinstein, H. (1969). Maternal care and infant behavior in Japan and America. *Psychiatry*, 32, 12-43.

Christensen, H. T. (1964). The intrusion of values. In H. T. Christensen (Ed.), *Handbook of marriage and the family* (pp. 969-1006). Chicago, IL: Rand McNally & Company.

Clark, R. A., Nye, F. I., & Gecas, V. (1978). Husband's work involvement and marital role performance. *Journal of Marriage and the Family*, 40, 9-21.

Conference Board. (1985). *Corporations and families: Changing practices and perspectives*. Report 868. New York: Conference Board.

Coverman, S., & Sheley, J. F. (1986). Change in men's housework and child-care time, 1965-1975. *Journal of Marriage and the Family*, 48, 413-422.

Crouter, A. C. (1984). Participative work as an influence on human development. *Journal of Applied Developmental Psychology*, 5, 71-90.

Deal, T. E., & Kennedy, A. A. (1982). *Corporate cultures: The rites and rituals of corporate life*. Reading, MA: Addison-Wesley.

Fernandez, J. P. (1986). *Child care and corporation productivity*. Lexington, MA: Lexington.

Franklin, J., & Scott, J. E. (1970). Parental values: An inquiry into occupational setting. *Journal of Marriage and the Family*, 32, 406-409.

French, J. R. P., Jr., Caplan, R. D., & Harrison, R. V. (1982). *The mechanisms of stress and strain*. Chichester, England: John Wiley & Sons.

Friedman, D. E. (1987, August). Work vs. family: War of the worlds. *Personnel Administrator*, 36-38.

Gecas, V. (1979). The influence of social class on socialization. In W. Burr, R. Hill, F. I. Nye, & I. Reiss (Eds.), *Contemporary theories about the family*, Vol. 1 (pp. 365-404). New York: Macmillan.

Glick, P. C. (1984). Marriage, divorce, and living arrangements. *Journal of Family Issues*, 5, 7-26.

Gutek, B. A., Nakamura, C. Y., & Nieva, V. F. (1981). The interdependence of work and family roles. *Journal of Occupational Behavior*, 2, 1-16.

Hayghe, H. (1986). Rise in mothers' labor force activity includes those with infants. *Monthly Labor Review, 109*, 43–45.

Harrison, R. (1972). Understanding your organizations character. *Harvard Business Review, 3*, 119–128.

Hertz, R. (1986). *More equal than others*. Berkeley: University of California Press.

Hoffman, L. W. (1986). Work, family, and the child. In M. S. Pallak & R. Perloff (Eds.), *Psychology and work: Productivity, change, and employment* (pp. 173–209). Washington, DC: American Psychological Association.

Juster, F. T., & Stafford, F. P. (1985). *Time, goods and well-being*. Ann Arbor, MI: Institute for Social Research.

Kagan, J. (1983, September). Work in the 1980s and 1990s. *Working Women*, 30–32.

Kamerman, S. B., & Kahn, A. J. (1987). *The responsive workplace: Employers and a changing labor force*. New York: Columbia University Press.

Kamerman, S. B., & Kingston, P. W. (1982). Employer responses to the family responsibilities of employees. In S. B. Kamerman & C. D. Hayes (Eds.), *Families that work* (pp. 144–208). Washington, DC: National Academy Press.

Kanter, R. M. (1977a). *Men and women of the corporation*. New York: Basic Books.

Kanter, R. M. (1977b). *Work and family in the United States: A critical review and agenda for research and policy*. New York: Russell Sage Foundation.

Kilmann, R. H. (1985, April). Corporate culture. *Psychology Today*, 62–68.

Kohn, M. L. (1963). Social class and parent child relationships: An interpretation. *American Journal of Sociology, 68*, 471–480.

Kohn, M. L. (1969). *Class and conformity: A study of values*. Homewood, IL: Dorsey.

Lamb, M. (1987, June). "Will the real new father please stand up?" *Parents*, 77–80.

LaRossa, R. (1988). Fatherhood and social change. *Family Relations, 37*, 451–457.

Levant, R. F., Slattery, S. C., & Loiselle, J. E. (1987). Father's involvement in housework and child care with school-aged daughters. *Family Relations, 36*, 152–157.

Levine, J. A. (1976). *Who will raise the children?* New York: Bantam.

Levinger, G. (1986). Compatibility in relationships. *Social Science, 71*(2/3), 173–177.

Louis Harris and Associates, Inc. (1981). *Families at work*. Minneapolis, MN: General Mills, Inc.

Mancini, J. A., & Orthner, D. K. (1988). The context and consequences of family change. *Family Relations, 37*, 363-366.

Mangam, I. L. (1981). Relationships at work: A matter of tension and tolerance. In S. Duck & R. Gilmore (Eds.), *Personal relationships. 1: Studying personal relationships* (pp. 197-214). London: Academic Press.

McBroom, W. H. (1984). Changes in sex-role orientations: A five-year longitudinal comparison. *Sex Roles, 11*, 583-592.

McCall, G. J., & Simmons, J. L. (1978). *Identities and interaction* (rev. ed.). New York: Free Press.

McGregor, D. (1960). *The human side of enterprise*. New York: McGraw-Hill.

McNeely, R. L., & Fogarty, B. A. (1988). Balancing parenthood and employment: Factors affecting company receptiveness to family-related innovations in the workplace. *Family Relations, 37*, 189-195.

Miller, D., & Swanson, G. (1958). *The changing American parent*. New York: Wiley.

Moos, R. H. (1986). Work as a human context. In M. S. Pallak & R. Perloff (Eds.), *Psychology and work: Productivity, change, and employment* (pp. 9-52). Washington, DC: American Psychological Association.

Nieva, V. F. (1985). Work and family linkages. In L. Larwood, A. H. Stromberg, & B. A. Gutek (Eds.), *Women and work: An annual review* (Vol. 1) (pp. 162-190). Beverly Hills, CA: Sage.

Orthner, D. K. (1981). *Intimate relationships*. Reading, MA: Addison-Wesley.

Orthner, D. K., Giddings, M. M., & Quinn, W. (1987). *Youth in transition: A study of adolescents from military and civilian families*. Washington, DC: Department of the Air Force.

Orthner, D. K., & Pittman, J. (1986). Family contributions to work commitments. *Journal of Marriage and the Family, 48*, 573-581.

O'Toole, J. J. (1979). Corporate and managerial cultures. In C. L. Cooper (Ed.), *Behavior problems in organizations* (pp. 7-28). New York: Prentice-Hall.

Ouchi, W. G. (1981). *Theory Z*, New York: Avon Books.

Ozawa, M. H. (1980). Development of social services in industry: How and why. *Social Work, 25*, 464-470.

Parke, R. D. (1981). *Fathers*. Cambridge, MA: Harvard University Press.

Perkins, C. A. (1989, June 4). Help for workers who care for their parents. *The New York Times*, p. F19.

Peters, T. J., & Waterman, R. H. (1982). *In search of excellence*. New York: Harper & Row.

Piotrkowski, C. S., Rapoport, R. N., & Rapoport, R. (1987). Families and work. In M. B. Sussman & S. K. Steinmetz (Eds.), *Handbook of marriage and the family* (pp. 251-283). New York: Plenum.

Pleck, J. H. (1977). The work-family role system. *Social Problems, 24,* 417–424.

Pleck, J. H. (1985). *Working wives/working husbands.* Beverly Hills, CA: Sage.

Raabe, P. H., & Gessner, J. (1988). Employer family-supportive policies: Diverse variations on the theme. *Family Relations, 37,* 196–202.

Repetti, R. L. (1987). Linkages between work and family roles. In S. Oskamp (Ed.), *Applied social psychology annual: Vol. 7. Family processes and problems* (pp. 98–127). Beverly Hills, CA: Sage.

Reubens, B. G., & Reubens, E. P. (1979). Women workers, nontraditional occupations and full employment. In A. F. Cahn (Ed.), *Women in the U.S. labor force* (pp. 103–126). New York: Praeger.

Schein, E. H. (1984). Coming to a new awareness of organizational culture. *Sloan Management Review, 25,* 3–16.

Schein, E. H. (1985). *Organizational culture and leadership.* San Francisco: Jossey-Bass.

Schwartz, F. N. (1989). Management women and the new facts of life. *Harvard Business Review, 67,* 65–77.

Segal, M. W. (1989). The nature of work and family linkages: A theoretical perspective. In G. L. Bowen & D. K. Orthner (Eds.), *The organization family: Work and family linkages in the U.S. military* (pp. 3–36). New York: Praeger.

Sekaran, U. (1986). *Dual-career families.* San Francisco: Jossey-Bass.

Silverzweig, S., & Allen, R. F. (1976). Changing the corporate culture. *Sloan Management Review, 17,* 33–49.

Stillman, F., & Bowen, G. L. (1985). Corporate support mechanisms for families: An exploratory study and agenda for research and evaluation. *Evaluation and Program Planning, 8,* 309–314.

Stryker, S. (1968). Identity salience and role performance: The relevance of symbolic interaction theory for family research. *Journal of Marriage and the Family, 30,* 558–564.

Taylor, F. W. (1947). *Scientific management.* New York: Harper & Row.

Teachman, J. D., Polonko, K. A., & Scanzoni, J. (1987). Demography of the family. In M. B. Sussman & S. K. Steinmetz (Eds.), *Handbook of marriage and the family* (pp. 3–36). New York: Plenum Press.

Voydanoff, P. (1985). Work/family linkages over the life course. *Journal of Career Development, 12,* 23–32.

Voydanoff, P. (1987). *Work and family life.* Beverly Hills, CA: Sage.

Whyte, W. H., Jr. (1956). *The organization man.* New York: Simon and Schuster.

Yankelovich, D. (1979). Work, values and the new breed. In C. Kerr & J. Rosow (Eds.), *Work in America: The decade ahead* (pp. 3–26). New York: Van Nostrand Reinhold.

9

Determinants of Family Culture: Effects on Fatherhood

Rudy Ray Seward

The concept of culture provides insights into the dynamics of families and the role of father. Application of the concept to the family is appropriate due to the important cultural transmission task it performs. The family's culture is a small slice of the society's culture. Families have major responsibilities for teaching, interpreting, and enforcing the culture's expectations. Many of the family's activities involving these responsibilities occur between parents and children. Thus, applying the concept of culture to the family contributes to an understanding of fatherhood.

Every family has its own culture. The culture consists of the interrelated norms shared by its participants, including their common values, rules, and expectations. Together these define the family's boundaries and direct its members' behavior. The major determinants of these norms are the family's location within society along with its members' contributions. These norms are largely a consequence of the family's cultural and subcultural setting within the larger social structure (macrolevel) and the distinctive social histories that each member brings to their family relationships (microlevel). But the family's culture is also affected by its composition, its

218

stage in the family life cycle, and the dynamics for each set of interpersonal relationships. Some of these norms proscribe how each man should go about enacting his father and family roles. But the proscription varies a great deal between subcultural settings. For example, the family culture for a Black, working class, single custodial father is much different from the family culture established and maintained by a White, middle-class, stepfather family.

This chapter demonstrates that each family is more than just a social group but is a cultural one as well. The major determinants of the family's culture are identified in society's social structure. Since these involve significant societal subcultures many families share similar cultures. Demographic and compositional differences also affect this culture. Family culture variation results in differences in the performance of the paternal role. Certain cross-cultural and historical patterns for fatherhood put these performances in perspective. Finally some practical and program implications for fathers based upon the concept of family culture are presented.

Family: A Social Group and a Culture

Human impulses are conditioned by society. Interactions between humans across generations produce a social order, that is, a society with an attached culture. This social order or ongoing structure shapes human behavior. In all societies when humans are born they are primarily conditioned by one subgroup within the larger system—the family.

This social group consists of those adults and children designated as relatives of a newborn child. The social positions (e.g. the father) held by each person are dictated by the culture. The culture's norms not only identify the parental and kinship positions but spell out how they should be performed. Like the larger society, the family social structure is in place when the child arrives. This structure is far from uniform. Families will vary in size, number of generations, and composition by age and gender.

In modern, complex societies many dimensions affect the family culture; of particular importance are dimensions of inequality within the society. Differences in power, prestige, and privilege are so great that they manifest themselves in significant subcultures. These consist of large groups of individuals whose opportunities and chances

in life vary a great deal. Individuals with similar opportunities frequently share norms and behavior which differ from others who are
either more or less fortunate than themselves. The family structure a
child is born into largely reflects its subcultural setting.

Because the family socializes or teaches the culture to the next
generation, it is in part a microcosm of the larger culture. The
mediating actions between family members and the larger society
entails socialization which exemplifies its role as a cultural unit
(Goode, 1964). A social perspective is necessary in understanding
fatherhood norms. A strictly situational approach, assuming each
situation is totally unique, or a purely psychological approach are too
narrow and do not lend themselves to a comprehensive study of
fatherhood (Benson, 1968). The social perspective searches for the
major determinants of families' cultures and the norms for fathers
they contain.

Major Determinants of Family Culture

The location of a family in society's social structure is a major
contributor to its culture (Goode, 1964; Parsons & Bales, 1955). In all
societies, the family handles many human problems. Some of these
concern only individuals within the family, while others deal with
the adaptation of its members and the family as a unit to the larger
society. The family can be viewed in two different ways. As a primary
group, it meets the personal needs of its members, operating much
like a self-contained social microcosm. At the same time, it is a
representative of a major social institution within the larger social
structure. The latter is concerned with cooperation or interdependence with other major institutional groups (e.g., school and work).

Each view of the family suggests a unique but not independent
role. As a primary group the family faces the problem of maintaining
its integrity, that is, its boundaries, solidarity, and satisfaction of
personal needs. As an institutional unit, the concern is with accommodation of the family's members to the more complex, external
order. The family plays these roles almost simultaneously with on-
going interpersonal relationships helping prepare its members to
perform social positions outside the family. Regardless of the role,
the major responsibility of the family remains the care for its children. This involves training offspring in the basic modes of social

cooperation, orienting them to more specialized adult tasks, and providing a social framework for managing the tensions of its members (Benson, 1968).

The family as a social institution includes broad ideological and normative proscriptions for a society. According to Bronfendbrenner's (1979) human ecosystem model, the family and other major societal institutions (e.g., economy) are macrosystems that affect individual behavior and their families. The proscriptions of these macrosystems are "blueprints" that guide the performances of participants in specific groups (e.g., the variety of families) throughout the society. The utility of the ecosystem model has been demonstrated as it relates specifically to childrearing (Garbarino, 1982) and varieties in the performance of fatherhood (Hanson, 1985).

When a new family is established, larger systems already in place contribute through various avenues to the culture it will develop. This is complicated because the family's culture is a modification of the "blueprints." The institutional norms never refer to a particular family unit but include all family varieties within a society. Many of these varieties share distinct subcultural norms. Since children are socialized first into a particular subculture and never the whole culture, the subcultural norms are crucial (Elkin & Handel, 1984).

A major contributor to family culture is the subculture or stratum to which it belongs. All societies are stratified with inequality occurring between certain subgroups in regard to power, prestige, and privilege. For some dimensions (e.g., gender and generation) different unequal subgroups are found within the same family and for other dimensions (e.g., social class, ethnicity, and community of residence) a family's members will all belong to the same subgroup or stratum. A family's gender and generation distribution results in compositional differences. A family's social class, ethnicity, and community provide its social address or coordinates, locating it in the social structure according to their particular strata (Berger, 1963). The latter dimensions are crucial as society's most significant subcultures represent particular social classes, ethnic groups and communities (see Chapters 3, 5, and 7). Specific subcultures often involve overlapping subgroups from different dimensions, for example the culture of poverty attributed to many lower class, Black, intercity neighborhoods (Rainwater, 1970; Stack, 1974).

If a middle-class, White family lives in the suburbs, this social address provides important information about its culture. If this household is headed by a divorced, middle-aged, single father who grew up during the counterculture of the 1960s, more insight is gained into its culture. The social context, as identified by its location on the inequality dimensions, contributes a great deal to a family's culture. Major social coordinates provide detail about family norms and consequent behavior without focusing upon an individual family. This is true for many large subgroups of families who share the same social address in society.

Family Microlevel Systems

Additional details on family culture come from the microlevel or analyzing the family as a primary group. This small intimate group, operating within and impinged upon by the larger social context, generates its own "culture" while performing its various tasks. This group does not appear to be as complex as the larger social structure yet in many ways it is. Compared to most other social groups (e.g., peers) it is much more heterogeneous. It is much more likely to contain persons representing different generations, genders, and backgrounds. More so than other social groups, the family is really a complicated, sometimes fragile, blending of human differences.

The family's organizational complexity is suggested in great detail by Kantor and Lehr's (1975) analysis of its space, time, energy, and other essential dimensions. The intricacies result from the three distinct, yet interrelated, family subsystems. Dividing the family into systems of decreasing size, the three subsystems include the entire family unit, the interpersonal subsystems (e.g., the father–son dyad), and each personal subsystem. Each family member is a unique individual participant who is related in dyads to all fellow members and part of the whole group. A typical family of four would contain eight subsystems, that is, four personal ones, three dyadic ones, and one for the entire unit. The sometimes contradictory needs and responsibilities of these subsystems and their interdependence provides useful details on family functioning on a day-to-day basis.

The number and complexity of subsystems depends upon the family's composition. Differences in size, number of generations, gender ratio, and marital status all have an impact. For example, a single-parent family lacks a marital dyad while a reconstituted family involves not only a household-marital dyad but potentially two additional divorced-marital dyads. The needs of and interest in children from former marriages require ongoing relationships with former spouses. At the same time, the number of parent–child and sibling dyads for children from the present marriage and previous ones, both inside and outside the household, are increased and meanings more complicated. Detailing the family's subsystems contributes to an understanding of its culture.

Impact of Macrosystems upon Fatherhood

The macrosystems of the social structure and the intricate interior of the family are tied together by the mediating function the family performs (Goode, 1964; Benson, 1971). The family acts as a link between the social order and family members. Parents teach their children the norms for their subgroups within the larger culture and encourage compliance to them. Using both positive and negative social sanctions family members direct and control its fellow members' behavior. In the process they create a culture reflective of the family's location within the larger social context. The intimacy, frequency, and continuity of family interactions provides the major means by which culture gets transmitted and social order maintained. The family's informal means of social control are more effective than the formal means used by other institutions, such as, the government (Berger, 1963). Family culture influences a father's performance more than state laws passed to guarantee certain rights for children (e.g., attempts to enforce child support payments).

Channeling society's culture to it members as modified by significant subcultures produces expectations on how the social position of father should be performed. But the actual performance is always somewhat variant. Behavior depends upon the individual's personal subsystem (e.g., being stern and rigid) and the dynamics for their interpersonal relationships (e.g., stress due to inconsistent approaches to childrearing between spouses) (Hanson, 1985).

Another link between the family as a primary group and the larger social structure is a consequence of the homogeneous membership patterns found typically in families. Individuals overwhelmingly select marriage partners more like themselves (Adams, 1986, 1988; Caplow & Bahr, 1982), especially when it comes to significant subcultural characteristics. Their spouses usually have the same ethnic background, social class membership, and community of residence. Hence, as parents they are likely to teach their children cultural norms consistent with their shared subculture.

The homogeneity of neighborhoods contributes to the same set of norms being taught. Most parents live in a neighborhood with other families who have similar social class standing and ethnicity, and who are in the same stage of the family life–cycle. Homogeneity exists in the children's elementary schools, peer groups, and so forth with regard to these significant subcultural characteristics. The social similarity of these groups is one of the supporting structural aspects leading to and helping maintain a family culture reflecting their particular location in the social structure. This also explains the sharing of a similar family culture by large segments of the population. Both macrolevel and microlevel factors, distinct yet clearly interdependent, play a role in producing this culture. (Heterogeneity is important in understanding both individuals and their families, and the changes in subcultures over time but is not essential to the focus here.)

Variety in the Performance of the Father Role

Fatherhood, like all primary social positions, is acted out in an endless variety of circumstances fulfilling a number of different social responsibilities. Although some expectations are spelled out, fathers are bound by few formal requirements. At an individual level the specific possibilities are almost endless. But the forces which generate a family culture, shared by families having a similar social composition and location, suggest a finite number of major approaches to fatherhood.

A family culture defines the father role for a particular family but a variety of elements affect its performance. Within the man's personal subsystem are the experiences of his own family of origin. Relations with his own father and his approach to the role are important. Additional role models, including grandfathers and peers' fathers; subcultural norms and demands from the larger social context (e.g., work role); and idiosyncrasies brought by the man to his family bear on his performance as a father. The dynamics of other microlevel systems and those at the macrolevel set the parameters for his specific performance.

Will he be an inquisitor, a martyr, an athletic coach, a teacher-counselor, everyday Santa Claus, authoritarian or buddy and pal, or a combination of these (Adams, 1986; Lasswell & Lasswell, 1982)? Colman and Colman (1981) present four archetypes of the father role. These possible choices are effectively drawn from legends, literature, dreams, and paintings in addition to personal and clinical data (including interviews with 15 fathers representing most socio-economic levels). The archetypes are not mutually exclusive or per-manent, as many fathers may combine aspects of two or more of these or change their approach over time. The archetypes are easily and consistently identified as the predominate approaches for partic-ular family cultures within specific subcultures. The vast research on families and childrearing by social class, ethnicity, and community lends itself to such designations.

Men who take the traditional approach to the role by achieving success outside the family but are more distant yet powerful within the family are termed "Sky fathers." Fathers who are so active in both the direction and details of childcare within the family that they become the ongoing nurturant provider are "Earth fathers." These represent two very different approaches with the latter being the most unfamiliar. The father who successfully combines both sky and earth father approaches may follow two different paths. The "Royal father" assumes complete control of every aspect of the family and child's life with a spouse, if present, being subordinate to his su-preme authority. In contrast, the Dyadic father chooses to balance the two approaches by attempting a partnership with his spouse. The chosen approach differs by social class, ethnicity, age or genera-tion, and community of residence.

Research findings have consistently documented differences in values, life styles and opportunities, and approaches to childrearing between social class groups (Elkin & Handel, 1984). The differences are so great and the patterns between these groups so distinct that the social classes are considered the most significant subcultures in the United States. Highly educated, upper-middle class professional men and their families express the values and exhibit behavior closely exemplifying the ideal culture with an interaction pattern characterized as adult-directed (Gans, 1982). In the past, the sky approach to fatherhood predominated among career-oriented men, but apparently this has changed. The dramatic increase in career-oriented mothers, as well as the emphasis upon the norm of equalitarianism has resulted in the dyadic approach being closer to the ideal. The arrival of children brings about pressures for many couples that result in a shift from a dyadic to a more traditional division of labor between father and mother (Adams, 1986). These career-driven, adult-directed families may emphasize one approach (dyadic) but actual performance probably comes closer to another (sky) (Araji, 1977; Haas, 1982).

Lower-middle class families exhibit less discrepancies between attitude and behavior. Compared to all other classes, these families are the most child-centered (Gans, 1982), with both parents subordinating their pleasures to the demands and happiness of their children. Companionship as a family is very important, and children may be the most easily shared interest for the couple. Without the high pressure demands of challenging careers, these fathers come closer to practicing the dyadic approach.

The less educated and less affluent working class fathers, despite having fewer resources than their middle-class counterparts, more likely emphasize and try to implement the sky father approach. Their adult-centered interaction pattern (Gans, 1982), emphasizes respectability and patriarchal authority (Rubin, 1976). Even though most of their spouses are employed, placing some restrictions on the fathers' authority, the ideology is very strong. The mother's employment and income are considered secondary to her family responsibilities.

The deprived, insecure, and unpredictable existence of the lower class subculture often results in incomplete families. Abandoned mothers often take the Royal parenting approach out of necessity. Fathers' roles may be primarily limited to conception and a sporadic, often unsuccessful attempt at being a sky father. Most of these men lack the resources to adequately fulfill this role and can often provide economically better for their family by leaving them (Adams, 1986; Cherlin, 1981). Their lack of interest in the role is demonstrated by cases where they do more fathering with the children of other men rather than their own (Liebow, 1967; see also Chapter 5.)

Differences by race in the approach to fatherhood have been documented but most disappear when social class is held constant. The distinctions often made between Black versus White families are primarily class-based differences. These are a consequence of a disproportionate segment of Black families located in the lower class along with a disproportinate segment of white families being in the middle-class. What differences remain are significant; for example, middle-class Black fathers are much more likely to practice the dyadic approach than their White counterparts (Willie & Greenblatt, 1978). In the lower class, due to greater discrimination and related factors, Black men are more likely than Whites to play a very limited or almost nonexistant father role (Cherlin, 1981; see also Chapter 3.)

Community of residence also produces differences many of which represent an intersection of class and ethnicity, such as, the lower class black intercity neighborhood. Due to a more urbanized population with less isolated communities, residential community is increasingly linked to social class and secondarily to ethnicity (Elkin & Handel, 1984). The distinct community examples which remain are likely to be found either in depressed rural areas (e.g., the Cumberland Plateau in the Appalachian Mountains) or specialized groups in large urban areas (e.g., communes). In the latter, the father role comes closer in some instances to the earth or dyadic approach. Even in these experimental communities, as both Haas (1982) and Colman and Colman (1981) point out, going beyond ideology and putting a role reversal or egalitarian approach into a practice is fraught with peril.

Finally, within each of these groups the composition of the family plays an important role in the approach to fatherhood. The royal approach most likely occurs by default when the father is left alone as the parent to provide childcare. The father's approach will vary somewhat depending on the contributing circumstances (e.g., getting divorced, being widowed, or being unemployed with a wage-earning wife). Since the 1960s, many families followed alternative forms besides the traditional nuclear family. The single-parent, divorced, reconstituted, extended, communal, and other variations effect interaction patterns and family culture (Cherlin, 1981; Elkin & Handel, 1984). How do these patterns in the United States compare to fatherhood in other cultures?

Fatherhood Across Cultures

Cross-culturally men in most societies want to succeed in becoming fathers. They usually have children with only one woman with whom they are mated for life. Most fathers live with their mate and offspring. While fathers most often are the key providers for the family, women tend to handle the daily care and nurturance of the children (Benson, 1985). These cross-cultural uniformities represent the typical patterns, but deviations occur in all known societies, often in persistent patterned ways. These patterns are determined by the processes that bring about a family culture. Also, the specific practices in any given society vary a good deal over time. The variety of fatherhood performance in the United States demonstrates this.

Typical male tasks related to fatherhood include the following: The father must reproduce and help sustain the life of his offspring during dependency, teach his children certain basic survival skills, model for them his unique means of accommodating to life, cope with a variety of real or potential family crises, and cooperate with other people both nonkinsmen and family in routine survival tasks (Benson, 1968).

Fatherhood Over Time in the United States

After industrialization, in the United States, the parental role was central in the lives of women and only peripheral for men. Fathers "cared" for their children primarily by succeeding in the work role and had little direct involvement with them. Expectations for both parents today but especially fathers are higher and the adjustments more complex.

The wide range of fathering styles today as compared to earlier views has been widely documented (Hanson & Bozett, 1985; Hanson, 1985). Major demographic trends like delayed marriage and parenthood, more employed mothers, and rising divorce have contributed to this variety. These various styles have occurred within and are accelerated by a cultural context emphasizing more individual choice and freedom. While tolerance is expressed more than practiced, diversity in fatherhood role performance is visable.

In the United States, the role of father has changed tremendously, but only recently has it become fashionable to focus attention upon this family social position. The traditional father was portrayed as an aloof and distant authority figure who only indirectly "cared" for his children by succeeding in work outside the family. He offered companionship and emotional support to his spouse but had little direct contact with his children after work roles moved outside the home (Demos, 1982; Rotundo, 1985; Seward, 1978).

In the past, several conceptual barriers prevented fathers from being considered significant in the parenting process (Pederson, 1980). Features of family life in the United States obscured concern for paternity. Foremost of these features is the stereotypic view emphasizing the husband's role as primary breadwinner and the wife's role as homemaker and mother. The predominant sociology textbook of the 1950s described fathers as the weak link in the family (Davis, 1949). Even after women became more involved in the labor force, employed mothers received more attention than employed fathers (Rapoport, 1978).

Another barrier was the exclusive focus of developmental theories upon the mother–child relationship. Early psychoanalytic scholars and others saw "no direct caring role for fathers with infants and young children" (Fein, 1978, pp. 123-124). At the same time research and theory on the marital relationship completely ignored its impact upon parenting. This chasm resulted in part from a division of research efforts between the disciplines of sociology and psychology. The former focused attention upon the marital dyad while virtually ignoring the parent–child relationship. Psychology ignored the marital dyad and focused upon mothers as if they were the only adults involved in parenting (Pederson, 1980).

Reflecting the traditional role distinctions, most research and writing was conducted on motherhood. The methods used in carrying out family research kept fathers in the background. Very often when studying parenting issues no data were gathered either from or about fathers. When information was collected about fathers it was usually obtained secondhand either from wives or children. Most early "family" research maintained these barriers by limiting respondents to suburban housewives and mothers, or their children at college, even when studying male family roles (Adams, 1986).

An additional barrier was the view which failed to appreciate early competencies of infants and very young children. They were considered incapable of interacting in either a complex, meaningful way or in a diverse setting. Hence the need for a single, consistent, constant, caring, caretaker, that is, the mother was stressed (Pedersen, 1980). Only after reaching 3 of age, it was incorrectly believed, could children successfully deal with others, including fathers, in the family.

New View of Fatherhood

A new view of fatherhood emerged along with an increasing interest in parent roles by social scientists which helped remove many of these barriers. Debates about how mothers should parent raged back and forth for decades, while fathers were virtually ignored until the early 1970s. One exception was the comprehensive analysis on fatherhood by Benson (1968). This work stimulated and directed much of the later research on fathers. Surveys of the parenting literature published in leading journals and manuals over three decades, starting in the 1950s, confirm the maternal emphasis and exceptional nature of Benson's work (LeMasters & DeFrain, 1983).

Social scientists tend to overlook the many roles that people play with detachment, shame, or resentment (Goffman, 1961) and fatherhood is one example. Historically, fatherhood has never been characterized by shame, but some resentment and considerable detachment do apply. The theoretical framework employed in early childrearing research which ignored the critical significance of the father supports this (Benson, 1968).

Recent research reflecting the new view of fatherhood suggests the necessity of the role. Fathers inculcate attitudes and behaviors their children need for educational and vocational attainment. They make important contributions to the child's socially appropriate gender-role identity, academic performance, and moral development (Fein, 1978; Lewis & O'Brien, 1987). Support is growing for the belief that fathers can assume a parallel role with mothers and are able to participate in a full range of parenting activities. Support for this belief is found in the literature on childbirth practices (Pedersen, 1980; Seward, Seward, & Natoli, 1984). Fathers are being reintegrated into the family unit after industrial development heightened their separation. This recent egalitarian or androgynous view is considered good for both parents and children.

The androgynous view reflects the dramatic changes in women's roles especially for those outside of the family. In the 1950s the least likely to be employed were mothers with children at home, today they are the most frequently employed among married women (Thornton

& Freedman, 1983). Even though employed mothers still spend more time with their children than their male counterparts, the amount of interaction has been exaggerated (Lamb, 1981). Time spent in caretaking does not always involve interpersonal interaction; hence the quality of the time spent together becomes an issue. The amount of time spent is not directly related to the amount of influence on the child's social and cognitive development. If having employed mothers does not hinder the development of children, the fathers daily absence should not be disruptive either (Hoffman, 1974).

A new view of fatherhood was also a response to the extreme imbalance of the earlier research. Those involved were "forced to ask whether fathers could legitimately be deemed irrelevant entitites in socialization." (Lamb, 1981, p. 4). The concern about the possible demise of the family added pressure for a reassessment of the father's role. Attitudes of both men and women increasingly stress the sharing of family responsibilities, especially childcare. Both young men and husbands say they want to be actively involved in the socialization and lives of their children (Lamb, 1981). At the same time, their actions have been less egalitarian than their beliefs. Occupational roles still take precedence over parental role in regard to men's prestige and power. They dynamics of the interpersonal relationships within families are complex. Unlike earlier circumstances when the father was a more distant figure, it is now difficult to be a good father if a man is not also a good husband. While "the maternal role has gained in power (if not prestige) . . . that of the father has been eroded" (LeMaster & DeFrain, 1983, p. 162). Expectations are higher, the role definitions less clear, outside role influence greater, and the adjustments more complex for todays fathers.

The kind of fatherhood role men follow is partially affected by the following: culture definitions, congruent marital role expectations between spouses, socioeconomic position, age cohort, timing, and perceptions of their own father. These contribute to the family's culture which in turn directs the father's specific performance.

Implications for Practice

Cultural (e.g., growing individualism), social (e.g., standard of living increases), and demographic (e.g., longer life expectancy) changes shape family culture and provide fathers with new opportunities.

Long-term, quality relationships within or outside the household and within or across generations have been enhanced. The family always has and will be one of the most meaningful groups in an individual's life. As the basis for relationships becomes increasingly voluntary, opportunities are provided for greater bonds in the family based upon warmth and intimacy. Some of the opportunities available to contemporary fathers include the following:

1. Transition from the aloof, distant, authority figure to experiencing positive emotional attachments produces in fathers a sense of self-effectiveness. This enables more risk taking behavior and creative adventuring for fathers in relationships with their children.
2. An open warm, and collaborative approach to childrearing increases the father's sense of well-being and higher morale in the face of other personal, social, and material challenges.
3. Active fathers help their families cope more successfully with the stresses of contemporary life by providing a cushion of support which absorbs family pressures, defuses social stresses, and provides needed assistance.
4. Dyadic fathers provide balanced and diverse role models for children to identify with and to learn about loving family relationships from.

To make these opportunities a reality several considerations must be kept in mind and relevant changes made. A key change must be raising the prestige of fatherhood in conjunction with a downplaying of the job as the only determinant of adult success. Also, family culture differences must be taken into account. The uniqueness of norms for families within distinct subcultures must be brought into play when promoting any changes. Finally, efforts must be directed toward the acceptance and involvement of the growing number of nontraditional fathers in addition to stepfathers (e.g., noncustodial).

Practical Suggestions to Augment the Ongoing Trends

Some trends suggest optimism about the future for many families. For example, many couples are deferring marriage, participating in family planning, having fewer but wanted children, and divorcing slightly less often than in the 1970s. Keeping in mind the diversity of family cultures and father roles, the opportunities for long-term, quality relationships would be enhanced by the following actions carried out by various educational and community organizations. (Johnson, 1983; Nute, 1987; Ochiltree, 1987; Robinson, 1987; Seward, Seward & Natoli, 1984).

1.   We need to continue to support, through literature and research, the critically important role of fathers during pregnancy, birth, and early contact with their infants.

2.   We need to direct family life education courses at the high school and college level towards improving the quality of father–child relationships, covering topics on conflict resolution, communication training, nurturing relationships, and fatherhood as a valuable resource.

3.   We need to develop divorce and blended family education programs to strengthen both old and newly developing father–child relationships by addressing the consequences of changes in the original family form. Topics covered should include the significance of original relationships, incorporating new parenting relationships, and understanding the socioemotional effects of changes in family form.

4.   We need to develop programs for the often ignored teenage, unwed, and noncustodial fathers. Provide opportunities for early and frequent involvement of these men. Develop and utilize their social networks including their (grand)parents and peers (Robinson, 1987).

5.   The significance of fatherhood in the family never has been addressed adequately in family life courses. We need to work to create a conscious awareness of its potential as a resource to families thereby stimulating family members to nurture and utilize this relationship.

6.   On a community level, we need to develop or encourage programs that team parents with children, such as, adult school volunteers, the Boy and Girl Scouts, Indian Guides, and others.

7.   Among employers we need to gain acceptance of fatherhood's importance and promote such benefits as paternity leave, leave for sick children, daycare facilities, and father's day off. These should enhance the status of fathers and enable them to better meet the demands of work and parenthood.

8.   We need to compile information on different fatherhood approaches and circumstances (e.g., strategies and available support services appropriate to each), and disseminate this information in appropriate ways and places (e.g., high schools, libraries, neighborhood centers).

Conclusion

Analyzing the family's culture and the impact of the larger social context augments our knowledge about fatherhood. In the past, many researchers studying parenthood ignored this topic. Previous research focused more on the mother's role and failed to acknowledge the importance of the family's social context. Recent demographic trends, changes in women's roles, and a new view toward parenting necessitate a more encompassing perspective. The practical implications of this perspective for richer father–child relationships have potential benefits for parental and other relationships in the family.

References

Adams, B. N. (1986). *The family: A sociological interpretation* (4th ed.). Boston: Little, Brown.

Adams, B. N. (1988). Fifty years of family research: What does it mean? *Journal of Marriage and the Family, 50,* 5–17.

Araji, S. K. (1977). Husbands' and wives' attitudes-behavior congruence on family roles. *Journal of Marriage and the Family, 39,* 308–321.

Benson, L. (1968). *Fatherhood: A sociological perspective.* New York: Random House.

Benson, L. (1971). *The family bond: Marriage, love, and sex in America.* New York: Random House.

Benson, L. (1985). Theoretical perspectives. *American Behavioral Scientist, 29,* 25–39.

Berger, P. L. (1963). *Invitation to sociology: A humanistic perspective.* Garden City, NY: Anchor.

Bronfenbrenner, U. (1979). *The ecology of human development: Experiments by nature and design.* Cambridge, MA: Harvard.

Caplow, T., Bahr, H. M., Chadwick, B. A., Hill, R., & Williamson, M. H. (1982). *Middletown families: Fifty years of change and continuity.* New York: Bantam.

Cherlin, A. J. (1981). *Marriage, divorce, remarriage.* Cambridge, MA: Harvard.

Colman, A., & Colman, L. (1981). *Earth father/sky father: The changing concept of fathering.* Englewood Cliffs, NJ: Prentice-Hall.

Davis, K. (1949). *Human society.* New York: Macmillan.

Demos, J. (1982). The changing faces of American fatherhood: A new exploration in family history. In S. Cath, A. Gurwitt, & J. Ross (Eds.), *Father and child: Developmental and clinical perspectives* (pp. 431–443). Boston: Little, Brown.

Elkin, F., & Handel, G. (1984). *The child and society: The process of socialization* (4th ed.). New York: Random House.

Fein, R. A. (1978). Research on fathering: Social policy and an emergent perspective. *Journal of Social Issues, 34,* 122–135.

Gans, H. J. (1982). *The urban villagers: Group and class in the life of Italian-Americans.* New York: Free Press.

Garbarino, J. (1982). *Children and families in the social environment.* New York: Aldine

Goode, W. J. (1964). *The family.* Englewood Cliffs, NJ: Prentice-Hall.

Goffman, E. (1961). *Encounters: Two studies in the sociology of interaction.* Indianapolis, IN: Bobbs-Merrill.

Haas, L. (1982). Determinants of role sharing behavior: A case study of egalitarian couples. *Sex Roles, 8,* 747–760.

Hanson, S. M. H. (1985). Fatherhood: Contextual variations. *American Behavioral Scientist, 29,* 55–77.

Hanson, S. M. H., & Bozett, F. W. (Eds.). (1985). *Dimensions of fatherhood.* Beverly Hills, CA: Sage.

Hoffman, L. W. (1974). Effects on child. In L. W. Hoffman & F. I. Nye (Eds.), *Working mothers: An evaluation review of the consequences for wife, mother and child* (pp. 144–157). San Francisco: Jossey-Bass.

Johnson, S. (1983). *The one minute father.* New York: William Morrow.

Kantor, D., & Lehr, W. (1975). *Inside the family.* San Francisco: Jossey-Bass.

Lamb, M. E. (Ed.). (1981). *The role of the father in child development* (2nd ed.). New York: John Wiley.

Lasswell, M., & Lasswell, T. E. (1982). *Marriage and the family.* Lexington, MA: Heath.

Liebow, E. (1967). *Tally's corner: A study of Negro streetcorner men.* Boston: Little Brown.

LeMasters, E. E., & DeFrain, J. (1983). *Parents in contemporary America: A sympathetic review* (4th ed.). Homewood, IL: Dorsey.

Lewis, C., & O'Brien, M. (Eds.). (1987). *Reassessing fatherhood: New Observations on fathers and the modern family.* Beverly Hills, CA: Sage.

Nute, M. (1987). Transition to fatherhood: A review. *Family Perspectives, 21*, 135-145.

Ochiltree, G. (1987). The sometimes forgotten parents. *Family Matters: AIFS Newletter, 19*, 23-25.

Parsons, T., & Bales, R. F. (1955). *Family, socialization, and interaction process.* New York: Free Press.

Pedersen, F. A. (Ed.). (1980). *The father-infant relationship: Observational studies in the family setting.* New York: Praeger.

Rainwater, L. (1970). *Behind ghetto walls.* Chicago: Aldine.

Rapoport, R. (1978). Sex-role stereotyping in studies of marriage and the family. In J. Chetwynd & O. Hartnett (Eds.). *The sex role system: Psychological and sociological perspectives* (pp. 62-75). Boston: Routledge & Kegan Paul.

Robinson, B. E. (1987). *Teenage fathers.* Lexington, MA: Lexington.

Rotundo, E. A. (1985). American fatherhood: A historical perspective. *American Behavioral Scientist, 29*, 7-25.

Rubin, L. B. (1976). *Worlds of pain.* New York: Basic.

Seward, R. R. (1978). *The American family: A demographic history.* Beverly Hills, CA: Sage.

Seward, R. R., Seward, J. A., & Natoli, V. (1984). Different approaches to childbirth and their consequences in Italy, Sweden, and United States. *International Journal of Sociology of the Family, 14*, 1-16.

Stack, C. B. (1974). *All our kin.* New York: Harper and Row.

Swetnam, B. (1984). Nurturing fatherhood. *Family Life Educator, 3*, 10-14.

Thornton, A., & Freedman, D. (1983). The changing American family. *Population Bulletin, 38*(4), 1-44.

Willie, C. V., & Greenblatt, S. L. (1978). Four "classic" studies of power relationships in black families: A review and look to the future. *Journal of Marriage and the Family, 40*, 689-693.

10
Internal Culture of the Family and Its Effect on Fatherhood

Anthony P. Jurich
Mark B. White
Carmel Parker White
Richard A. Moody

If you ask a colleague or a friend or an acquaintance how that person's family celebrates Christmas or Hanukkah or some other family religious holiday, you will most likely get a detailed description of the family's ritual surrounding the celebration of that holiday. If you ask where the pieces of that ritual originated, you will most likely find three sources: (1) the culture at large; (2) the tradition of previous generations; and (3) the newly created rituals of the family which exists presently as a unit. Similarly, if you were to question the origin of the rituals associated with the role we call "father," you should find pieces of that ritual originating in the same three sources. However, when we in the "scientific community" seek to define "fatherhood," we typically stop at the first source, "the culture at large," or pay only a nodding recognition to the second source, "the tradition of previous generations." It is the purpose of this chapter to explore the nature of fatherhood within the second and third sources of definition: the internal family culture.

Changing Nature of Fatherhood

American society's beliefs about the nature of fatherhood have typically been based upon the definitions handed down to us by Western Culture (Bloom-Feshback, 1981). Lamb (1981) described this cultural influence as the "disappearance of fatherhood" (p. 2). Rigid sex roles, which were born out of preindustrial revolution labor necessities (e.g., fathers working difficult manual jobs away from the family), were described by the culture as being necessary, despite the fact that the labor market conditions had long since changed. Scientists and scholars reinforced this rigidity by arguing that these sex roles were "natural" and a direct result of "biological predispositions and imperatives" (p. 3). Fathers' role prerogatives, under this cultural mandate, were limited to occupational and economic arenas (Lamb, Pleck, & Levine, 1985). In such a system, where social roles are so rigidly defined by the culture, there is little room for idiosyncratic variations fostered by individual families.

However, with the advent of the late 1960s, several cultural changes have brought about a change in these traditional cultural definitions (Lamb, 1981). The women's movement has challenged many of the cultural assumptions of the role of women. In doing so many of the rigidities of the male gender role have been similarly challenged. If women could work out of the home, why could men not spend more time in the home to nurture their children? Fathers began to demand a greater role in the raising of their children (Lamb et al., 1985). Social scientists began to question old assumptions upon which many rigid gender-role stereotypes were based (Lamb, 1981). For example, the quality of the time spent with the children seemed to be more important than the quantity of the time. Consequently, women did not have to outweigh their husband's influence on the children just because he spent less time with the children. Scientists began to view the child as having a reciprocal role with their parents, rather than just being a passive recipient of the parents' socialization. These changes raised doubt about rigid, culturally based systems of parental roles, such as the "mother as expressive leader and father as instrumental leader" hypotheses of Parsons and Bales (1955). Those hypotheses appeared too simplistic and culturally deterministic. Factors which defined and determined the role of fatherhood in a given family were then thought to be much more complex than had previously been assumed (Barnett & Baruch, 1988). The previous conceptualizations of fatherhood were bounded by rigidly defined cultural imperatives. This new and more complex view of fatherhood was more subject to the influence of both families of origin and present families of residence in defining the nature of fatherhood for an individual father and elaborating the rituals, attitudes, and behaviors associated with that role definition. Therefore, social science must turn to the influences exerted within the family constellation to study this increasingly important factor upon the definition of fatherhood.

In undertaking this endeavor to study internal family dynamics, many problems arise. Because each family's influence is so idiosyncratic, the study of the intrafamily influences on fatherhood lacks the clarity, specificity, and universality of cultural definitions, such as those of Parsons and Bales (1955). This has been an ongoing problem in the field. Social scientists have tried to study the nature of fatherhood by studying father absence (Brown, 1988; Orthner & Bowen, 1985). This "definition in absentia" attempts to study what fatherhood is by seeing what happens to the family when the father has gone. Likewise, social and behavioral scientists have tried to define fatherhood by studying the effects of fatherhood, namely the implications of fatherhood on child development or behavior (Watkins, 1987). There is a budding body of knowledge on fathers in single-parent families (Greif, 1985), stepfamilies (Pink & Wampler, 1985), and nontraditional family forms (Macklin, 1987). While these studies give valuable information in their respective topic areas, they are problematic in defining fatherhood. The scientific community has provided more information on fatherhood by telling us what happens when it is not there, what its effects are on children, or what it is like under special circumstances than it does by describing it as it typically is. A major reason for this trouble is that once we get beyond the cultural definition of fatherhood as a sex role, there is so much variance among family definitions and prescriptions that it becomes difficult to study in any way other than a series of case studies.

The rest of this chapter will address the intrafamily influences upon the definition and practice of fatherhood within the family context. The authors will utilize four types of theoretical perspectives in this process. These perspectives were taken from the field of family therapy as defined and elaborated in Furman and Kniskern's *Handbook of Family Therapy* (1981). They are (1) Intergenerational

Approach; (2) Structural Approach; (3) Behavioral Approach, and (4) Strategic Approach. All of these draw upon a systems theory of family relations. There are several disadvantages to utilizing these theoretical perspectives:

1. These theories do not lend themselves to defining content but instead are much more "process-oriented."
2. There is no previous research to guide social scientists in this endeavor.
3. There may be a generalizability to the *process* of defining fatherhood but there is little to generalize about the *content* of fatherhood.

However, using these theories in this way has one major advantage to the study of fatherhood: It lets us look into the internal process of the family in order to better understand the family's creation and continuation of its definition of father.

Intergenerational Approach

The *intergenerational approach* to marriage and family therapy looks at the process of family relations within the context of previous generations of that family. Intergenerational family therapists such as Framo (1981), Boszormenyi-Nagy and Spark (1973), and Bowen (1978) all emphasize the legacy that is handed down from previous generations to the family. Families translate societal rules to their descendants. Therefore, it is through the eyes of their parents and their parents' parents that a young married couple understand societal roles.

Translating Cultural Norms

We know that the societal norm for fatherhood is that a father should be more instrumental in his orientation and the mother should focus on the expressive elements of childrearing (Parsons & Bales, 1955). However, how that societal norm gets translated to a young couple is highly dependent upon both the husband's and wife's parents' views of that norm, which in turn were products of their parents' views. Therefore, a tradition-bound father who is rigidly traditional in his gender role will translate the societal gender-role norm to his son in such a way that will push him to be similarly traditional in his gender role (Bradley, 1985). Consequently, the young father will spend less time and be less emotionally expressive with his child than a father who was raised by less rigidly traditional parents. The young father will reinforce that which is traditionally gender-stereotypical in their sons by playing with them in a more physical manner, while they encourage stereotypical female behavior by being less physical and more verbal with their daughters (Bronstein, 1988). In this way, the traditional gender-role norm of society is translated from one generation to the next.

If all families were as rigid in their sexual stereotyping of fatherhood, there would be little need to consider the internal culture of the family. This is not the case. Some parents of the present generation of parents were much more androgynous in their own gender-role orientation, despite the societal norm of rather rigid masculinity in fatherhood. These parents translated to their children a modified societal norm that was much more flexible in its gender-role orientation than did parents who were more traditional (Brayman & DeFrain, 1979). The children of these androgynous parents fostered a definition of fatherhood for themselves which included more time spent with their children and more involved caregiving and play than the definitions of fatherhood fostered by more traditional families. Although the societal norm is the same for fathers who were raised by traditional gender-role parents and those raised by more androgynous parents, the families of origin and the generations that spawned them will translate that norm to the next generation of fathers in quite a different way. Therefore, the family of origin will interpret the content or "message" of the social norm in a way which is idiosyncratic to their family history.

Dancing the Family Dance

The influence of previous generations on the formulation of the definition of fatherhood, however, is not limited to this straightforward process of interpretation of societal norms. The new father has listened to more than just the "message" of fatherhood from his parents. He has also listened to the "metamessages" about fatherhood. Metamessages are the messages the family transmits about the message or the content of the social norm (Watzlawick, Wenkland,

& Fisch, 1974). This is part of the rich tapestry which Bowen (1978) refers to as the "dance" of the family. Each family has its own "dance." For some it is a slow waltz. Others fox trot. Still others just get down and boogy. Each child has not only watched this family dance but has lived as a part of it. They were and still are a vital part of that family system. Therefore, the influence of previous generations is more than intellectual; it is also highly emotional.

Bowen (1978) believes that the central task of individuals is to "differentiate" themselves from their parents. Individuals who are "differentiated" from their parents achieve a balance between the forces of "individuality" and "togetherness" within the family context. If people are too needy of "togetherness," they will become "emeshed" with their family. If they are too individualistic, they will be "cut off" from the family. If individuals are in a highly anxious emotional state about their family, they will tend to drift to one of these extremes (Kerr, 1981). If adults had warm, caring relationships with effective parents in the context of a happy marriage, those individuals would have less emotional anxiety about their family and be able to differentiate well, striking a balance between individualistic and togetherness forces (Block, van der Lippe, & Block, 1973). Young parents, who exhibit differentiated patterns, will be fairly independent in choosing which aspects of their parents' definitions of fatherhood they wish to incorporate into their own rituals of fatherhood. However, individuals who were raised in a problematic household in which they either felt distanced by their parents or smothered by them will be much more prone towards anxiety surrounding the family of origin. This will tie those individuals to the parents' style of parenting in one of two ways. Either these new parents will attempt to duplicate the exact pattern of parenting received or they will try to "do the opposite" of the parents' poor parenting technique. In either case, these individuals are closely tied to the parents' behavior as a determinant of their own behavior.

When attempting to define fatherhood for their family, spouses who are differentiated from their parents will have more freedom to blend each spouse's family's conception of fatherhood into their own, while adding specific touches which each has drawn from their own life experience outside the realm of their families. This will give them maximum flexibility in self-determining their own definition of fatherhood. Emeshed young parents will often duplicate their parents' role of fatherhood in an underlying "loyalty" to the family, even if they view the parents' parenting style as dysfunctional. An example of this would be the intergenerational "cycle of violence" from the child abuse literature (Silver, Dublin, & Lourie, 1969). If a young parent's spouse previously had defined fatherhood as including physical abuse, there is a strong chance that the new parents will also define fatherhood in their family of procreation as including abuse. In this way, the two definitions of fatherhood from each generation are emeshed with one another. A second possibility is that the spouses presently formulating their definition of fatherhood might cut themselves off from their family of origin in a concerted effort not to repeat past problems of poor fathering. If the couple can remain relatively unemotional about this decision, they may break the maladaptive cycle and create a better definition of fatherhood. For example, a significant predictor of greater involvement in fathering is dissatisfaction with the fathering which the new parents had received when they were children (Barnett & Baruch, 1988; Radin, 1988). However, if the young couple is highly emotionally invested in countering their parents' maladaptive fatherhood patterns, they could very well choose an equally dysfunctional but opposite pattern of fathering. For example, a father, who experienced his own father as too distant, could become too emeshed and smother his children psychosocially. A father, who felt smothered by his own father, could become very distant from his children in an effort to allow them more freedom. In any of these cases the parents' fatherhood definitions will be altered by the young parents' perception of the metamessage of the family dance and the degree of anxiety which that dance elicits.

Coping with Disagreements

Young couples are not always in agreement about their definition of fatherhood. If such a disagreement should arise, Bowen (1978) hypothesized four basic ways of handling the situation:

1.   The couple could engage in conflict and openly discuss the situation. If the emotion is kept to a minimum, this can be quite helpful in arriving at a compromise definition of fatherhood. However, if the emotion runs too high and there is no room for compromise, conflict can turn to open hostility, making the situation worse, and often leading to a hostile definition of fatherhood.

2.   The couple may distance from each other. Although some distancing may be useful to "cool things down," too much distancing can lead to a cold marriage, and either a distant fathering style or an overinvolved fathering style which is used to compensate for a cold marriage.

3.   The couple could engage in "emotionally complementarity." In this situation, one spouse takes the role of the competent, powerful partner who must overcompensate for the other family members, while the other spouse plays the role of the weak, incompetent individual who underfunctions in the family. If the father takes on the overfunctioning role, the definition of "fatherhood" will include overtaking responsibility for the other family members. If the father is the underfunctioner, "fatherhood" will be seen as a weak role with very little power.

4.   The couple could engage in "triangulation," in which case the parents would reduce their anxiety over their differences by using their children, for instance, as a shield to deflect the anxiety. This is a couple who would blame their children for their inability to come to a spousal consensus on the definition of "fatherhood." When they have marital problems, they will drag the children into their problems to "take sides" or will try to resolve their spousal difficulties by working on the "children's problems." These types of couples will often come into therapy with a child-focused problem as the presenting problem when they are really having marital difficulties.

Each of these coping mechanisms has its origin in the young parents' families of origin. Therefore, the legacy of the couples' families translates the culture's normative values about fatherhood, involves the couple in the ongoing "family dance" about the nature of fatherhood, and supplies coping mechanisms, either functional or dysfunctional for the couple to use when they disagree about the nature of fatherhood. The structure of the family also provides crucial clues to the nature of fatherhood.

Structural Approach

The *structural approach* to marriage and family therapy is based upon the assumption that the family can only be understood in terms of the relations which exist between the parts (Lane, 1970). Even a family member's sense of self definition and individuation occurs "through participation in different family subsystems in different family contexts, as well as through participation in extrafamilial groups" (Minuchin, 1974, pp. 47–48). Since their classic study of *Families of the Slums* (1967), Minuchin, Montalvo, Guerney, Rosman, and Schumer and other Structural Therapists, such as Aponte and Van Densen (1981), have worked with individuals and families by examining the structure of the family and how that structure interacts with the development of both the individual and the family. A major family structural change is precipitated by the birth of a child (Minuchin, 1974). The physical care and emotional nurturance of the new child changes the spouses' interactions with each other, precipitates a change in the spouses' transactional patterns beyond the family, and initiates an entirely new set of subsystems within the family, delineating a different set of functions for parents and children. These changes and how the individual family carries them out will define the role of "fatherhood" within that family.

Boundaries

Every system, be it mechanical, biological, or social, has a boundary which demarcates what is internal to the system and what is external to the system (Buckley, 1967). As a social system, the family has its own boundary and also has a set of boundaries which demarcate subsystems within the families, such as husband–wife, father–child, and mother–child subsystems. "The boundaries of a subsystem are the rules defining who participates, and how" (Minuchin, 1974, p. 53). Boundaries may be clear, diffuse, or rigid. If the young husband and wife are clear about their definitions of fatherhood and have defined those boundaries between the father–child subsystem and the husband–wife subsystem, for example, in clearly understood and mutually agreed-upon terms, "fatherhood" will have a set of clear expectations with the flexibility to creatively alter those boundaries should the situation demand it. With the advent of the new child, the spousal subsystem will need to differentiate in order to perform the roles associated with child-rearing, while maintaining the mutual support that should be a characteristic of the spousal subsystem (Minuchin, 1974). A clear boundary must be drawn that allows the child to have access to both parents in their parent–child subsystems, but excludes the child from invading the spousal subsystem.

If the boundaries are too rigid, the family will become dis-engaged. In this situation, either the child, the father, the mother, or any combination of those family members will feel a lack of closeness and a general sense of family distancing within the family. This sense of disengagement may permeate the entire family, creating a feeling of distance and coldness as a predominant family motif. There is a push from the external culture for the man to primarily function as "breadwinner" (Bradley, 1985) and "disciplinarian" (Lamb et al., 1985). Because many men lack the training and interest to develop other parenting skills (Brown, 1988), they rely upon the cultural prescriptions to define their role for them. Therefore, when the family has established rigid boundaries, the role of "father" often is reduced to a disciplinarian and breadwinner from whom little affec-tion and caring is forthcoming to either spouse or child.

If the boundaries are too diffuse, the family will become emeshed. In this situation, the family members find it hard to distinguish who is in which subsystem, which task is to reside in which subsystem, and what behaviors are improper in which context. If a child cries in the middle of the night, the family with clear boundaries may send the father or mother in to comfort the child in the child's bedroom. The emeshed family will invite the child into the parents' bed to sleep on a regular basis. In this example, the boundary between the conjugal bed and the father's role of comfort-ing the child is blurred to such a degree that one role, the father's comforting, invades the spousal turf. If this continues on a regular basis, the spouse's alone time, sleep patterns, and even sex life will be altered, becoming emeshed with their parent–child role.

Some families may create a set of subsystem boundaries which are rigid in certain areas and diffuse in others. A family which has an emeshed spousal subsystem, in which the husband and wife become overinvolved with each other, may find little time for parenting and, therefore, create a rigid boundary between the parents and the chil-dren. In this "marriage-focused family," the spousal dyad may flour-ish at the expense of the children and the parent–child role bond. Without the guidance and nurturance of a parent–child bond, the child will suffer developmentally. In other families, both parents may become so involved in their parenting duties that the boundary between each of them and the child become diffused. This emesh-ment between parents and child may create a rigidity in the boundary between the spouses. This "parenting-focused family" will encourage the father to pursue his overinvolved fathering role at the expense of his role as husband. In either of these families, one subsystem gains at the expense of the other, creating an unnecessary loss.

Once these boundaries are defined, they must be maintained (Buckley, 1967). The task of boundary maintenance is typically a shared task among family members but most families choose one member to fulfill the boundary maintenance role in a given set of circumstances. In our society the mother seems to fulfill the role of boundary maintainer *within* the family. It is mother who acts as gatekeeper between subsystems within the family, often not only defining "fatherhood" within the family but also regulating the father's involvement with the child (Yogman, Cooley, & Kindlon, 1988). In many families, it is only when the mother relinquishes some of this role, such as under conditions of maternal employment, that the father can reestablish a fathering role (Barnett & Barach, 1988).

The role of maintaining the boundary around the family and mediating the transactions that the family has with the outside world has traditionally fallen to the father in the family. He has been the family's link to the outside world (Parsons & Bales, 1955). It is the father who is expected to maintain the boundaries between the family and the economic institutions of the society through his occupational role as breadwinner (Lamb et al., 1985). Fathers have a primary role in fostering academic success in their children (Lamb, 1981). In fact, the child's entry into school "involves a shift from caregiver and organizer of experiences to that of mediator and guide in a broader social-cultural context" (Bradley, 1985, p. 148). Therefore, the mother carries out the boundary maintenance function *within* the family, while the father performs the boundary maintenance functions *between* the family and the outside world. In this way, the father completes the role he started when he was the first significant relationship outside the mother–child bond in infancy (Watkins, 1987), thereby helping to complete the separation-individuation process of the child.

Alignment

Alignment is the ". . . joining or opposition of one member of a system to another in carrying out an operation" (Aponte, 1976, p. 434). When two or more family members join in an "alliance," they seek to create some mutual benefit (Haley, 1976). For example, father and son might join in an alliance to watch a football game on the family television set on a Sunday afternoon, an activity in which mother has no desire to partake. However, family members may also join in a "coalition" in which two or more members specifically join together against a third family member. For example, mother and daughter might join in a coalition to watch a movie on the family television on a Sunday afternoon, in a concerted effort to keep father from watching a football game which they dislike. This pattern of alliances and coalitions will have a powerful effect upon the definition of the nature of the fatherhood role.

If a stable coalition is formed against the father in the family, the role of father will be less powerful in the family and the concomitant isolation will become a dominant, inflexible characteristic of the spousal and parent–child relationship. A stable coalition between the mother and the children *against* the father will lessen his effectiveness in his fathering role. Consequently, this will either escalate into repeated conflict or result in the lessening and eventual termination of the father's fatherhood role. If that mother-child coalition is strong enough it could also bring about the end to the spousal relationship, either through divorce or the effective retreat of the father from the whole family. For example, the father could become a "workaholic" and begin to ignore both his wife and the children. If it is the father who helps to form the stable coalition against another family member, his fathering role will be most influenced by those with whom he has formed that coalition. If that coalition is with his wife against the children, his fatherhood role will often lack the insight of seeing the world through the child's point of view. If that coalition is with the other male members of the family (e.g., his sons) against his wife and/or daughters, his fatherhood role will tend to be more "traditionally masculine." If the father joins another family member in a "detouring stable coalition," he will seek to reduce "the stress between the members of a coalition by designating another party as the source of their problem and assuming an attacking or solicitous attitude toward that person" (Aponte & Van Densen, 1981, p. 314). By this "scapegoating" mechanism the father is able to reduce his responsibility for the family and lessen the obligations of his fatherhood role. Whether the father is included within a coalition or is the object of a coalition, the existence of a stable family coalition will heavily influence the role of the father in the family.

Power

The power dimension in a family system refers to "the relative influence of each (family) member on the outcome of an activity" (Aponte, 1976, p. 434). Power is an important structural dimension of a family because it lets the theorist gauge the effectiveness of each role in a given context. For example, a father may exert a great deal of influence over his adolescent's choice of career but little influence on his adolescent's choice of clothes, hairstyle, or music. Even though a father may have a great deal of power over the very important area of occupational development, he may have almost no power in such relatively trivial areas as style or music. A mother may have total power over her husband in the kitchen but no power when it comes to the barbecue pit. Parents may be able to control their son's behavior in the house when he is by himself but have no control over him when he is out with his friends. Therefore, power is not a single trait but varies considerably according to time, place, and content of the situation.

When the child is an infant, a father has a relatively absolute level of power in the life of the child. Moreover, as the child develops, the demands for autonomy place demands upon the parenting skills of the parents (Minuchin, 1974). The child is no longer as totally reliant upon his or her parents as he or she was before. A daughter, who obeyed her father at age four, has a wider support system at age seven and may, therefore, not comply with her father's wishes as readily. An order that went unquestioned by a son at age eight may be challenged for a rational explanation of the rule at age fourteen. Rules that may be self-evident to the parents may need a lot of explanation before they are accepted by a teenager. Power shifts with the age of the child and the definition of "fatherhood" must also shift if power is to be maintained.

The last dimension of power revolves upon the nature of the alliances and coalitions which help support a power base (Aponte & Van Densen, 1981). A mother might take on the role of the disciplinarian, but she is effective or powerful in that role only as long as her husband supports her efforts in his fathering role. A father who was the sole provider for his family must form an alliance with his wife if she takes on a job in order to maintain his power base without having it subverted by his wife's new income. Such alliances must be carefully and overtly discussed among spouses. Often in parenting, if the mother and father can keep a "unified front," their power is enhanced. However, if the parents are at odds with each other, the authority of one parent might weaken the authority of the other (Shulman & Klein, 1984). When the parental coalition, the executive system of the family, loses power, the family has a tendency to lose direction and order (Minuchin, 1974). When this happens, fathers lose their power to influence family decision-making and "fatherhood" becomes an impotent role.

Changes in Family Structure

In addition to the changes of structure of the interactions among family members, there are also changes in the structural composition of the family that might affect the family's definition of fatherhood. For example, among dual-career couples, the fathers took a more active role in childcare, displayed more nurturant behavior as a father, and demonstrated fewer gender-role stereotypes than did their counterparts from more traditional homes (Carlson, 1984). In this case, the wage-earner, career mother increased the number of adults fulfilling that function for the system, which allowed for a broadening of the fatherhood role.

In some cases, such as divorced families, family members are removed from the family, causing a major upheaval in the fatherhood role. For the noncustodial father, his fatherhood role may become more optional, especially if he feels inadequate at parenting (Brown, 1988). Despite this attitude among some fathers, the noncustodial father remained a significant person to his children, even if there were *no* contact (Peck & Manocherian, 1988). Many men withdraw from their fatherhood role in order to ease the pain of losing day-to-day contact with their children. They feel that their ex-wife will enter into a coalition with their children against them and leave them disengaged from the family. However, research has shown that all parties, father, mothers, and especially children, benefit greatly when there is continued shared parenting, provided that there is a mutually supportive, cooperative parental alliance (Peck & Manocherian, 1988). In approximately 11% of divorces, the father receives custody of the children (Bronstein, 1988). In this situation, there is no person to shoulder the mothering role for the children. In most cases, the single father takes on both the more instrumental role of fathering and the more expressive role of mother (Bradley, 1985). Although fathers report some difficulty in balancing the demands of both work and fatherhood (Greif, 1985), becoming a single parent intensified the parental bonding experience (Bradley, 1985) and greatly improved the father's relationship with his child (Greif, 1985).

In some cases, family members are added to the structure of the family, such as in the case of stepfamilies. The addition of stepchildren to a father is a difficult situation. Unlike the natural father, whose role was ascribed, the stepfather has to achieve his role with his stepchildren and prove his worth (Lewis, 1985). This is particularly difficult when the task that the stepfather must achieve is the blending of two different family cultures and identities (Pasley, 1985). Issues surrounding different family rules, distribution of resources, and loyalty conflicts place a heavy burden upon the stepfather to cope constructively with his new fatherhood identity. Discipline becomes very difficult as the father tries to make the transition from "good friend" to "parent" (Robinson & Barret, 1986). Stepfathers consequently reported a more negative image of themselves as fathers, as compared to intact families (Macklin, 1987). Stepfathers reported lower cohesion, adaptability, regard, and unconditionality than members of first-time marriages (Pink & Wampler, 1985). They had trouble with their boundary maintenance tasks (Pasley, 1985). These structural changes placed the stepfather under great stress in his fatherhood role and consequently contributed to the stress of the stepfamily. However, even under these stressful conditions, social behavior of stepchildren was found to be no less competent than that of children from intact or divorced families (Santrock, Sitterle, & Warshak, 1988) and, in fact, the stepfather–stepchild relationship did improve over time (Amato, 1987). Therefore, even under these most extreme structural handicaps, the family was able to define fatherhood in such a way as to enhance the development of the child. Within the family structure, the behaviors of family members also play an important role in determining the nature of fatherhood.

Behavioral Approach

The *behavioral approach* to marriage and family therapy focuses upon the behaviors that take place within the family system and serve as the connecting tissue which holds that system together. Behavioral family therapists, such as Patterson (1971) and Gordon and Davidson (1981) seek to apply the principles and philosophy of behaviorism to the study and therapy of families and individuals within a family concept. Therefore, through the lens of the behavioralist, the role of fatherhood would be defined by both the behaviors of the parents and the behaviors they elicit in the children.

Assessment of Family Behaviors

Within each family, both parents make an assessment of the way the family behaves. The parents' perception of these behaviors, their antecedents, and their consequences enables them to define their roles, fatherhood and motherhood, in such a way which will produce the desired behaviors in the child (Gordon & Davidson, 1981). For example, if a young couple with an infant son would like the infant to stop his crying, the parents' observation of the situation is of paramount importance. They must first observe when the behavior occurs and try to pinpoint both the antecedent and consequent behaviors which surround the infant's crying. If the infant son cries when he is put down for a nap but stops crying if he is picked up and rocked, both parents will observe this pattern and change their behaviors to correspond to their newly observed pattern, in order to stop the baby's crying. The accuracy of these observations is crucial in establishing an effective fatherhood role. If these observations are inaccurate or "miss the mark", the father may engage in behaviors which only serve to exacerbate the problem behavior, such as crying, thereby frustrating both parents and the child and becoming a negative fathering experience. This is the root of many cases of child abuse. In some cases one parent is accurate, while one parent repeatedly has faulty observations. For example, if the mother is accurate in her perception and the father is not, the father may quickly be labeled as incompetent and asked to limit his participation in fatherhood. However, if the observations of the father are "on target" with the feelings and strategies of the child, the father can alter his antecedent and consequent behavior in order to provide the desired results. In this case, the positive outcome of a parenting encounter will encourage both parents to expand the role of fatherhood in the family.

Changing Behaviors

A parent may change the child's behaviors in one of several ways:

1. Positive punishment—presenting an aversive stimuli which will decrease the occurrence of an unwanted behavior
2. Negative punishment—removing a pleasant stimuli which will decrease the occurrence of an unwanted behavior
3. Positive reward—presenting a pleasant stimuli which will increase the occurrence of a desired behavior
4. Negative reward—removing an aversive stimuli which will increase the occurrence of a desired behavior

If a father is going to achieve maximum efficiency as a father who regulates his child's behavior, he will need to be aware of all four types of reinforcement and be able to shift the type of reinforcement to accommodate the situation. If he only is able to use positive rewards or punishments, he will find situations in which he is powerless to affect a change in his child's behavior and will consequently withdraw from his fathering role. If he becomes only punishment-oriented and forgets that there is a reward side to discipline also, he will define his fatherhood role as the executioner and will restrict his fathering role to interactions with a negative emotional tone. Furthermore, he will be paid back in kind by his children. Under the principle of reciprocity, in which there is an equitable exchange of positive and negative emotional interactions between family members (Patterson & Reid, 1970), the punishing father's negatively toned behaviors will be returned by the child in the form of negative affect and bitter feelings. Fatherhood will lose its appeal quickly. A rewarding father is more likely to receive positive affect back from his child. Therefore, the father who has a facility in all four types of reinforcement techniques will be most likely to define fatherhood in both an effective and caring way.

Even with a facility in all four types of reinforcement, a father may not feel rewarded for his fatherhood role by obtaining the child's compliance. Fathers are often inconsistent in providing support and discipline for their children (Easterbrooks & Goldberg, 1984). This inconsistency will confuse the child as to the real meaning of the rule to be enforced. For example, a father, who imposes a curfew of 10 o'clock p.m., and sometimes enforces it and sometimes doesn't, is sending a very confusing message to his adolescent daughter. She becomes confused as to the importance of the rule and ultimately the importance of her father in his fatherhood role. In this way, the father may actually be reinforcing her breaking of her curfew. Furthermore, he is intermittently reinforcing her breaking her curfew and intermittent reinforcement is the most difficult to extinguish (Patterson, 1971). In this way, a father who is inconsistent in his reinforcement may render himself impotent or counterproductive in his fatherhood role.

The circumstances may also serve to subvert a father in his parenting role. A father who handled a situation with his son very well may be quite pleased with his fatherhood role because his son complies with his wishes when disciplined. However, family dynamics change as the child grows older and broadens his field of alternatives (Richer, 1968). To the preschool child at home, the sun rises and sets in his dad's eyes. However, once that child goes to school or has a favorite aunt come to visit, his range of alternative sources of gratification and support has increased. Similarly, the child's alternative gratifications increase as he broadens his circle of friends. In these circumstances, the child's dependence upon his father for support and nurturance is diminished. Therefore, the father's power to reinforce behaviors is also diminished. What used to take a scowl to make the child comply now will take a scolding. With increasing alternative sources of gratification, the scolding may escalate into physical discipline. In this way, a child, who was highly compliant to a father's disciplinary rules may rebel against those same rules because of a change in his extrafamilial relationships, despite his father's consistency. Consequently, if the father is going to be an effective parent, he is going to have to adjust his discipline to the changing nature of the family.

A final way to bring about change in the children is through the father's modeling of the behavior which he wishes the child to adopt (Bronstein, 1988). Actions *do* speak louder than words. If the father wants his children to be honest he may talk about it until he's blue in the face, but it will all be lost if his children see him lying. Consequently, many fathers define their fatherhood role in a way which they hope will be a positive influence upon their children. For example, if a father wants his son to follow a fairly traditional male gender role, as defined by the culture, the father himself may take on a traditional gender role in an effort to model that behavior for his son (Lamb, 1981). Modeling that same gender-role behavior to his daughter will teach her how to complement the male role and assist her in her feminine gender-role behavior (Lamb, 1981). In this way, the father's modeling may bring about the desired consequences, a son who acts masculine and a daughter who acts feminine. Realizing this, a father may act out more masculine behaviors in hopes of helping his children's gender-role learning or he may specifically engage in more traditionally "feminine behavior," such as doing the laundry, in order to specifically model a more androgynous gender role for his children to emulate. In either case, the father's role of fatherhood is changed to achieve a desired outcome with his children.

If the father is aware of some of these principles of behavioral family therapy, he can increase his fatherhood role and reap the rewards of a richer relationship with an increase in nurturant feelings and behavior, even in the face of the costs of slower career advancement (Lamb et al., 1985). In a true behavioral sense, he will have weighed the costs and benefits of expanding his fatherhood role. However, some patterns of family interaction do not lead themselves easily to a behavioral analysis. To study these patterns and their effect on the development of fatherhood, we turn to strategic therapy as an approach.

Strategic Approach

The *strategic approach* to marriage and family therapy situates therapists so that they may initiate the course of therapy and design a specific, tailor-made approach to each problem in each family context (Haley, 1973). The therapist studies the situation, creates his or her own hypotheses about the family's functioning which he or she does *not* share with the family, and creates an intervention to help the family cope with the idiosyncratic nature of the family and its presenting problem. Major proponents of the strategic approach, such as Haley (1976), Madanes (1981), Stanton (1981), and the Italian school of Strategic Therapy, headed by Palazzoli-Selvini (Palazzoli–Selvini, Boscolo, Cecchin, & Prata, 1978), all focus upon the interactional sequence of behaviors which are present in the family. The focus is upon circular, rather than linear, causality (Stanton, 1981). Sequences of interaction and not roles are the factors to be studied when we are trying to understand the family system (Haley, 1973). This poses a major problem for this chapter in that the strategic approach does not lend itself to the study of a role such as fatherhood. Definitions and formulations of fatherhood would lend themselves to the study of "first-order change." "First-order change" is the movement within an unchanging system (Watzlawick, Weakland, & Fisch, 1974). In first-order change, the emphasis is on stability and constancy over time and across families. The strategic approach to marriage and family therapy is much more interested in "second-order change," which is a shift which actually alters the system itself (Watzlawick et al., 1974). Second-order change is idiosyncratic to a specific family at a specific point in time. Therefore, it is difficult to focus upon the family's definition of fatherhood through the eyes of the strategic therapist.

However, the strategic approach to marriage and family therapy can offer some insight on the formulation of the fatherhood role within a specific family by studying the recursive patterns of behavior which may influence how fatherhood roles are enacted. Haley (1976) presents several cases in which the fatherhood role is impacted upon by a sequence of behaviors. For example, Haley presents the "One Parent Against Another" scenario. Since fathers are often more distant from their children because of commitments to outside activities (Lamb et al., 1985), a mother often develops an intense relationship with her child. This intensity exaggerates the importance of both positive and negative responses for both mother and child. Since this is a difficult situation for the child, the child may begin to develop symptomatic behavior. The mother then attempts to deal with the child" with a mixture of affection and exasperation" (p. 115). The child's symptomatic behavior is exacerbated by this "double message" and his or her symptoms become more extreme. Consequently, the mother calls upon the father for assistance. The father steps in to take charge of the situation and cope with the child. However, the mother reacts against the father by telling him that he is not dealing with the situation properly. If the father persists in his course of action to take charge of the child, the mother will escalate her attack upon the father by threatening to distance herself from the father or even break off the relationship by bringing up the subject of divorce. Consequently, the father withdraws, giving up on his attempt to separate the mother and child from a relationship which he views as too intense. Both the mother and child then continue their relationship which has been characterized by a mix-ture of extremes of affection and exasperation. This sequence can continue *ad infinitum* unless someone (e.g., a therapist) or some-thing (e.g., mother's employment) (Lamb et al., 1985) interrupts the cycle to stop it.

The strategic marriage and family therapist utilizes several concepts in analyzing this sequence of interactions. All three family members (mother, father, and child) have now linked the child's maladaptive behavior with the parent's potential separation and even divorce. The child begins to overtake responsibility for the parent's marriage and creates a metaphor that the child is the savior of the parent's marriage (Madanes, 1981). When the child misbe-haves, the parents are occupied with the child's problems and, for a while, must act like a "team" in order to overcome the child's problems. Therefore, the symptoms of the child have taken on a function within the marriage. The mother scapegoats the father, pulling him into the mother-child dyad and then blaming him for his lack of efficacy in coping with the daughter's problem. For the mother, this recursive cycle is quite functional. It exonerates her from taking responsibility for her own part in the dysfunctional mother-child relationship. In this way, the mother can continue to be the loving mother who is cursed with a dysfunctional child and an incompetent husband. The father is subverted and distanced from any viable fatherhood relationship with his child. His fatherhood role becomes severely curtailed. In this way the father's fatherhood role is impacted upon by the other members of the family (Lamb et al., 1985) and by both the mother-child relationship and the hus-band-wife relationship (Yogman et al., 1988).

If the strategic marriage and family therapist was asked to intervene in this situation, there are several avenues which might be pursued. The therapist may ask the family to perform a task, such as asking the father to have a conversation with the child without interruption from the mother (Haley, 1976). This intervention shifts the pattern of communication within the family, thereby, prompting second-order change of the system itself. The child's behavioral problems could be reframed into a more positive connotation of trying to keep the parents together. This disrupts the parents' nega-tive interpretation so that they can no longer see only the negative aspects of the symptom of the child. This new forced insight also precipitates second-order change (Madanes, 1981). Finally, the therapist may simply make the covert overt. If the therapist can expose some of the covert motivations to everyone, these covert motivations lose their power. This forces the family members to seek another method of achieving the same goals. In this manner, second-order change is also fostered. Any of these interventions will serve to enhance the role of fatherhood in the case study family. In this way, although the strategic approach to marriage and family therapy does not address the nature of fatherhood in the same way as the other three approaches, it still can shed some light on the internal family culture and how it contributes to the process of defining fatherhood.

Summary and Conclusions

This chapter explored the internal family environment upon the family's definition of fatherhood. In a time of changing societal trends concerning definitions of family roles and gender roles, the internal influences of the family upon the definition of fatherhood has become more influential than in previous times. Using family therapy to explore the internal dynamics within families, the authors chose four theories to explore the internal family environment. From the *intergenerational approach*, the authors demonstrated how generations of families translate cultural norms about fatherhood to their youngest members and create methods of coping with disagreements about cultural norms. The *structural approach* elucidated the importance of boundaries, alignment, and power upon the formulation of fatherhood roles. The *behavioral approach* focused upon the behavioral aspects of family dynamics and the role of reward and punishment upon the development of the fatherhood role. Lastly, the *strategic approach* was utilized to highlight the importance of interactional patterns in developing a role of fatherhood within a family.

From these theories and the application of them in the area of fatherhood, it can be seen that the internal dynamics within the family are of crucial importance in determining the nature of the fatherhood role within a given family. Broad cultural influences have their place as the background upon which this drama is played. However, in an increasingly pluralistic society, the ability of a cultural explanation to fully explicate the development of a fatherhood role within a family is becoming more and more limited. As social scientists turn to future research into the fatherhood role in today's society, it is of increasing importance that they look on a more microscopic and perhaps idiosyncratic level at the internal dynamics within the family and focus upon their power to mutually create a sense of fatherhood. This chapter is but a springboard in that process.

References

Amato, P. R. (1987). Family processes in one-parent, stepparent, and intact families: The child's point of view. *Journal of Marriage and the Family*, 49, 327–337.

Aponte, H. J. (1976). Underorganization in the poor family. In P. J. Guerin (Ed.), *Family therapy: Theory and practice* (pp. 432–448) New York: Gardner.

Aponte, H. J., & Van Densen, J. M. (1981). Structural family therapy. In A. S. Gurman & D. P. Kniskern (Eds.), *Handbook of family therapy* (pp. 310–360). New York: Brunner/Mazel.

Barnett, R. C., & Baruch, G. K. (1988). Correlates of father's participation in family work. In P. Bronstein & C. P. Cowan (Eds.), *Fatherhood today: Men's changing role in the family* (pp. 66–78). New York: Wiley.

Block, J., van der Lippe, A., & Block, J. H. (1973). Sex roles and socialization: Some personality concomitants and environmental antecedents. *Journal of Consulting and Clinical Psychology*, 41, 321–341.

Bloom-Feshback, J. (1981). Historical perspectives on the father's role. In M. E. Lamb (Ed.), *The role of the father in child development* (2nd ed., pp. 71–112). New York: Wiley.

Boszormenyi-Nagy, I., & Spark, G. (1973). *Invisible loyalties: Reciprocity in intergenerational family therapy*. New York: Harper & Row.

Bowen, M. (1978). *Family therapy in clinical practice*. New York: Jason Aronson.

Bradley, R. H. (1985). Fathers and the school-age child. In S. M. H. Hanson & F. W. Bozett ((Eds.), *Dimensions of fatherhood* (pp. 141–169). Beverly Hills: Sage.

Brayman, R., & DeFrain, J. (1979). Sex role attitudes and behaviors of children reared by androgynous parents. Paper presented to the Groves Conference on Marriage and the Family, Washington, D.C., April.

Bronstein, P. (1988). Father-child interaction: Implications for gender-role socialization. In P. Bronstein & C. P. Cowan (Eds.), *Fatherhood today: Men's changing role in the family* (pp. 107–126). New York: Wiley.

Brown, F. H. (1988). The postdivorce family. In B. Carter & M. McGoldrick (Eds.), *The changing family life cycle* (2nd ed., pp. 371-398). New York: Gardner Press.

Buckley, W. (1967). *Sociology and modern systems theory.* Englewood Cliffs, NJ: Prentice-Hall.

Carlson, B. E. (1984). The father's contribution to childcare: Effects on children's perceptions of parental roles. *American Journal of Orthopsychiatry, 54,* 123-135.

Easterbrooks, M. A., & Goldberg, W. A. (1984). Toddler development in the family: Impact of father involvement and parenting characteristics. *Child Development, 55,* 740-752.

Framo, J. (1981). The integration of marital therapy with sessions with family of origin. In A. S. Gurman & D. P. Kniskern (Eds.), *Handbook of family therapy* (pp. 133-158). New York: Brunner/Mazel.

Gordon, S. B., & Davidson, N. (1981). Behavioral parent training. In A. S. Gurman & D. P. Kniskern (Eds.), *Handbook of family therapy* (pp. 517-555). New York: Brunner/Mazel.

Greif, G. L. (1985). *Single fathers.* Lexington, Massachusetts: D. C. Heath.

Gurman, A. S., & Kniskern, D. P. (1981). *Handbook of family therapy.* New York: Brunner/Mazel.

Haley, J. (1973). *Uncommon therapy.* New York: Norton.

Haley, J. (1976). *Problem-solving therapy.* San Francisco: Jossey-Bass.

Kerr, M. E. (1981). Family systems theory and therapy. In A. S. Gurman & D. P. Kniskern (Eds.), *Handbook of family therapy* (pp. 226-266). New York: Brunner/Mazel.

Lamb, M. E. (1981). Fathers and child development: An integrative overview. In M. E. Lamb (Ed.), *The role of the father in child development* (2nd ed., pp. 1-70). New York: Wiley.

Lamb, M. E., Pleck, J. H., & Levine, J. A. (1985). The role of the father in child development: The effects of increased paternal involvement. In Laney and Kazdin (Eds.), *Advances in clinical child psychology* Vol. 8 (pp. 229-266). New York: Plenum.

Lane, M. (1970). *Introduction to structuralism.* New York: Basic Books.

Lewis, H. C. (1985). Family therapy with stepfamilies. *Journal of Strategic and Systemic Therapies, 4,* 13-23.

Macklin, E. (1987). Nontraditional family forms. In M. B. Sussman & S. K. Steinmetz (Eds.), *Handbook of marriage and the family* (pp. 317-354). New York: Plenum.

Madanes, C. (1981). *Strategic family therapy.* New York: Jossey-Bass.

Minuchin, S. (1974). *Families and family therapy.* Cambridge, Massachusetts: Harvard University Press.

Minuchin, S., Montalvo, B., Guerney, Jr. B., Rosman, B., & Schumer, F. (1967). *Families of the slums.* New York: Basic Books.

Orthner, D. S., & Bowen, G. L. (1985). Fathers in the military. In S. M. H. Hanson & F. W. Bozett (Eds.), *Dimensions of fatherhood* (pp. 307-326). Beverly Hills, CA: Sage.

Palazzoli-Selvini, M., Boscolo, L., Cecchin, G., & Prata G. (1978). *Paradox and counterparadox: A new model in the therapy of the family in schizophrenic transaction.* New York: Jason Aronson.

Parsons, T., & Bales, R. F. (1955). *Family, socialization, and interaction process.* Glencoe, Illinois: Free Press.

Pasley, K. (1985). Stepfathers. In S. M. H. Hanson & F. W. Bozett (Eds.), *Dimensions of fatherhood* (pp. 288-306). Beverly Hills, CA: Sage.

Patterson, G. R. (1971). *Families: Applications of social learning to family life.* Champaign, IL: Research Press.

Patterson, G. R., & Reid, J. B. (1970). Reciprocity and coercion: Two facets of social systems. In C. Neuringer & J. Michael (Eds.), *Behavior modification in clinical psychology* (pp. 133-177). New York: Appleton-Century-Crofts.

Peck, J. S., & Manocherian, J. R. (1988). Divorce in the changing family cycle. In B. Carter & M. McGoldrick (Eds.), *The changing family life cycle* (2nd ed., pp. 335-370). New York: Gardner.

Pink, J. E. T., & Wampler, K. S. (1985). Problem areas in stepfamilies: Cohesion, adaptability, and the stepfather-adolescent relationship. *Family Relations, 34,* 327-335.

Radin, N. (1988). Primary caregiving fathers of long duration. In P. Bronstein & C. P. Cowan (Eds.), *Fatherhood today: Men's changing role in the family* (pp. 127-143). New York: Wiley.

Richer, S. (1968). The economics of child rearing. *Journal of Marriage and the Family, 30,* 462-466.

Robinson, B. E., & Barret, R. L. (1986). *The developing father.* New York: Guilford.

Santrock, J. W., Sitterle, K. A., & Warshak, R. A. (1988). Fathers in stepfamilies. In P. Bronstein & C. P. Cowan (Eds.), *Fatherhood today: Men's changing role in the family* (pp. 144-165). New York: Wiley.

Russell, G. (1978). The father role and its relation to masculinity and androgyny. *Child Development, 49,* 1174-1181.

Shulman, S., & Klein, M. M. (1984). Resolution of transference problems in structural therapy of single-parent families by a male therapist. *The American Journal of Family Therapy, 12,* 38-44.

Silver, L. B., Dublin, C. C., & Lourie, R. S. (1969). Does violence breed violence?: Contributions from a study of the child abuse syndrome. *American Journal of Psychiatry, 126,* 404-407.

Stanton, M. D. (1981). Strategic approaches to family therapy. In A. S. Gurman & D. P. Kniskern (Eds.), *Handbook of family therapy* (pp. 361-402). New York: Brunner/Mazel.

Watkins, K. P. (1987). *Parent–child attachment: A guide t* [ ] *research.* New York: Garland.

Watzlawick, P., Weakland, P., & Fisch, R. (1974). *Change:* [ ] *problem formation and problem resolution.* New York [ ] Norton.

Yogman, M. W., Cooley, J., & Kindlon, D. (1988). Father [ ] toddlers: A developing relationship. In P. Bronstein & [ ] (Eds.), *Fatherhood today: Men's changing role in the f* [ ] 65). New York: Wiley.

11
Cultural Change and the Future of Fatherhood and Families

Frederick W. Bozett
Shirley M. H. Hanson

The variations of fatherhood and families described in this volume are impossible to separate out as distinct entities responsible for influencing father behavior in one way or the other. They interact and intersect in almost infinite ways to produce attitudes toward fathering and specific fathering behaviors that are unique to each man. Moreover, it is clear that certain beliefs about fathering, or specific father behaviors, such as methods of child discipline, may be directly influenced by various aspects of one's cultural and family heritage such as social class and religion. Yet it is also our point of view that the whole cannot be understood without understanding the component parts. It is the responsibility of family theorists, researchers, and family therapists/practitioners to incorporate the components into workable wholes so that cultural variables that influence individual fathers within their family context can be understood and applied.

It is the purpose of this chapter to identify some broad themes that are threaded throughout the previous chapters, and to make statements that synthesize the previous content while also making projections into the future.

Fathering in families is carried out within multiple cultures and subcultures; individual men may or may not conform to the fatherhood role prescribed by the subculture. Bowen and Orthner (Chapter 8) point out that the culture may not necessarily be healthy or productive for the individual. For example, the current wave of drug addiction has fostered a surprising number of men who have taken responsibility for their drug-addicted newborn infants who have been abandoned by their addicted mothers (Seligorann & Abramson, 1989). These men, both Black and White, refuse to allow their children to be reared in a cultural context that continues to perpetuate the cycle of addiction and poverty. These men often seek the assistance of their own mothers or other relatives to help in daily caretaking responsibilities. Although they probably would not have taken on the primary parenting responsibility if it were not for the addiction of their children's mothers, even so they are proving to be responsible parents. Also, this evidence helps support Mirandé (Chapter 3) who points out that Black fathers are neither invisible, absent, nor peripheral to families.

Also, men and fathers are autonomous beings; not objects acted upon by external forces over which they have no control. Marciano (Chapter 6) discusses the voluntaristic nature of religious beliefs and conformity to religious teachings; that the outcomes of religious beliefs for fatherhood may be less a matter of denominational effect than the man's consent to the denomination's teaching. Likewise, many aspects of fatherhood are chosen or voluntaristic, primarily those considered to be *extrinsic*, that influence men's enactment of the paternal role such as occupation, commitment to religious teachings and beliefs, or choice of living environment. Marciano makes the point that voluntarism is to be viewed as an outcome of experiences and roles in a man's life, not as the independent variable. This point of view is crucial to understanding that the conscious choices men make in their lives have a direct effect upon how their enactment of fatherhood is played out in families.

In contrast to external factors are *internal* elements over which little control can be exerted. Examples are the culture of socialization, and genetic makeup and inherited qualities that predispose men to carry out the father role in unique ways. It is not that one never has control over the effect of these factors, but their influence is often more subtle, and thus more difficult to identify and oversee.

Another important learning from the foregoing chapters are that there are many assumptions about fatherhood and families not based in reality. For example, it is wrongly assumed that it is easier to rear children in the rural more bucolic environment than it is in the pluralistic and fast paced environment of the city (DeFrain, LeMasters, & Schroff, Chapter 7), that Black families are necessarily matriarchal (Mirandé, Chapter 3), and that Hispanic males are distant and aloof from their children (Mirandé, Chapter 3). Similarly Marciano (Chapter 6) cautions against assuming religion as a cause or even a correlate of specific father behaviors. Moreover, Mirandé (Chapter 3) is convincing in his admonition against considering Anglo families the norm against which all others should be compared. He instructs us that Black, Hispanic, Native American, and other ethnic families units *are* adaptive and viable when analyzed within their own sociohistorical, political, and structural frameworks; that to consider them deficient and maladaptive because they somehow vary from Anglo-American norms is ethnocentric, stereotyping, and unduly prejudicial. The United States is not a melting pot in which everyone blends; it is time that myth was laid to rest. We simply cannot assume homogeneity or monolithic cultural effects on parental and paternal roles. While attitudes and behaviors may be maladaptive by white middle class standards, they may be quite adaptive under conditions of lower class family life (Erickson & Gecas, Chapter 5). Focusing on dominant societal patterns while ignoring the substantial diversity within and between cultural and social class groupings makes any generalization suspect. The study and practice of fathering in families demands that we be alert to assumptions in order to avoid the pitfalls and falsehoods they often generate.

Contrary to broad, sweeping generalizations that are of questionable merit, then, are more narrow "bytes" of data that may be useful to help us understand fatherhood in more limited circumstances. For example, fathers with careers have less time for their family role than do men with jobs, and middle class men tend to stress independence and self-direction in their children whereas lower class fathers tend to emphasize obedience (Erickson & Gecas, Chapter 5). While we recognize the potential for misuse of even these types of generalizations, nevertheless they help us to understand and interpret father behaviors and family characteristics within certain cultural contexts and under particular circumstances. Similarly, it is crucial to determine the nature of the fatherhood role with a given family if the role of individual fathers is to be understood (Jurich, White, White, & Moody, Chapter 10).

Whenever the future of fatherhood is discussed there is often the tendency to urge the "more and better" approach; that fathers find more time to be with their children, and that the time spent be of quality. But this admonition, if it has any validity, does not rest solely upon decisions of individual fathers. Rather, it depends, among others, on policies of the workplace (Bowen & Orthner, Chapter 8), public policy in general, as well as other cultural considerations such as the individual family's internal dynamics, religious affiliation, ethnic factors, and others. We would hope that organizations as well as public policy formulations would have more respect for the importance of the family, and that policy makers understand that taking family matters into consideration when establishing policy is in the best interest of business as well as families and thus the country in general. At the same time, we also recognize that the absence of family policy in the workplace is not necessarily or solely at fault if time fathers spend with their families is limited. Multiple factors are etiologic.

Men and fathers owe a great deal to the women's movement, a major cultural phenomenon of the 20th century. Had it not been for women's demands for equality, it is doubtful men would have sought out (to the extent they have) a greater role for themselves in family life. As Jurich, White, White, and Moody (Chapter 10) point out, the rigidities of the male gender role have been challenged as have women's roles, as a result of the challenge of current cultural assumptions regarding men and women, mother and father, and the whole nature of families and what constitutes families. Each family creates its own culture, and because of what appears to be an almost infinite variety of family structures, it is almost impossible to rely on any generalizations to understand the family. Increasingly it is crucial to understand broad cultural influences that impinge upon the family in order to understand changes occurring in implementation of the fatherhood role. And, as changes occur in father role enactment, so do they become reflected in the society's culture.

A major way of changes being reflected in society is the media, particularly television. For example, the movement toward "androgynous fatherhood" (Rotundo, 1985) is increasingly apparent in more than one successful TV series. "Who's the Boss" (ABC) chronicles the life of a father who is a full-time live-in housekeeper for an upwardly mobile female executive; he has a teenage daughter, and she has a teenage son. "Full House" (ABC) is a story of a father who lives with his three young daughters and two male friends. These and other similar television series reflect today's culture, in which child-care and child and family household activities are considered acceptable as masculine activities. The emphasis on both fatherhood and family life in television productions like the ones mentioned above reflect the shift in cultural values in the United States toward responsible, active fatherhood and the importance and capability of men in American homes and family life.

Model: Impact of Culture on Fatherhood

There is a need to conceptualize just what is the impact of selected cultural variables upon the enactment of fatherhood in families. A conceptual model can serve as a road map for the next iteration of writers and researchers in the area of fatherhood, families, and cultural variations. In an earlier book edited by Hanson and Bozett, *Dimensions on Fatherhood* (1985), Pedersen discussed how any theoretical/conceptual model depicting paternal behavior should contain at least four elements (pp. 437–450). These same elements guided the development of the model described herein. First, there should be provision for considering *internalized concepts* of paternal behavior, including what is culturally normative as well as idiosyncratic variations in normative behavior (i.e., gender-role identification, experiences with children, and conceptions of children's needs at different developmental stages). There are usually role scripts that evolve in considerable part prior to parenthood. Second, a useful theory should recognize that there are *modifying constraints* in the environment that exert selective influences upon the father—influences that in concert modify role constructions and affect whether or not they are enacted as behavior. These constraints include family structural variables, or the social context in which interactions occur; for example, perinatal events, characteristics of the child, interactional context, supports from wife/mother, mother–child relationship, or other roles of parents and family structure. Third, a theory should include some kind of *integrator mechanism* that reconciles discrepancies between role constructions and situational constraints. This usually refers to the psychological processes that are involved in comparative and evaluative processes and subjective events (thoughts, emotions, attributions) or how a person receives, processes, and sends out signals to others. Fourth, and finally, the overall model must be explicitly developmental in character by recognizing the influence of two different aspects of time. One is developmental time and the other is historical time. Changes in culture and society influence both shared concepts of paternal roles and circumstances that constrain or modify its expression.

Figure 11.1 is a beginning schematic map displaying some similar features in regard to the impact of culture on fatherhood in

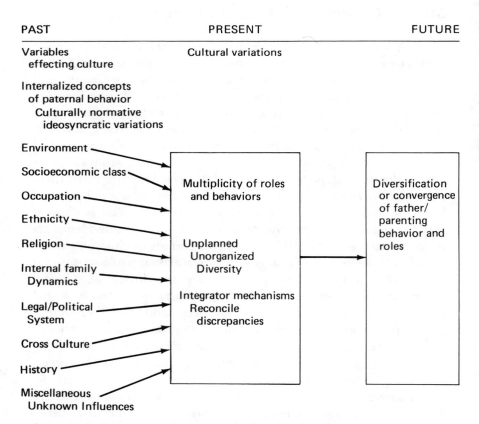

Figure 11.1 Impact of culture on fatherhood in families.

families over time and over man's developmental history. The area on the left represents the historical past and variables that impact the roles and behaviors of males as they move from childhood to adulthood and then become parents. Although this list is not all encompassing, it includes such variables as the environment in which one lives, a person's socioeconomic class, the occupation and the organization in which they work, religious values, ethnic origin, internal family dynamics, legal/political mileau, history, and cross-cultural perspectives. Additionally, it may include other miscellaneous influences that constitute what is called the culture; other factors may include time and events within historical time, and peculiar socialization patterns of males in different societies. These variables are usually innate or internalized (culturally normative as well as ideosyncratic variations) to males and their families when they are born and they may or may not exercise some control over their impact on their parenthood status as they grow and develop.

The middle part of the model depicts the present roles and behaviors that men may enact by virtue of their unique and individual past endowments. These roles may be unplanned, unorganized, although diverse. Individual men may ameloriate the impact of the past internalized value as it impacts their present lives but usually only a certain amount of what people are born with is truly changeable. A certain amount of discrepancies must be integrated or reconciled. The admixture of all the cultural variables on the present role are infinite and this is what makes each father unique in the way they interact with their children and family.

Finally, the right side of the model depicts the future of fatherhood in families. If we understand what constitutes the heritage which men carry from their past to the present, we ought to be able to predict some of the future of American families and fatherhood. Although it is not possible to predict with accuracy the future occurrance of major sociohistorical events that will impact on parental behaviors, there are some who believe that society in the United States is becoming more homogenized resulting in similar and more predictable behavior and events. They believe that there is a confluence of impacting variables effecting how people behave. Other family scholars purport that diversity is even more rampant, and they call for more acceptance of the deviations and variations in the way that families come together (Spanier, 1989). In the first instance, homogenization, we are going from a wider more complex schema to a narrower simpler schema. In the second case, diversity, each generation over time creates an increasingly wider or complicated schema. In sum, the model—Impact of culture on fatherhood in families, is an effort to depict graphically how the cultural variables with which men are born, may change or remain the same over historical time and men's developmental history.

Future of Families and Fatherhood

To understand what the future of fatherhood might bring, we can summarize what theorists and researchers are predicting as future trends for families in general (Cherlin & Furstenberg, 1982; Chilman, 1986; Perch, 1987; Spanier, 1986, 1989). The literature on the future is vast and its application to fatherhood only hypothetical.

First, it is projected that families will continue to take on diverse forms. Fewer Americans will spend most of their lives in a "nuclear" family. By the year 2000, three kinds of families will dominate the personal lives of most Americans: families of first marriage, single parent families, and families of remarriage (Cherlin & Furstenberg, 1982). There is evidence that these three family structures occur despite the "cultural" background of the family.

For families of first marriage, couples will have cohabitated before marriage. The desire to have children will cause them to marry but will not necessarily enhance or prolong their marriage. Most of these families will have one or two children. A sizeable minority will remain childless. It is predicted that about one-fourth of all women currently in childbearing years will never bear children. Childbearing will be compressed with years of working/career before and after childbearing. More families will have both spouses employed. Today one out of two women work but this will rise to three out of four. Families will continue to be faced with how to balance work and family responsibilities. There is ample evidence that men in these kinds of marriages continue their roles and participation in family life, much as it has always been. That is, they have not taken on much more in terms of household work and childrearing responsibilities. As women have evacuated homes, men have not rushed in to fill the vacuum.

The second major type of family structure will be single-parent families. Divorce will continue to occur early in marriage while three-fifths of all divorcing families will continue to include children. Although joint custody is on the rise, it is still uncommon. It is likely to remain the exception rather than the rule because ex-spouses cannot get along well enough to coparent. Mothers will continue to obtain custody after divorce. Children will continue to grow up in these homes without much involvement on the part of their fathers. As divorce will continue to become more common, co-parenting will remain difficult for most families. If current rates continue, more than 60% of all children will spend time in a single-parent family before they reach age 18. The most detrimental effect for children living in single-parent families is not the lack of male presence, but the lack of male income. Single-parent families will become more intentional and less transitional in nature. Family structure will become a choice—a choice away from an unhappy marriage, a choice never to marry, or a choice to marry but remain voluntarily childless. There will be increased numbers of single-parent families due to incidence of never-married birth and adoptive parents. Although the incidence of single fathers will continue to increase, they will represent proportionally fewer single parent families. Single parents will be younger due both to teen pregnancy and earlier divorce after marriage.

Families of remarriage will be the third predominant family lifestyle. The experience of living as a single parent is temporary for many divorced people, especially in the middle class. Three out of four divorced people remarry, and about half of these remarriages occur within three years of divorce. Recently, the incidence of remarriage has dropped reflecting the tendency of divorced people to postpone remarrying. Remarriage relieves the financial difficulties and role overload, but it frequently creates additional problems. Also, the divorce rate for remarriage is higher than for first marriages, and this trend is expected to continue.

People in the United States today, despite their particular cultural background, are living in a larger number of family settings during their lives than was the situation in past generations. Children born in the 1980s could possibly follow this projected course of events and live in as many as ten different family configurations: (1) live with both parents for several years; (2) live with mother after parental divorce; (3) live with mother and stepfather; (4) live alone or communally in early twenties; (5) cohabit without marriage; (6) marry and perhaps have children; (7) get divorced; (8) live alone again; (9) remarry; and (10) live alone again following the death of a spouse. The number of these life course events will be less for men than women because women have a longer life expectancy (Cherlin & Furstenberg, 1982).

Differences in family lives in the United States have and will vary according to factors such as class, ethnicity, and religion, yet less in the future than now because there is evidence of convergence among class, ethnic, religious, and regional groups in many features of family life. In contrast, there is some evidence of a movement that supports a return to patterns of family life like those characterized by middle-class families in the 1950s: early marriage, sexual chastity, fewer divorces, larger families, and a sharper sexual division of labor (Cherlin & Furstenberg, 1982). These traits form what has been called "the classical family of Western nostalgia." But it is unlikely that society will go backwards in time. There has been a maelstrom of social change in the past decades and we can expect the same in the future. Unlike the 1950s, which in retrospect appears to be an anomalous decade in a demographic transition that was otherwise consistent with long-term social and familial change (Cherlin, 1981), the 1980s reflect demographic changes that appear consistent with trends that started or accelerated in the 1960s and that will likely continue into the 1990s and the future. "Patterns of mate selection, cohabitation, fertility, divorce, remarriage, household living arrange-ments, labor force participation among women, child care, and other family related events have been on largely logical and predictable courses, given our increasingly well-documented social history." Fluc-tuations are a given, but significant trends almost always have deep historical and cultural roots (Sweet & Bumpass, 1987, pp. 8–12).

Families of the future will represent both convergent and divergent characteristics. Divergency in the lives of families in the United States have and will vary according to such factors as class, ethnicity, and religion. For example, the latest immigrants from Latin America and East Asia will introduce increasingly greater variations in family patterns. There is much diversity among differ-ent kinds of Hispanic families as there is between Hispanic and non-Hispanic families.

There will also be substantial convergence among class, ethnic, religious, and regional groups that will continue, although it will fall short of eliminating all social class and subcultural differences in family practices. For example, there is strong evidence that styles of marriage, childrearing, and kinship obligations will continue to differ by social class.

A few general and final comments can be made for the future of families in the United States and its impact on fatherhood. Men will become more affective in their relationships. Although "machismo" is not dead, men are beginning to put more time and energy into their relationships including relationships with their wives and children.

There is a need for a men's mental health movement in this country. This men's health care movement may need to be similar to the women's health care movement of earlier decades (Bozett & Forrester, 1989). The focus of this movement should be on mental health of men which will in turn effect their physical health as well as the mental and physical health of women. Our society does not do a good job of socializing males in a way that leads to either good physical or mental health. When men need help, they often turn to work, illness, suicide, or addictive behaviors instead of seeking the help they need, and the help that is generally available in the community.

As values in our culture continue to change, reflecting greater emphasis on both the acceptability and expectation that women will work as well as have careers, there will be a concurrent expectation that men will participate, more than in the past, in childcare, and in home and family-life activities. These obligations and expectations of both men and women, mothers and fathers, will continue to emphasize the importance of both sexes in the rearing of children. Moreover, more men will want to participate both in quantity and quality in the lives of their children and families. While at first, this trend may be more evident among the middle class, it will gradually continue to spread to all social classes as well as to most ethnic groups in the United States.

The future of fatherhood is intrinsically tied to the future of families in the United States, so the story has yet to be written. Speculation can be made based on the past and present cultural variables described in this volume, but many factors can intervene between now and the future. As family scientists studying culture, fatherhood, and families, we are excited by the future possibilities and will continue to chronicle and analyze the development and the future of American fatherhood.

References

Bozett, F. W., & Forrester, D. A. (1989). A proposal for a men's health nurse practitioner. *Image: Journal of Nursing Scholarship, 21,* 158–161.

Cherlin, A., & Furstenberg, F. F. (1982). *The shape of the American family in the year 2000.* Washington, DC: Social Research Services, American Council of Life Insurance.

Chilman, C. S. (1986). Some critical issues facing the United States in the 1980's and (if we're lucky) beyond. In P. W. Dail & R. H. Jewson, *In praise of fifty years: The Groves Conferences on the conservation of marriage and the family* (pp. 94–100). Lake Mills, IA: Graphic Publishing.

Hanson, S. M. H., & Bozett, F. W. (1985). *Dimensions of fatherhood.* Beverly Hills: Sage Publications.

Pedersen, F. A. (1985). Research and the father: Where do we go from here: In S. M. H. Hanson & F. W. Bozett's *Dimensions of fatherhood* (pp. 437–450). Beverly Hills: Sage Publications.

Perch, K. L. (1987). The economics of changing household composition and family roles. *Family and Community Health, 9*(1), 1–9.

Rotundo, A. (1985). American fatherhood. *American Behavioral Scientist, 29,* 7–23.

Seligorann, J., & Abramson, P. (1989, April 17). Crack pushes dads to duty. *Newsweek,* pp. 64 and 66.

Spanier, G. B. (1986). The changing American family: Demographic trends and prospects. In P. W. Dail & R. H. Jewson (Eds.), *In praise of fifty years: The Groves Conferences on the conservation of marriage and family* (pp. 86–93). Lake Mills, IA: Graphic Publishing.

Spanier, G. B. (1989). Bequeathing family continuity. *Journal of Marriage and the Family, 51,* 3–13.

Sweet, J. A., & Bumpass, L. L. (1987). *American families and households.* New York: Russell Sage.

Author Index

Subject Index

Boys
  father differentiation in care of, 18–19
  fatherless, 16
  masculine guidance for, 44–45
  in military families, 196
Breadwinning role. *See* Provider role
Bureaucratic settings, 194
Bushmen fathers, 14
Business life, readying boys for, 44

Caregiving patterns, 14–15
Catholicism, 37
Chicano families, 74. *See also* Latino families
Child abuse, 243
  colonial times, 33
  premodern, 31
  rural areas, 174
Child behavior
  changing, 253–255
  strategic therapy and, 257
Childbirth practices, 230, 233
Child care
  employers and, 207
  paternal participation in, 20
  socialization and, 117–118
  summertime, 166–167
Child custody, 250–251
  black fathers and, 99
  industrial era, 42
  joint, 85, 88, 271
  legal changes and, 84–85
  mothers and, 87–88
  social change and, 87–89
  tender years doctrine, 42
  unwed fathers and, 92
Child labor, colonial times, 32
Child rearing
  African-American, 56–58
  Asian American, 68, 96
  class differences, 117
  father's employment and, 187–188, 201
  manuals and, 41
  Native American, 72
  quality of time spent, 231

social class and, 225–226
social structure components and, 5
20th century standards, 46
Children
  abandoned, 39, 48
  character formation, 15–17
  early competencies of, 229–230
  emancipated, 16
  emotional involvement with, 45
  gender characteristics among, 44–45
  illegitimate, 39–40, 91
  launching, 16
  leisure of, 166–167
  as property, 87
  as servants, 34
  step-, 251
  urban versus rural, 166–167
Child socialization, 220
  African-Americans and, 56, 57
  child care and, 117–118
  father's occupation and, 119–121
  father's role, 16, 231
  religious, 141–142
  social class and, 116, 118
  subcultural norms and, 221
  See also Value transmission
Child support
  enforcement of, 89–90
  prevalence of, 12
Chinese Americans, father role and, 64–65
Christian beliefs
  authority and, 33
  manhood ideals and, 35
Colonial families, 31–32
Community programs, 233
Company welfarism, 198
Concern, fathering function and, 13
Consumption, 115
Cooperative social modes, 47
Courtship, 36
Couvade, 6, 20–21
Cuckoldry, 8
Cultural norms
  man/child dyads, 17
  translating, 240–241